Getaway Plans

Published by Hanley Wood
One Thomas Circle, NW, Suite 600
Washington, DC 20005

Distribution Center
29333 Lorie Lane
Wixom, Michigan 48393

Group Vice President, General Manager, **Andrew Schultz**
Editor-in-Chief, **Linda Bellamy**
Managing Editor, **Jason D. Vaughan**
Senior Editor, **Nate Ewell**
Associate Editor, **Simon Hyoun**
Senior Plan Merchandiser, **Morenci C. Clark**
Plan Merchandiser, **Nicole Phipps**
Proofreader/Copywriter, **Dyana Weis**
Graphic Artist, **Joong Min**
Plan Data Team Leader, **Ryan Emge**
Production Manager, **Brenda McClary**
Contributing Editor, **Elena Marcheso Moreno**

Vice President, Retail Sales, **Scott Hill**
National Sales Manager, **Bruce Holmes**
Director, Plan Products, **Matt Higgins**

Most Hanley Wood titles are available at quantity discounts with bulk purchases for educational, business, or sales promotional use.
For information, please contact Bruce Holmes at bholmes@hanleywood.com.

BIG DESIGNS, INC.
President, Creative Director, **Anthony D'Elia**
Vice President, Business Manager, **Megan D'Elia**
Vice President, Design Director, **Chris Bonavita**
Editorial Director, **John Roach**
Assistant Editor, **Tricia Starkey**
Senior Art Director, **Stephen Reinfurt**
Art Director, **Mary Ellen Mulshine**
Production Director, **David Barbella**
Photo Editor, **Christine DiVuolo**
Graphic Designer, **Jacque Young**
Graphic Designer, **Maureen Waters**
Graphic Designer, **Billy Doremus**
Assistant Photo Editor, **David Halpin**
Assistant Production Manager, **Rich Fuentes**

PHOTO CREDITS
Front Cover: **Photo by Mark Samu.**
Back Cover Left: **Photo by Mark Samu.**
Back Cover Center: **Photo by Northlight Photography.** For details, see page 95.
Back Cover Right: **Photo Courtesy of: Arthur Manns Harden Architects.** For details, see page 74.

10 9 8 7 6 5 4 3 2 1

Printed in the United States of America

Library of Congress Control Number: 2004099003

ISBN: 1-931131-37-6

Getaway Plans
250 Home Plans
for Cottages,
Bungalows, & Capes

Contents

4 Introduction
Discover the joys of your own
getaway plan

6 Retreat in Style
We'll provide the secrets to a
successful second home

25 Open Plans
Homes with Open Floor Plans

77 Comforts of Home
Homes with Multiple
Bedroom Suites

129 Outdoor Living
Homes with Outdoor Rooms

181 Room to Grow
Homes with Storage and
Bonus Spaces

233 Sunny Days
Homes with Patios or Decks

278 Order Plans
Information on purchasing
blueprints

Plan Your Getaway

F ew events are more magical than the time you spend on vacation, disconnected from home and busy schedules. Nothing can interfere with the rhythm of the day as it spreads out before you. And there is time, plenty of it, for family members to spend together rather than leaving messages for each other as they head out to separate responsibilities. It is on vacation that relatives bond, kids learn about nature, new sports are conquered, entertainment is at the ready, good cheer abounds, and friends are reminded why they want to keep company.

It is also a time to just lean back and relax. Having your own vacation house makes getting away so much more comfortable. How exciting it is to be surrounded by beautiful scenery in a warm and inviting retreat

where family and friends want to gather together on the weekends.

By 2010, the number of vacation homes in the United States is expected to increase to nearly 10 million. That growth is driven in large part by the aging baby boomers who have gained enough wealth for a second home. And it is true that vacation homes are taking on a new importance as a top symbol of success. But they also represent a greater need to disconnect, to make getaway plans that accommodate long-term needs for rejuvenation or just a long weekend for a quick break.

When time off is on the agenda, when you need a regular dose of down time, and when you are convinced there is no place like home, consider the house plans in this book. With so many to choose from and the breadth of different styles, there is surely a home here for you. ■

For more details on these beautiful homes, see (from left to right): page 76, page 74, page 30, page 242, page 234, page 273, page 95, and page 249.

Retreat in Style

The very best vacation homes begin with smart planning at the building stage

A gabled roof, screened-in porches, built-in cabinets, and fine stonework are all hallmarks of the Craftsman style.

It's vacation time and that means its time to get away, kick back, and relax. A vacation home of one's own makes that ever so much easier and so much more comfortable. There is something truly special about a vacation home when beautiful scenery and a retreat from the normal routine are on the agenda or when family and friends want to gather together on the weekends.

If everyone enjoyed the same vacations, vacation homes would probably all look alike. But vacation means different things to different people, which is why there is no perfect architectural style that meets all needs and tastes.

The best designs for getaway homes are not complex or fussy, but rather focus on convenience and function. While sometimes rambling, more often than not vacation homes are not large. As you choose your home plan, celebrate all the qualities that make vacation homes so special. It is true that getaway retreats often come in small packages, but they are always inviting and memorable.

Vacation idylls are guaranteed when your getaway is a comfortable home in a beautiful setting, like this new house that looks old. Historical details and fine craftsmanship extend inside, where the lifestyle is thoroughly modern.

How do you want to get away? Whether you see yourself on the deck of a cottage by the water or in a ski lodge with double height windows overlooking the slopes, your vision of relaxation will determine where you wish to be when you get away. And the location of your retreat can help you select the right plans.

Lots of light and an open plan make this rendition especially inviting.

The overall architecture is an important consideration when building a new vacation home or renovating an existing one. Getaway homes are frequently in locations with distinct regional character, the type of character that draws vacationers there. So blending the design of a new home with the local architectural style is a proven approach to creating a welcoming retreat.

But the perfect architectural style for your getaway house is really the one that pleases you. So consider the home plans in the following sections of this book as you decide on the outside appearance of your vacation place, and remember that exterior design often has a large impact on the interior architecture.

Some of the most sought-after second homes are Craftsman-style cottages, with their gabled roofs and inviting entryways. This style home is characterized by its use of organic materials such as wood siding, clay bricks, and metal wrought as ornamental hardware. These cottages are characterized by uncomplicated interiors, clean lines, and exposed beams. In the Craftsman style, exterior and interior architecture are treated almost as one.

Borrowing ideas from regional architecture can make a home feel like it's part of the community, and this approach works for homes of all sizes.

Above: This farmhouse captures rural American design that can be found in a number of vacation retreats, especially in the Northeast. **Below:** Shingle siding, a variety of window treatments and a sprawling porch help this gorgeous home blend with the landscape.

The local design tradition often is what makes a vacation spot or resort area so charming.

A second-floor sunroom, above the porch overlooks a stone bridge and private island.

REGIONAL CHARACTER

Selecting home plans in keeping with the regional character will guarantee that a getaway fits its setting. And if the local identity is charming, why not embrace it? After all, any architectural style can be adapted to meet the needs of a modern lifestyle. Sometimes building a house in keeping with the surrounding aesthetic is as simple as including exterior trim and roof overhangs or selecting compatible window, door, or garage door styles.

Left: Lights from a beach house at night beckon guests forward. **Below left:** A perfect spot to enjoy the sun and the views is a necessity in any good vacation home. **Right, and below right:** Expansive vistas of lake and forest were the driving force behind this lodge-like bungalow. Local materials like granite and fine architectural details like the paneled walls add up to welcoming a rustic retreat.

Bungalows, just another Arts and Crafts rendering of the cottage, are also popular. With a low-pitched roof, simple structure, covered porch, and understated design, this home style is known for its efficient use of space, where dining areas, kitchen, and bedrooms are typically clustered around central living spaces. Part of the bungalow genre, Prairie-style homes typically hug their sites with a visually low-to-the-ground, horizontal spread to their design. They have hipped roofs and porches with deep eaves.

Capes are another American style home with great appeal for vacation property. Known for their conservative appearance, steep roofs with side gables and no overhangs, little exterior ornamentation other than shutters, and multipane windows, Cape Cod homes historically are designed with small rooms around a central hall. Another enduring American home style is the Colonial. Colonial architecture really encompasses a number of variations, but most are symmetrical, with a central entryway punctuated by columns, medium-pitched roofs and multipaned windows.

Many retreats are contemporary in style. Contemporary homes can have large expanses of window area, open spaces, and interior structural elements that are left exposed. One type of inexpensive contemporary getaway home observed on a rambling drive through beach and mountain areas is the A-frame. The steep slope of the A-frame roof is intended to shed snow to the ground and creates a half-floor at the top for sleeping lofts or extra storage space.

Many vacation home styles hail from an earlier period in history, when homes were smaller. Today's new retreats are generally bigger, though not necessarily large, and have interior spaces designed for modern lifestyles.

Two very different homes located on the water provide equal amounts of relaxation and every opportunity to get away in your own unique style.

OPEN DOOR POLICY

The front door announces a home's character and extends an invitation to come inside. Your choice of door could be formal or casual, but either way it will be more than a division between the public and private spaces. Many homeowners prefer wood doors for their enduring appeal and style that equally complement a rustic cabin, casual beach house, or more elegant entryway. Other homeowners, with an eye to security or energy conservation, will select foam-insulated steel doors or fiberglass doors—especially in coastal regions where wood doors may not meet building codes. Exterior doors can be clad with aluminum, vinyl, or wood. Glass panels in the door or glass sidelights let in light and can reflect lots of charm. And French or double doors would be twice as nice!

Left, and below left: Open plans offer a relaxed welcome to beachcombers and keep people engaged in different activities gathered together. Simple but effective detailing and hard-wearing materials make maintenance a breeze.

Long before they start to contemplate an exterior look, many prospective vacation home buyers dream about floor plans. They think about extra bedrooms, plan for family-centered kitchens, and wonder if there should be stairs to climb. They want interior spaces to be arranged to reflect the way they expect to relax and to accommodate the daily patterns of their life while on vacation.

Recent developments in home plans are helping buyers realize their dreams. New floor plans are adaptable without dictating the size and placement of the rooms by strict adherence to old rules about architectural styles. And these plans concentrate on flexibility, not excessive space. Getaway plans don't have to be super-sized. Instead of excessive space, vacation homes can feel much larger than they are when designed properly.

The trend in today's best new home designs is to turn away from the seemingly endless rooms of wasted space toward more compact home designs where the boundaries of individual rooms are erased and the larger context of the home becomes pliable, adapting to living needs as they arise.

APPEALING DETAILS

Even a modest home design can sing with the right architectural details. When adding details to building plans, first be sure they complement the house style and any period that it references. Arts and Crafts homes, for example, often exhibit low-pitched roofs with gables, decorative braces, and front porches with columns. Meanwhile, Colonial homes tend to be symmetrical right down to the placement of windows and have understated entrances. Bold or subdued, architectural detailing on any style of house plan can pay big design dividends, even on a limited budget.

Blurring the distinction between indoors and out can be a key to success in a getaway plan. If you can, don't limit outdoor spaces to public areas; give yourself a private getaway off the master suite.

The focus instead is on the rooms used every day, and on making them as comfortable and spacious as possible in a reasonably sized home.

A few guiding design principles help make this work. Open, free-flowing floor plans are growing in popularity because they connect rooms to each other and create large living spaces. Plans where the great room flows easily into the dining room and kitchen generate the sense that there is much more space than one might expect when looking at the house from the outside.

These floor plans are especially popular in getaway plans, which have little need for formal living and dining rooms. When several rooms are connected, activities become communal, letting families spend time together even when working on several different tasks, and creating a hub for social gatherings rather than forcing social groups to separate into several different rooms.

WINDOW WISDOM

Windows bring natural light inside and also provide a unique view on the world beyond. When selecting windows for your vacation home, consider the following:

■ Is the window style in harmony with the architecture of the house? Double hung windows would look out of place on a contemporary home, but large expanses of glass would not.

■ Windows come with energy ratings. Pick the right one for your climate.

■ Orientation counts. While views to the east and west might be desirable, the energy required to counter heat gains or heat losses will be greater. South-facing windows provide the best energy savings and also the best quality of daylight.

■ Window materials include wood, aluminum, and vinyl, all with different maintenance issues and weathering properties.

■ Windows can be one of the most expensive components of a new house, but they can also contribute most to its architectural character. Choose wisely.

retreat in style

A grand sense of space keeps open plans in high demand, for rustic as well as more formal retreats.

LOOKING OUT

The living space of a good getaway plan doesn't stop with its four walls. Include the outdoors in your plans, and almost endless additional space will open up to enjoy. Here a timeless flagstone patio provides extra sitting areas, whether for entertaining or a quiet spot to read a book. Porches and decks can accomplish the same thing.

Making the transition

Opening up interior spaces into combined living areas is a winning solution for your getaway. But without the right planning, vast undifferentiated rooms can be cold and uninviting. The trick to making open floor plans welcoming is to define more intimate areas within the larger overall interior context with knee walls, columns, or arches that suggest a boundary while leaving the views unobstructed, or with islands between kitchen work space and entertaining areas so that people in the midst of different activities are still gathered together. To make these smaller places flow seamlessly together they should visually relate to each other with unifying elements such as paint colors, fabrics, and furnishings, and they should have consistent window shapes and sizes, moldings and trim, and flooring materials.

The inherent flexibility of open plans is what makes them so appealing. Just moving furniture around creates new "rooms," and this multifunction aspect of open plans is hard to beat. But one word of caution—architects and designers say that eliminating all hallways is not the way to go. When bedrooms or baths open directly into a public space, privacy is sacrificed. While long narrow corridors with bedrooms on both sides have the feel of a large impersonal apartment building, shorter corridors, corners, or vestibules help separate the private areas of the home from the major activity and allow for quiet places to retreat.

Here, the structural elements of the house define its transitions, where a closet in an alcove identifies the progression from kitchen to sitting room and sitting room to great room. Railings along the circulation path for an upper level further enhance the sense of open walls.

The open floor plan and high ceilings of this rustic retreat are warm and inviting due in large part to the use of transitional strategies like the change of one space to another identified only by open timbers (page 272).

Whether open or intimate, the space in a getaway house must be put to good use.

Rather than restricting space, built-in cabinets and bookcases actually open it up. Combined with high windows and natural materials, the built-ins in this home reaffirm its contemporary interpretation of rustic style.

Transitional space is important for other reasons as well. If all the public spaces in the home are open, noise becomes an issue. Soft finishes such as carpeting and window treatments can absorb some of the sound, and strategically placed breaks in the open space, where perhaps the special volume turns a corner, will help reduce unwanted noise as well. Plus, these in-between places are good spots to include some extra storage.

Design efficiency in a small house pays big dividends. In addition to putting transitional spaces to use for storage, well-planned details like built-in bookcases, cabinets, and window seats will boost the performance of an open plan. Many of the plans in this book provide unfinished or partly finished space for future expansion. When your dreams include more rooms than the construction budget for your second home allows, selecting house plans with bonus space could be the perfect solution.

Bonus rooms hold great potential as multifunctional spaces to allow for

INTERIOR ARCHITECTURAL DETAILS

Interior details add the kind of style and character that can help boost the relaxation value of a vacation home. Moldings and trim define windows, doors, and walls. Some details, like a bulkhead that lowers the ceiling in just a part of the space, can provide intimate style or hide unsightly transitions or building systems. Chair railings, built-in bookcases and cupboards, as well as wall panels can visually correct the scale of a room. Custom and off-the-shelf architectural details are readily available, and often reasonably priced.

Built-ins are a great solution to keep everything in its place and organized, even in a small area.

unique designs that can be tailored to your current or future lifestyle. There will be room to spread into, more places to relax or to create an additional bedroom suite. The options for using this extra space are almost limitless, but one of the most appealing is as additional storage for all the paraphernalia that makes a vacation memorable, but that can get in the way when not in use. From snowboards to inflatable rafts to extra kitchen supplies, there can be a place for everything in a bonus room.

The best vacation places are sure to attract overnight guests. So if your getaway plans include visitors, make sure they feel especially welcomed. A gracious way to do just that is to provide a nice place for family and friends to stay. Guest rooms and multiple extra bedroom suites let your visitors have some privacy. Give guests ample space for sleeping, reading, and storing their personal items. If at all possible, provide a separate bathroom so that guests and hosts both have more privacy. Designed with overnight guests in mind, some house plans go a step farther, and include separate entrances and porches just for them.

Bonus rooms can easily be converted into guest suites when the need arises. A small but colorful bathroom sits under the eaves, right next to the guest room sitting area.

What's the Program?

Building a vacation home can be an exciting challenge. Each idea about the size, shape, or amenities of this second home brings you one step closer to realizing the dream of your own getaway, a place to relax, disconnected from work, busy schedules, and daily responsibilities.

Whether you expect to hire an architect or take advantage of pre-drawn home plans, the first step in the process of building a house is to create a plan. Compile a wish list of everything you envision, from the look and feel of your new house, to the way you want to use it. Then create a set of priorities, identify a budget, and cull down the list, separating the things that must be included from the things that would be nice to have, but could be eliminated without too much regret.

This process of determining the priorities—what is required for the house—is known as programming. This is when decisions are made about the kinds of rooms that are needed and how big they should be, how the house will look and feel and flow. Armed with a program of what you need and want for your vacation home, you can select a floor plan that suits your unique situation.

SITE PLANS

Matching a vacation home to its site is an important design consideration that requires thinking ahead. If you already own a lot, you'll want to assess it with a critical eye before you select a house plan.

Study the site; examine its physical characteristics like slope, access to the sun or to views, soil type, and whether there are naturally occurring features that will restrict building in certain areas. Learn about local zoning ordinances, such as setback from the property line and building height restrictions.

Find a design for your vacation house that suits your site and blends naturally into the lot. Then work with what is available. Don't fight the site. Rather, take advantage of what it has to offer, be it a steep hillside that promises great views, tree stands that offer privacy, or immovable boulders that can be used as a foundation. Consider the regional building style, which has often evolved from local conditions, such as the steeply-pitched roofs common to the snow-prone mountains of New England or the deep porches with high roofs found on Southern homes, where a buffer from the hot sun helps keep interior spaces cool.

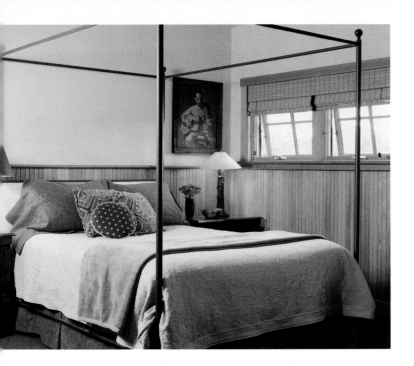

Space must be allocated for public areas, such as kitchens and family gathering places, as well as private bedroom areas and quiet spots for contemplation. But even before that, determine the overall feel of the floor plan so that your getaway house becomes a place that is truly meaningful to you. While many people envision their vacation home as a place to wind down and let the day unfold, others like a more formal approach with some structure.

Is your retreat to be an open, airy place where friends and family gather, or a collection of small, intimate spaces where privacy reigns? How many bedrooms are needed and how many baths? Which rooms should be close together and which far apart? For some people, vacation means not cooking much, but other people cook to relax. This first group doesn't need an elaborate kitchen, but the second set would probably benefit from a large kitchen or combination kitchen and family room for gatherings large and small.

Getaway homes are often in scenic spots, so enjoy the view. Will you need tall windows to contemplate expansive vistas, groups of small windows clustered together for visual access to a garden, or high windows for privacy? What about the sun? A common and successful solar

VACATION HOME FINANCING

If you are building or purchasing a second home and need financing, here are a few things to keep in mind:

- About 400,000 vacation properties are purchased each year, and that number is expected to increase. The application process is just like that for a primary residence, but lenders consider these properties to be luxury items and the loans to be riskier, so rates could be a little higher.
- The magic debt-to-income ratio of 38 percent still holds—and that includes all of your debt (mortgages for two houses, credit cards, and loans)
- It is easier to secure financing for an existing home than it is to get a loan to purchase property and then a construction loan. If you can purchase the property first and borrow against it and any equity that has built up to build a new house, you will likely come out ahead.
- A getaway home can also be an investment property that is rented part of the time. But the IRS insists the income be reported if the home is rented more than 14 days each year. Tax deductions and mortgage interest write-offs are allowed in any case.
- All houses need maintenance and updating. Factor these costs into your budget, along with operating expenses for things like heating and cooling. And expect insurance to be greater on a second home that is only periodically occupied than on a primary residence.

Outdoor rooms come in many shapes and sizes, but they all offer an invitation to come outside and relax for awhile, although sometimes a lap blanket might be required.

strategy is to locate rooms that are used most during the day with a southern exposure. Breakfast rooms could face east, dining areas west in order to capitalize on natural daylight. Bedrooms can typically face north, but if they will be used regularly in the daytime, a brighter location might be desired.

Once you have addressed what a great floor plan for your getaway looks like, turn your sights outside. It is time to decide on an architectural style. Will your vacation house be a cottage, shingle, contemporary, or perhaps Arts and Crafts style? Are you committed to blending in with the regional architecture, or more comfortable with a different style? Give some thought to which materials will give the exterior of your vacation house the charm and inviting look you seek.

Every decision made in the programming stage affects the budget. Search in plan books for your dream getaway place; it may be helpful to talk to some builders about what it will cost to build. If you plan to work directly with an architect or designer, get their input right away. Once you have prioritized your wants and needs, settled on a design, and have a clear idea of construction costs, it is time to line up financing. Then be patient. It will take awhile, but soon you will be enjoying your own getaway. ■

Take It Outside

Outdoor living calls for a leisurely lifestyle, so as the weather warms up, bring gatherings outside. Outdoor living spaces become extra rooms in most vacation spots. The key to creating inviting rooms outside is to design the space in keeping with the architectural style of the house.

Patios, porches, courtyards, and atriums are some of the most popular forms of outdoor living rooms. The most inviting provide comfortable furniture, and many feature a complete outdoor kitchen or outdoor fireplace as the centerpiece of the space.

To seamlessly extend the useable boundaries of the house, design outdoor rooms as complements to indoor spaces. One easy way to that is with flooring: use brick or stone tile on the floor of an open plan, and extend similar materials to the patio. Another approach is to repeat some interior details outside, like columns, arches, or pilasters. Some of the means of blending spaces together are inexpensive. For example, use paint to finish patio or deck furniture in shades similar to the colors used inside. Whether these outside retreats are large or small, they will be perfect for relaxation, cooking, and entertaining—the very definition of a getaway house.

Outdoor fireplaces, among the most popular features in new homes, draw the crowd outside.

THE OUTDOOR LIVING ROOM

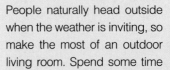

People naturally head outside when the weather is inviting, so make the most of an outdoor living room. Spend some time creating a comfortable retreat that welcomes family and friends. Smooth the transition to the outdoors by borrowing some of the colors and finishes from the house. Think about how you will use the space, what form it will take, and whether there will be surrounding gardens. Come to grips with your entertaining style: if you only have room to host a small picnic, plan your large gatherings for another area. Make sure to include a space to eat meals cooked outside.

MEANDER ALONG

The hardscape around entryways and the walkways that lead to intimate spots in a getaway garden should always beckon. Gently curving paths are often pleasing, providing a sense of movement and the opportunity to group plants in an imaginative way. But straight paths can be a powerful garden design element when there is a statue, water feature, or other focal point at their end. Wood chips, rocks, even low-growing plants used as ground cover can all control weeds and limit maintenance.

When outdoor living includes a trellised deck, the native plantings nearby create a living wall.

The right landscaping will enhance your getaway. It blends the design of the house to its natural setting. Of particular interest are features known as "hardscapes," such as walkways, retaining walls, patios, fences, arbors, and trellises. These are the components that give structure to a landscape plan, mark an entrance, or identify an approach to the house. Wood, stone, brick, and concrete are the materials used to construct these features and they provide nice textures to contrast with plants. The object when installing a new garden or renewing an old one is to balance the form of the garden and all of its hardscape with plantings in a harmonious way.

Backyards and patios are where everyone wants to be. They can help combine the inside and the outside into one big comfortable space or into distinct areas for various family activities. Provide comfortable and durable furniture and protection from the sun and wind to transform the backyard into a retreat that suits your getaway plans.

The brick path, wooden garden gate, and cottage garden all complement the established appearance of this home.

TEAM BUILDING

The success of your building project depends in large part on the team of professionals you assemble. Finding qualified design and construction service providers to help you build your vacation home will help you get away sooner. The services provided vary depending on the expert.

Architects work on the whole scope of a project, from overall aesthetics to space design to structural soundness. While they can design a whole house, they are also good sources to turn to when you have found house plans you like a lot, but which require some changes to meet your needs. An architect can make additions, changes, or deletions to the plans without compromising the architectural integrity of the original design or the function of the home. Part of their job is to make sure your plans meet building codes and local zoning regulations. Another part is to help you make wise choices on everything from room sizes to sight lines to products and materials so that the home you build has all of the inviting charm you dream about.

Architects are often hired to oversee construction and help find the best solutions to the inevitable changes that arise. Architects most often charge a fee as a percentage of the cost to build the house. These fees typically range from 7 to 10 percent.

General contractors coordinate the construction of a house based on construction drawings. They will be familiar with building codes and obtain all the necessary permits. They also hire and coordinate all the subcontractors who actually build the house. You pay the general contractor and they in turn pay the subcontractors.

Contactors charge fees for their services in a variety of ways. Cost-plus fees include overhead and profit fees for the contractor, plus all the costs for materials and labor to build the house. Fixed fees set the overall cost to build the house in advance. Percentage fees mean you pay the builder some specified percentage of the overall cost of construction.

Interior designers can bring a lot of design ideas to a project and can oversee some of the subcontractors who build the house. While their aesthetic opinions are as respected as those of architects, interior designers are limited in their ability to adjust floor plans. They are not trained to make structural changes, and many states limit their ability to move plumbing or electrical components without oversight of a licensed architect or engineer. Interior designers have access to materials and products that could be difficult to obtain on your own. In addition to charging hourly fees, interior designers typically mark up the price of the products they help you select.

Find the Right Pro

Getting the house built and getting the job done right is all a matter of assembling the right team for your project. The following organizations can provide the names of qualified and licensed professionals in your area:

American Institute of Architects: 202-626-7300, www.aia.org

Society of Registered Architects: 888-385-7272, www.sara-national.org

National Association of Home Builders: 800-368-5242, www.nahb.org

National Association of the Remodeling Industry: 800-611-6274, www.nari.org

American Society of Interior Designers: 202-546-3480, www.asid.org

Open Plans:
Homes with Open Floor Plans

Style in a vacation home comes in many forms. From cottage to farmhouse to contemporary home, the place where you go to get away says a lot about you and the way you live. Vacation homes typically are not as large as primary homes, but they can still "live large." Opening up the public areas by joining living room, family room, and kitchen is a strategy that works well for family-friendly getaway plans. Open floor plans with their large central areas are perfect gathering places to cook, eat, play games, watch TV, or entertain. An informal great room provides a sense of spaciousness, and an open floor plan makes entertaining more enjoyable. It is easier for everyone to spend time together and when the furniture is arranged to create separate rooms and functions, kids can play while guests relax by the fire and the hosts cook dinner.

This coastal home features fantastic views and a smart layout (page 74).

This home will be the envy of the neighborhood with its stone-and-stucco facade and graceful archway.

Spacious Retreat

An intelligent floor plan brings everyone together—and sets this three-bedroom home apart

With a layout that makes the very most of every room, you'll be swept away by the generous living space that this 2,293-square-foot home provides. Whether you want to relax with family or entertain large groups, this plan provides comfort and convenience, thanks to its open design and expansive living area. The exterior has a classy style you'll love. The gently sloping hipped roof and stone-and-stucco facade lend a European look with hints of Floridian style. A soaring entry, highlighted by a keystone and an

The kitchen's island offers additional work space, plus a convenient spot to enjoy informal meals.

arched window above, draws attention and beckons visitors inside.

Intelligent interior details abound, such as the built-in entertainment center in the family room, the good-sized and perfectly located laundry room, and a decorative wall niche in the foyer.

As you enter the home, double doors to your left open to a cozy den. Further inside, the dining room features an open design that connects to the foyer and the family room. The dining room's coffered ceiling lends a distinguished, elegant air.

The spacious family room has a well-deserved commanding location, connecting easily to every corner of the house. It includes plenty of space for entertaining, opening to the covered patio on one end, and connecting to the kitchen on the other.

You'll appreciate the view from the breakfast nook, even if you use the space to pay bills or do homework.

Varied ceiling treatments help set spaces like the dining room apart without adding unnecessary walls.

A snack bar and cozy breakfast nook, surrounded by windows, offer two convenient serving options. The kitchen has plenty of room not only for the cook, but for some helpers as well—or for snack-seekers, who can get to the fridge without getting in the way! You'll find plenty of storage space, with cabinets galore and a walk-in pantry in the corner.

The master suite occupies the left side of the plan and offers everything you could hope for. French doors to the patio highlight the large

The grand foyer flows effortlessly into the dining room and family room.

The home provides convenient outdoor access to the covered patio.

bedroom, which also features a tray ceiling. In the master bath you'll discover a garden tub, separate shower, and two walk-in closets.

The split-bedroom design places two other bedrooms on the right side of the plan, at the front of the house. They share a full bath in the hallway nearby.

A bonus room or fourth bedroom sits above the two-car garage and provides a perfect oasis for an in-law or guest. It includes its own full bath and French doors opening to a balcony that overlooks the backyard. ■

plan# HPK0900001

Style: European Cottage
Square Footage: 2,293
Bonus Space: 509 sq. ft.
Bedrooms: 3
Bathrooms: 2
Width: 51' - 0"
Depth: 79' - 4"
Foundation: Slab

SEARCH ONLINE @ EPLANS.COM

Balc.

Bonus/Bedrm 4
21⁴ · 16⁴

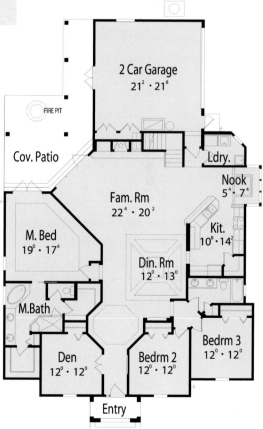

2 Car Garage
21² · 21⁸

FIRE PIT

Cov. Patio

Ldry.

Nook
5⁴ · 7⁴

Fam. Rm
22⁴ · 20²

Kit.
10⁸ · 14²

M. Bed
19⁰ · 17⁴

Din. Rm
12⁰ · 13⁰

M.Bath

Bedrm 3
12⁰ · 12⁰

Den
12⁰ · 12⁰

Bedrm 2
12⁰ · 12⁰

Entry

This fine three-bedroom home is full of amenities and will surely be a family favorite! A covered porch leads into the great room/dining room. Here, a fireplace reigns at one end, casting its glow throughout the room. A private study is tucked away, perfect for a home office or computer study. The master bedroom suite offers a bayed sitting area, large walk-in closet, and pampering bath. With plenty of counter and cabinet space and an adjacent breakfast area, the kitchen will be a favorite gathering place for casual mealtimes. The family sleeping zone is upstairs and includes two bedrooms, a full bath, a loft/study area, and a huge storage room.

plan# HPK0900002

First Floor: 1,896 sq. ft.
Second Floor: 692 sq. ft.
Total: 2,588 sq. ft.
Bedrooms: 3
Bathrooms: 2½
Width: 60' - 0"
Depth: 84' - 10

SEARCH ONLINE @ EPLANS.COM

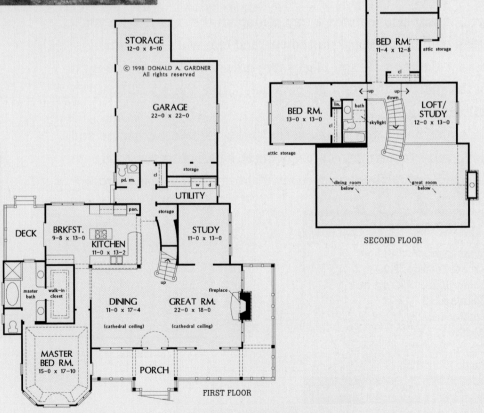

This fine bungalow, with its multiple gables, rafter tails, and pillared front porch, will be the envy of any neighborhood. A beam-ceilinged great room is further enhanced by a through-fireplace and French doors to the rear terrace. The U-shaped kitchen features a cooktop island with a snack bar and offers a beam-ceilinged breakfast/keeping room that shares the through-fireplace with the great room. Two secondary bedrooms share a full bath; the master suite is designed to pamper. Here, the homeowner will be pleased with a walk-in closet, a separate shower, and access to the terrace. The two-car garage has a side entrance and will easily shelter the family fleet.

plan# HPK0900003

Style: Bungalow
Square Footage: 2,489
Bedrooms: 3
Bathrooms: 2½
Width: 68' - 3"
Depth: 62' - 0"
Foundation: Walkout Basement

SEARCH ONLINE @ EPLANS.COM

Master Bedroom
17⁹ x 14⁰

Terrace

Great Room
21⁹ x 16⁰

Breakfast/Keeping
12⁰ x 19³

Kitchen
11⁰ x 16⁰

Foyer

Dining Room
13⁹ x 15³

Bedroom #2
10⁹ x 14³

Bedroom #3
10⁹ x 14⁰

2 Car Garage
23⁹ x 23⁹

Craftsman-style windows with a bit of Palladian flair enhance the exterior of this home. Inside, a vaulted ceiling accents the formal living room; the adjoining dining room includes columns and a built-in display cabinet. The family room and nook, also with vaulted ceilings, serve as charming informal gathering areas. Sleeping quarters, to the left of the plan, include the vaulted master suite and two additional bedrooms. All three bedrooms are conveniently close to the utility room, which offers a wash sink and counter space.

plan # HPK0900004

Style: Craftsman
Square Footage: 2,218
Bedrooms: 3
Bathrooms: 2
Width: 50' - 0"
Depth: 70' - 0"
Foundation: Crawlspace

SEARCH ONLINE @ EPLANS.COM

A **New-Age contemporary** touch graces the exterior of this impressive yet affordable home. The entry leads to the formal areas in the open dining room and vaulted living room. The kitchen overlooks a quaint morning room, which leads to a rear deck that's a perfect spot for outdoor activities. With a walk-in closet and private bath, homeowners will be pampered in the master suite. The second bedroom, the two-car garage, and a utility room complete the plan.

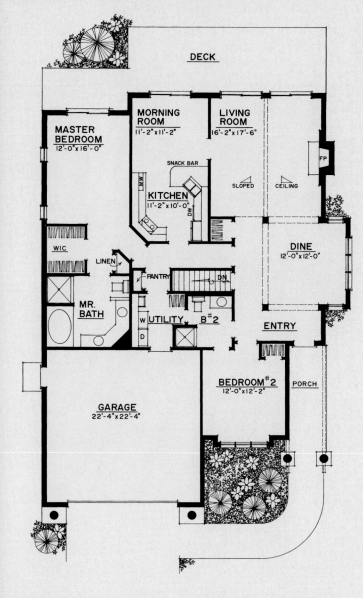

plan # HPK0900005

Style: Mediterranean
Square Footage: 1,723
Bedrooms: 2
Bathrooms: 2
Width: 45' - 0"
Depth: 62' - 6"
Foundation: Basement

SEARCH ONLINE @ EPLANS.COM

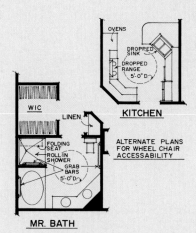

Vaulted ceilings highlight the foyer, great room, dining room, and master suite of this charming one-story home. A fireplace further enhances the great room, and the master suite boasts a sumptuous private bath. Two family bedrooms and a full bath occupy the right wing of the plan.

plan # HPK0900006

Style: Country Cottage
Square Footage: 1,290
Bedrooms: 3
Bathrooms: 2
Width: 46' - 0"
Depth: 53' - 4"
Foundation: Crawlspace,
Slab, Basement

SEARCH ONLINE @ EPLANS.COM

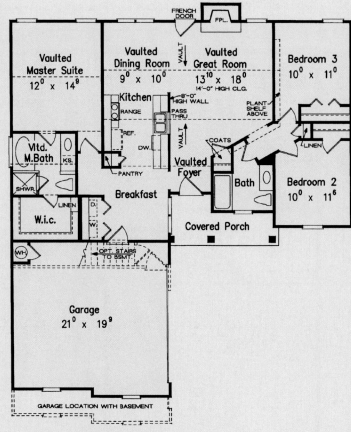

Relax in this sweet-faced bungalow featuring Craftsman details and charm. The main floor is open and modern without any wasted space. The large kitchen is set to the front of the plan with the dining and family areas just a few steps away. The master suite offers a full bath and walk-in closet. The screened porch and adjoining deck make this cottage live larger than its modest square footage. The lower level provides guests with two secondary bedrooms, a full bath, and a game room.

Christine Canova 3/02
© Copyright 2003, Garrell Associates, Inc.

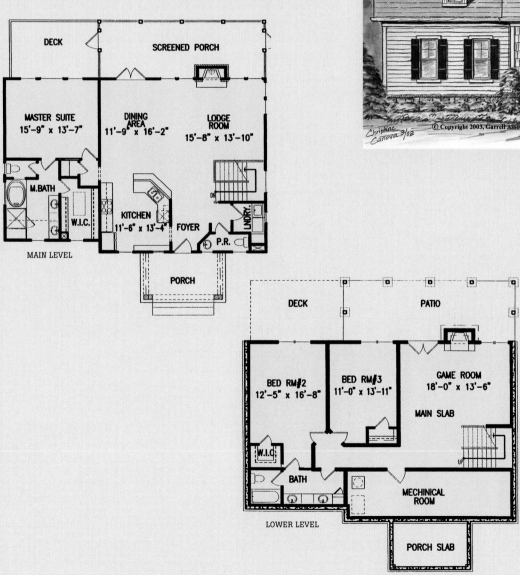

plan # HPK0900007

Style: Craftsman
Main Level: 1,288 sq. ft.
Lower Level: 1,242 sq. ft.
Total: 2,530 sq. ft.
Bedrooms: 3
Bathrooms: 2½
Width: 44' - 0"
Depth: 30' - 0"
Foundation: Basement

SEARCH ONLINE @ EPLANS.COM

What appears to be a traditional brick country farmhouse on the exterior is actually a luxurious home, filled with all the decadent elements that new homeowners desire. French doors lead to the two-story foyer; a living room/study greets guests on the right. Columns to the left define a formal dining room. A butler's pantry makes service from the open island kitchen effortless. To the rear, a vaulted keeping room is hearth-warmed and filled with natural light. The two-story grand room surveys the rear property, courtesy of a prominent bowed window wall. The right wing is devoted to the master suite, rich with a trayed foyer, vaulted sitting room, and magnificent spa bath. Three generous upstairs bedrooms each enjoy unique amenities.

plan # HPK0900008

Style: Farmhouse
First Floor: 2,928 sq. ft.
Second Floor: 1,296 sq. ft.
Total: 4,224 sq. ft.
Bedrooms: 4
Bathrooms: 3½
Width: 67' - 0"
Depth: 70' - 10"
Foundation: Crawlspace, Basement

SEARCH ONLINE @ EPLANS.COM

SECOND FLOOR

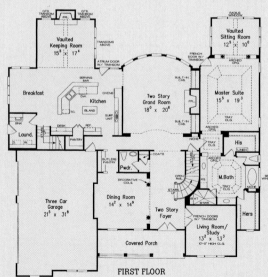

FIRST FLOOR

Three dormers and a welcoming porch greet visitors
into this four-bedroom home. The foyer—note the charming plant shelf above—introduces a dining room to the right with easy access to the pantry and kitchen. This flexible design also offers an optional study with French doors opening to left of the foyer. The vaulted grand room features a fireplace and is open to the kitchen area. Two family bedrooms and an optional bonus room share a bath on the second level, while the master suite and one additional bedroom reside on the first floor.

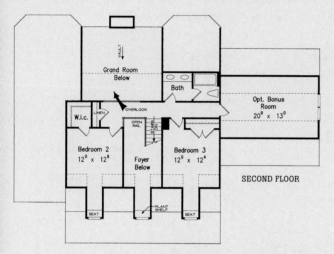

SECOND FLOOR

FIRST FLOOR

plan# HPK0900009

Style: Cape Cod
First Floor: 1,771 sq. ft.
Second Floor: 627 sq. ft.
Total: 2,398 sq. ft.
Bonus Space: 285 sq. ft.
Bedrooms: 4
Bathrooms: 3
Width: 65' - 0"
Depth: 49' - 0"
Foundation: Crawlspace, Basement

SEARCH ONLINE @ EPLANS.COM

This handsome bungalow is very practical, yet comfortable, for the active family. The kitchen, dining area, and living room are organized for great efficiency in preparing and serving meals and snacks, and for warm social and family gatherings. The dining nook opens to the rear patio through a sliding glass door, and the living room looks through a bay window onto the front covered porch. Columns separate the kitchen and dining area from the living room, which features a vaulted ceiling and fireplace. A vaulted ceiling soars above the master bedchamber; the adjoining private bath enjoys a dual-sink vanity and a combined shower/tub. Two other bedrooms share a bath.

plan# HPK0900010

Style: Bungalow
Square Footage: 1,275
Bedrooms: 3
Bathrooms: 2
Width: 40' - 0"
Depth: 58' - 0"
Foundation: Crawlspace

SEARCH ONLINE @ EPLANS.COM

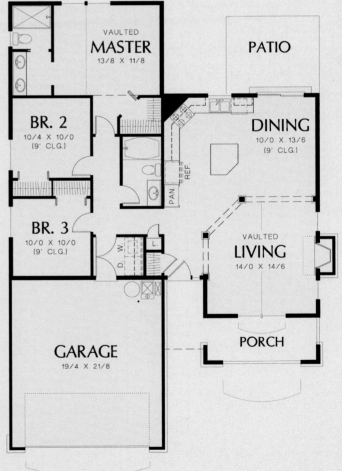

Modest living at its best, this unassuming exterior reveals a practical, contemporary design. A fireplace in the vaulted family room warms the space. A side patio and covered porch offers outdoor living space. The kichen bar conveniently serves the adjoining dining room. A hallway leads to the master suite on the left and a second bedroom and hall bath on the right. The vaulted master suite boasts sliding door access to a private sitting room. An optional layout offers a sunroom.

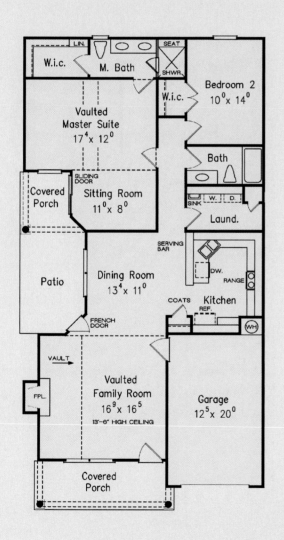

OPTIONAL LAYOUT

plan# **HPK0900011**

Style: Craftsman
Square Footage: 1,393
Bedrooms: 2
Bathrooms: 2
Width: 32' - 0"
Depth: 63' - 0"
Foundation: Slab, Basement

SEARCH ONLINE @ EPLANS.COM

A quaint cottage for seasonal use or year-round, this design is appealing, yet practical. The open floor plan combines the living spaces, allowing the kitchen to serve the dining and great rooms and a central fireplace to warm the entire space. The first-floor master bedroom enjoys a dual-sink vanity, a spa tub with separate shower, a compartmented toilet, and a walk-in closet with built-in shelves. Upstairs, two additional bedrooms share a full bath. A workshop area in the garage is an added bonus.

plan # HPK0900012

Style: Craftsman
First Floor: 1,603 sq. ft.
Second Floor: 471 sq. ft.
Total: 2,074 sq. ft.
Bedrooms: 3
Bathrooms: 2½
Width: 50' - 0"
Depth: 56' - 0"
Foundation: Crawlspace

SEARCH ONLINE @ EPLANS.COM

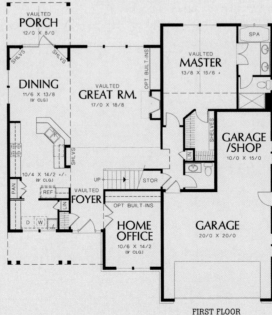

SECOND FLOOR

FIRST FLOOR

This charming one-story plan features a facade that is accented by a stone pediment and a shed-dormer window. Inside, elegant touches grace the efficient floor plan. Vaulted ceilings adorn the great room and master bedroom, and a 10-foot tray ceiling highlights the foyer. One of the front bedrooms makes a perfect den; another accesses a full hall bath with a linen closet. The great room, which opens to the porch, includes a fireplace and a media niche. The dining room offers outdoor access and built-ins for ultimate convenience.

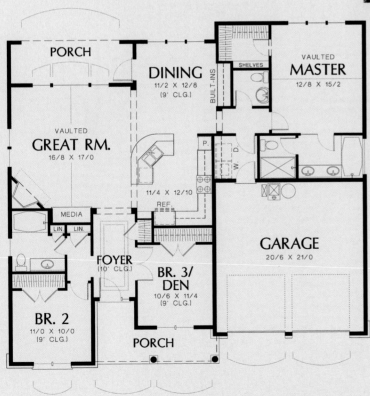

plan # HPK0900013

Style: Country Cottage
Square Footage: 1,580
Bedrooms: 3
Bathrooms: 2½
Width: 50' - 0"
Depth: 48' - 0"
Foundation: Crawlspace

SEARCH ONLINE @ EPLANS.COM

Don't be fooled by the small-looking exterior. This plan offers three bedrooms and plenty of living space. Notice that the screened porch leads to a rear terrace with access to the breakfast room. A living room/dining room combination adds spaciousness to the floor plan. Other welcome amenities include boxed windows in the breakfast room and dining room, a fireplace in the living room, a planning desk and pass-through snack bar in the kitchen, a whirlpool tub in the master bath, and an open two-story foyer. The thoughtfully placed flower box, beyond the kitchen window above the sink, adds a homespun touch to this already comfortable design.

plan # HPK0900014

L

Style: Country Cottage
First Floor: 1,111 sq. ft.
Second Floor: 886 sq. ft.
Total: 1,997 sq. ft.
Bedrooms: 3
Bathrooms: 2½
Width: 32' - 8"
Depth: 50' - 0"
Foundation: Basement

SEARCH ONLINE @ EPLANS.COM

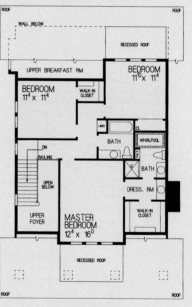

SECOND FLOOR

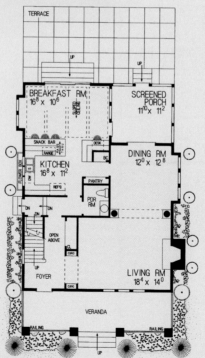

FIRST FLOOR

This uniquely designed home, which will win applause from your neighbors, very effectively breaks down the boundary between indoors and outdoors. Walls of windows facing the expansive rear deck not only bring superb views from all the living areas; they also bring in cascades of sunlight. From the living room, a bumped-out sunroom extends onto the deck—a perfect place for your favorite plants. The master suite is large enough for a sitting area and enjoys a resplendent bath with all the comforts designed to please. An island snack counter and open space to the dining area make serving meals a breeze. The upstairs bath with a dual-sink vanity serves two bedrooms with a hallway entry. Both rooms share access to a cozy sitting room. A laundry and nearby half-bath are located on the first floor.

SECOND FLOOR

FIRST FLOOR

plan# HPK0900015

Style: Contemporary
First Floor: 1,405 sq. ft.
Second Floor: 695 sq. ft.
Total: 2,100 sq. ft.
Bedrooms: 3
Bathrooms: 2½
Width: 60' - 0"
Depth: 46' - 0"
Foundation: Basement

SEARCH ONLINE @ EPLANS.COM

For sheer comfort and relaxation, this quaint two-story country home fills the bill. Tired and want to be soothed? Slip into the hot tub surrounded by windows and easily entered from the covered front porch or the master suite. Want to lay back and read? Settle into a comfy chair on the second-floor mezzanine between two family bedrooms. Looking for a snack? Sit up at the island counter in the country-size kitchen. Luxury reigns in the master bath, which boasts an oversize garden tub, double-sink vanity, compartmented toilet, and pentagonal shower. A sunny alcove in the front living room adds a special touch.

plan # HPK0900016

Style: Lakefront
First Floor: 1,539 sq. ft.
Second Floor: 705 sq. ft.
Total: 2,244 sq. ft.
Bedrooms: 3
Bathrooms: 2½
Width: 54' - 0"
Depth: 50' - 0"
Foundation: Basement

SEARCH ONLINE @ EPLANS.COM

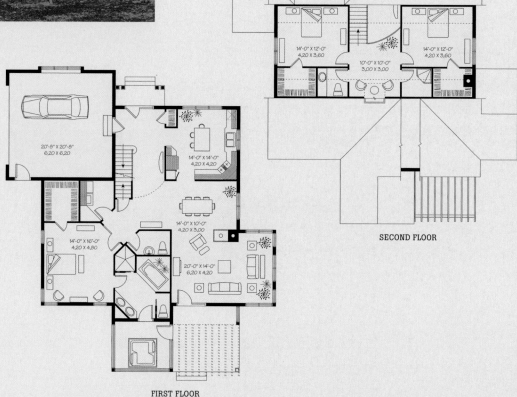

SECOND FLOOR

FIRST FLOOR

rear exterior

As a cozy mountain cabin or a refreshing lake retreat, this comfy home is designed for privacy and total relaxation. Highlighting the home is a gourmet kitchen with a cooktop island and an adjoining snack bar for casual meals. A dining room is nearby and opens to the spacious gathering room with a fireplace and side-porch access. A grand master suite uses unique angles and a luxury bath to add subtle style. Up the central stairs, a bedroom enjoys a full bath and quiet loft reading area. Above the garage (but accessed from the interior) apartment-style sleeping quarters include a separate bedroom and living area and a full bath.

plan # HPK0900017

Style: Farmhouse
First Floor: 1,232 sq. ft.
Second Floor: 987 sq. ft.
Total: 2,219 sq. ft.
Bedrooms: 3
Bathrooms: 3½
Width: 67' - 0"
Depth: 40' - 0"
Foundation: Basement

SEARCH ONLINE @ EPLANS.COM

SECOND FLOOR

12'-8" X 11'-8"
3,80 X 3,50

11'-8" X 12'-0"
3,50 X 3,60

9'-4" X 12'-0"
2,80 X 3,60

10'-0" X 13'-0"
3,00 X 3,90

FIRST FLOOR

22'-0" X 23'-8"
6,60 X 7,10

14'-8" X 12'-0"
4,80 X 3,60

16'-0" X 22'-8"
4,80 X 6,80

14'-8" X 12'-0"
4,40 X 3,60

Under hipped roofs and behind a rustic brick facade is a cozy living area your family will want to call home. An unexpectedly extravagant bath with both a shower and tub is sure to soothe. Two bedrooms, the larger with a walk-in closet, are on the right side of the house. The family chef will go wild with the walls of counter space and cabinets. A peninsula counter with a snack bar separates the kitchen from the combined dining and living rooms. Large windows on two sides of this area will let in plenty of sunshine. A front-entry, one-car garage completes this plan.

plan # HPK0900018

Style: Contemporary
Square Footage: 1,138
Bedrooms: 2
Bathrooms: 1
Width: 34' – 0"
Depth: 48' – 0"
Foundation: Basement

SEARCH ONLINE @ EPLANS.COM

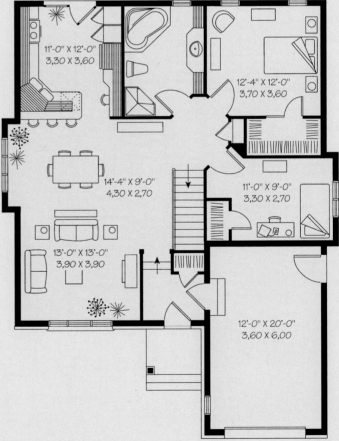

11'-0" X 12'-0"
3,30 X 3,60

12'-4" X 12'-0"
3,70 X 3,60

14'-4" X 9'-0"
4,30 X 2,70

11'-0" X 9'-0"
3,30 X 2,70

13'-0" X 13'-0"
3,90 X 3,90

12'-0" X 20'-0"
3,60 X 6,00

Looking for the perfect starter home? How about a great retreat? For anyone who wants a budget-friendly plan, this brick-and-siding design is a dream come true. The foyer is adorned by columns and a half-wall that gracefully separate it from the living room. The kitchen flows easily from here, with a step-saving layout and sliding glass doors that let the light in. Four bedrooms line the left side of the house and share a marvelous spa bath.

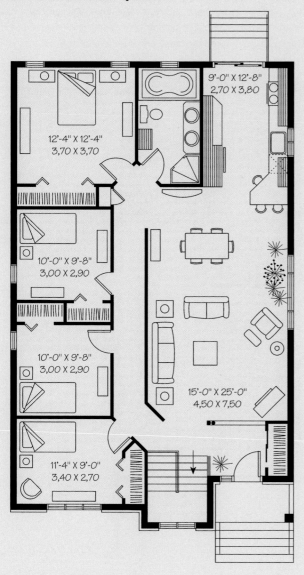

plan# HPK0900019

Style: Contemporary
Square Footage: 1,433
Bedrooms: 4
Bathrooms: 1
Width: 30' - 0"
Depth: 50' - 0"
Foundation: Basement

SEARCH ONLINE @ EPLANS.COM

For a starter home, this smart, compact plan makes good use of its nearly 1,200 square feet to provide comfort and convenience. Two good-sized bedrooms share hallway access to a luxurious bath. With a large corner garden tub, walk-in shower, and double-basin vanity, the bath is designed to pamper. The living room and dining area are separated by an impressive column; a bow-bay window floods the dining area with sunshine. With plenty of elbowroom, the kitchen makes food-preparation a joy. A snack bar handily serves breakfasts and light lunches. Extending across the front of the house, the handsome covered porch with stately pilasters beckons friends and neighbors to stop and stay awhile.

plan # HPK0900020

Style: Bungalow
Square Footage: 1,191
Bedrooms: 2
Bathrooms: 1
Width: 34' - 8"
Depth: 48' - 0"
Foundation: Basement

SEARCH ONLINE @ EPLANS.COM

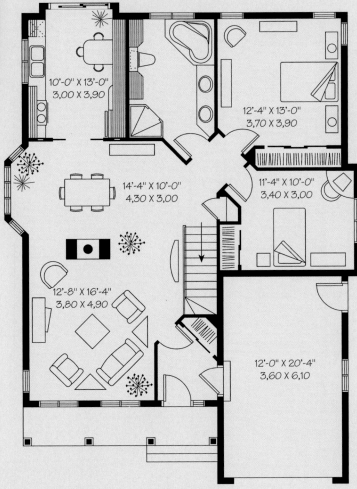

10'-0" X 13'-0"
3,00 X 3,90

12'-4" X 13'-0"
3,70 X 3,90

14'-4" X 10'-0"
4,30 X 3,00

11'-4" X 10'-0"
3,40 X 3,00

12'-8" X 16'-4"
3,80 X 4,90

12'-0" X 20'-4"
3,60 X 6,10

A traditional design with untraditional amenities, this mid-size home is sure to please. The front-facing den, enhanced by French doors, is bathed in natural light. The great room sits at the heart of the home with an optional media center in the corner and a central fireplace along the right wall. The open design leads nicely into the adjoining dining room and kitchen. An island cooktop/serving bar conveniently serves the area. A future deck is accessible from the breakfast nook. Upstairs, the spacious master suite boasts a dual-sink vanity, a spa tub, a separate shower, a compartmented toilet, and an enormous walk-in closet. Two additional family bedrooms share a full bath. A bonus room and a practical second-floor laundry room complete this level.

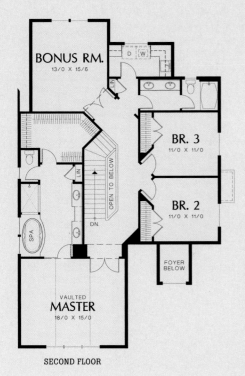

SECOND FLOOR

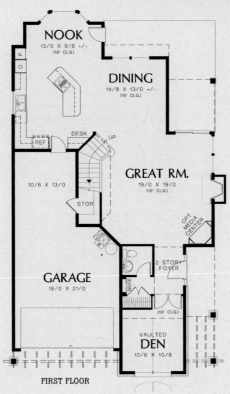

FIRST FLOOR

plan# HPK0900021

Style: Craftsman
First Floor: 1,204 sq. ft.
Second Floor: 1,264 sq. ft.
Total: 2,468 sq. ft.
Bonus Space: 213 sq. ft.
Bedrooms: 3
Bathrooms: 2½
Width: 35' - 0"
Depth: 63' - 0"
Foundation: Crawlspace

SEARCH ONLINE @ EPLANS.COM

Rustic details complement brick and siding on the exterior of this home. The interior features vaulted living and family rooms and a convenient kitchen separating the dining and breakfast rooms. The living room provides a fireplace flanked by radius windows, while a French door in the breakfast room opens to the rear property. A bedroom to the back could be used as a study. Second-floor bedrooms include a master suite with a sitting area.

plan # HPK0900022

Style: Country Cottage
First Floor: 1,279 sq. ft.
Second Floor: 1,071 sq. ft.
Total: 2,350 sq. ft.
Bedrooms: 4
Bathrooms: 3
Width: 50' - 0"
Depth: 42' - 6"
Foundation: Crawlspace, Basement

SEARCH ONLINE @ EPLANS.COM

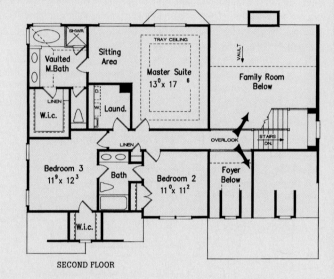

SECOND FLOOR

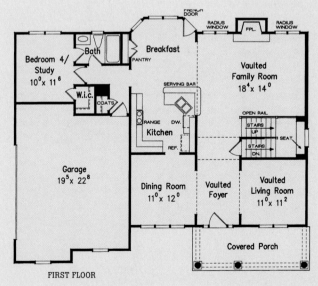

FIRST FLOOR

A combination of stone, siding, and multiple rooflines creates a cottage feel to this large home. Inside, the grand room and keeping room feature fireplaces and vaulted ceilings—the grand room adds built-in cabinets and windows with transoms. A sumptuous master suite enjoys a sitting room, a tray ceiling, and a lavish private bath featuring a shower with a built-in seat. The gourmet kitchen enjoys an island countertop, a serving bar, and a walk-in pantry, which accesses the three-car garage. Three additional bedrooms are found upstairs with two full baths—Bedrooms 3 and 4 each include large walk-in closets.

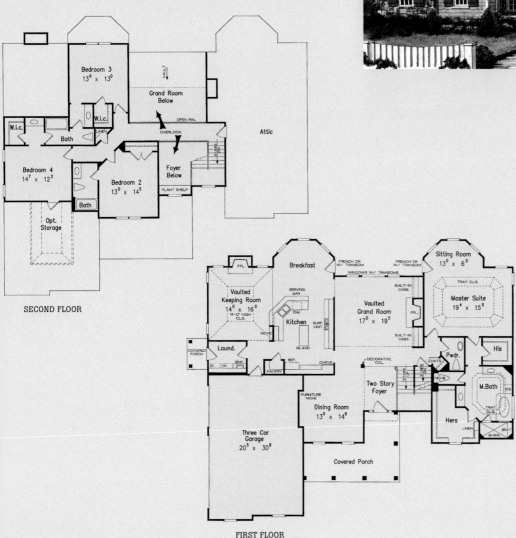

SECOND FLOOR

FIRST FLOOR

plan# HPK0900023

Style: Country Cottage
First Floor: 2,293 sq. ft.
Second Floor: 992 sq. ft.
Total: 3,285 sq. ft.
Bonus Space: 131 sq. ft.
Bedrooms: 4
Bathrooms: 3½
Width: 71' - 0"
Depth: 62' - 0"
Foundation: Crawlspace, Basement

SEARCH ONLINE @ EPLANS.COM

A covered porch welcomes family and friends to this appealing plan. Inside, arches create a formal air in the dining room and a vaulted ceiling adds space to the family room. A bay window brightens the breakfast room, which opens to the rear property. The first-floor master suite features a tray ceiling and a large private bath with a walk-in closet. Two second-floor family bedrooms, both with walk-in closets, share a full bath.

plan# HPK0900024

Style: Country Cottage
First Floor: 1,458 sq. ft.
Second Floor: 516 sq. ft.
Total: 1,974 sq. ft.
Bonus Space: 168 sq. ft.
Bedrooms: 3
Bathrooms: 2½
Width: 50' - 0"
Depth: 46' - 0"
Foundation: Crawlspace, Basement

SEARCH ONLINE @ EPLANS.COM

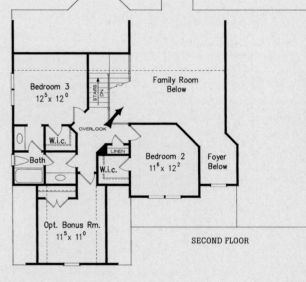

SECOND FLOOR

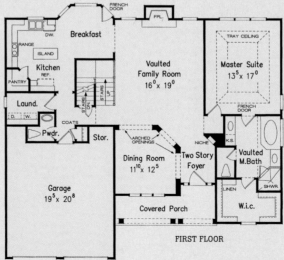

FIRST FLOOR

Stone accents and sturdy columns highlight this traditional home's facade. Interior highlights include a fireplace in the two-story family room, a French door in the breakfast nook, and a central work island in the kitchen. Upstairs, three family bedrooms and a full bath surround the lavish master suite—a tray ceiling adds elegance to the bedroom, and a vaulted ceiling enhances the private bath. An alternative layout converts one of the family bedrooms into a cozy master-suite sitting room with built-in cabinets.

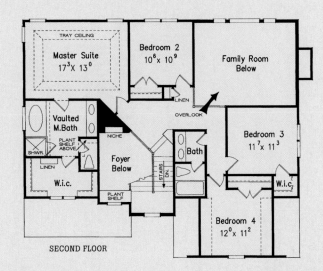

SECOND FLOOR

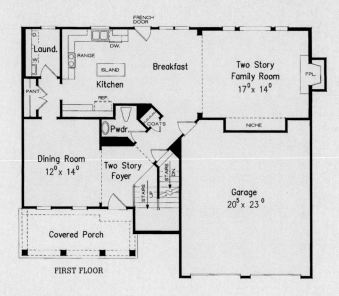

FIRST FLOOR

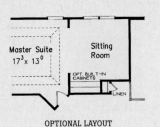

OPTIONAL LAYOUT

plan# HPK0900025

Style: Country Cottage
First Floor: 1,094 sq. ft.
Second Floor: 1,128 sq. ft.
Total: 2,222 sq. ft.
Bedrooms: 4
Bathrooms: 2½
Width: 48' - 4"
Depth: 40' - 0"
Foundation: Crawlspace, Basement

SEARCH ONLINE @ EPLANS.COM

Shingles and stone decorate the exterior of this charming design. Inside, decorative columns separate the living and dining rooms. The kitchen includes a pantry and a work island; the breakfast nook is conveniently nearby. Built-in cabinets flank the fireplace in the two-story family room. One family bedroom resides on the first floor, while the master suite and a second family bedroom are upstairs. An optional bonus room completes the second floor.

plan# HPK0900026

Style: Country Cottage
First Floor: 1,293 sq. ft.
Second Floor: 922 sq. ft.
Total: 2,215 sq. ft.
Bonus Space: 235 sq. ft.
Bedrooms: 3
Bathrooms: 3
Width: 40' - 0"
Depth: 57' - 0"
Foundation: Crawlspace, Basement

SEARCH ONLINE @ EPLANS.COM

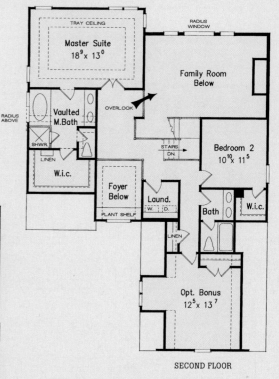

SECOND FLOOR

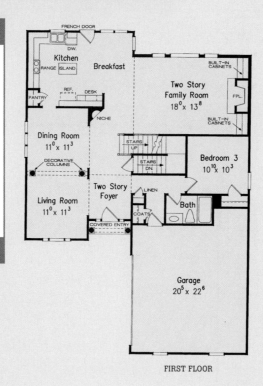

FIRST FLOOR

Shingle siding and quaint shutters open this three-bedroom plan. The interior revolves around a vaulted family room, which opens to a formal dining room. The island kitchen easily serves the breakfast area and the dining room. A vaulted study sits to the front of the first floor; the master suite sits to the back. Note the vaulted master bath with His and Hers walk-in closets, a separate shower and tub, and two vanities. Two family bedrooms on the second floor share a full bath. An optional bonus room of 235 square feet can become a fourth bedroom later.

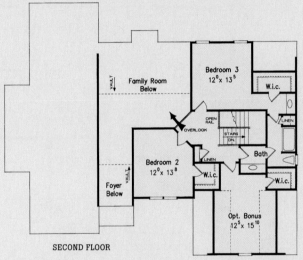

SECOND FLOOR

FIRST FLOOR

plan # HPK0900027

Style: Cape Cod
First Floor: 1,788 sq. ft.
Second Floor: 639 sq. ft.
Total: 2,427 sq. ft.
Bonus Space: 235 sq. ft.
Bedrooms: 3
Bathrooms: 2½
Width: 59' - 0"
Depth: 51' - 0"
Foundation: Crawlspace, Basement

SEARCH ONLINE @ EPLANS.COM

This cozy Craftsman plan conveniently separates living and sleeping quarters, with family living areas on the first floor and bedrooms on the second. The plan begins with a vaulted living/dining room, and moves on to a great room that provides a fireplace flanked by built-ins. The adjacent kitchen includes a built-in desk and adjoins a breakfast nook that opens to the rear property. To the rear of the plan, the den can be converted to a fourth bedroom. Upstairs, a master suite—with a spa tub and walk-in closet with built-in shelves—joins two bedrooms and a vaulted bonus room.

plan # HPK0900028

Style: Craftsman
First Floor: 1,252 sq. ft.
Second Floor: 985 sq. ft.
Total: 2,237 sq. ft.
Bonus Space: 183 sq. ft.
Bedrooms: 4
Bathrooms: 3
Width: 40' - 0"
Depth: 51' - 0"
Foundation: Crawlspace, Basement

SEARCH ONLINE @ EPLANS.COM

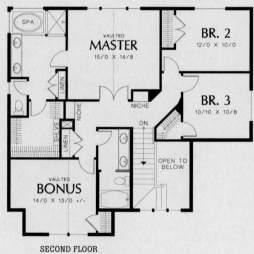

SECOND FLOOR

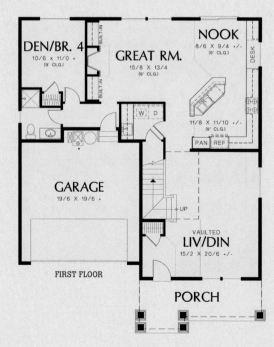

FIRST FLOOR

Ideal for a narrow lot,

this Bungalow offers an open design with a practical flow. The first floor is highlighted by an island-cooktop, U-shaped kitchen that conveniently serves the adjacent family room, breakfast nook, and nearby dining room. Upstairs houses the master suite, two additional family bedrooms, a full bath, and an optional fourth bedroom/loft. A built-in bench on the front porch is perfect for outdoor gatherings.

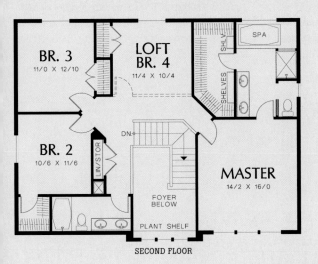

BR. 3
11/0 X 12/10

LOFT
BR. 4
11/4 X 10/4

SPA

SHELVES

BR. 2
10/6 X 11/6

LIN/STOR

DN

MASTER
14/2 X 16/0

FOYER
BELOW

PLANT SHELF

SECOND FLOOR

NOOK
9/0 X 10/0
(9' CLG.)

FAMILY
16/0 X 14/0
(9' CLG.)

BUILT-IN

DINING
10/8 X 13/10
(9' CLG.)

REF.

10/0 X 14/0
(9' CLG.)

DESK

O.

PANTRY

STOR

W/D

LIVING
14/2 X 15/8
(9' CLG.)

UP

GARAGE
22/0 X 21/6

BENCH

FIRST FLOOR

plan# HPK0900029

Style: Craftsman
First Floor: 1,255 sq. ft.
Second Floor: 1,128 sq. ft.
Total: 2,383 sq. ft.
Bedrooms: 4
Bathrooms: 2½
Width: 47' - 0"
Depth: 48' - 0"
Foundation: Crawlspace

SEARCH ONLINE @ EPLANS.COM

Triple dormers highlight a

perfectly modern twist of historic style with this stately country facade. Formal rooms frame the two-story foyer, which leads to an open great room. This airy space, capped with a vaulted ceiling, is anchored by a fireplace and enhanced by outdoor views. Decorative columns define the gourmet kitchen and vaulted breakfast nook, which leads out to the rear property. A private master suite offers plenty of wardrobe space and a walk-in closet, as well as a dual vanity. Upstairs, three secondary bedrooms share a compartmented bath and a gallery hall that leads to a spacious bonus room.

plan# HPK0900030

Style: Farmhouse
First Floor: 1,719 sq. ft.
Second Floor: 1,589 sq. ft.
Total: 3,308 sq. ft.
Bonus Space: 515 sq. ft.
Bedrooms: 4
Bathrooms: 4
Width: 65' - 0"
Depth: 52' - 0"
Foundation: Crawlspace

SEARCH ONLINE @ EPLANS.COM

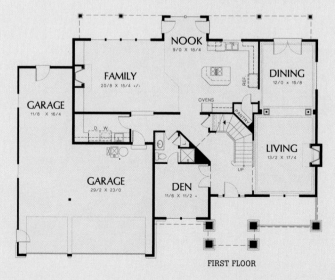

SECOND FLOOR

FIRST FLOOR

Perfect for a sloping lot, this Craftsman design boasts two levels of living space. Plenty of special amenities—vaulted ceilings in the living, dining, and family rooms, as well as in the master bedroom; built-ins in the family room and den; a large island cooktop in the kitchen; and an expansive rear deck—make this plan stand out. All three of the bedrooms—a main-level master suite and two lower-level bedrooms—include walk-in closets. Also on the lower level, find a recreation room with built-ins and a fireplace.

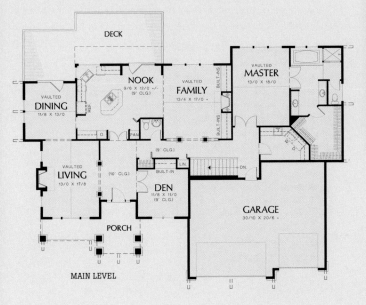

MAIN LEVEL

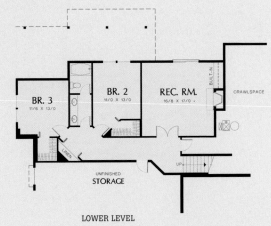

LOWER LEVEL

plan# HPK0900031

Style: Craftsman
Main Level: 2,170 sq. ft.
Lower Level: 1,076 sq. ft.
Total: 3,246 sq. ft.
Bedrooms: 3
Bathrooms: 2½
Width: 74' - 0"
Depth: 54' - 0"
Foundation: Slab, Basement

SEARCH ONLINE @ EPLANS.COM

Each room outdoes the next in this amenity-filled design. The spacious family room enjoys a central fireplace and access to a rear patio. The island kitchen features abundant counter space, a built-in desk, and access to a rear porch from the breakfast nook. A nearby butler's pantry services the dining room. The master suite, enhanced by a tray ceiling, boasts two walk-in closets, a dual-sink vanity, a compartmented toilet, a separate shower, and a garden tub. Upstairs houses a second family bedroom, a full bath, a cedar closet, and a bonus room. The basement features bedrooms 3 and 4, each with a full bath, two large storage spaces, a recreation room complete with a fireplace and wet bar, and a wine closet. A workshop in the garage is an added bonus.

plan ⊕ HPK0900032

Style: Craftsman
Main Level: 2,191 sq. ft.
Upper Level: 384 sq. ft.
Lower Level: 1,642 sq. ft.
Total: 4,217 sq. ft.
Bonus Space: 354 sq. ft.
Bedrooms: 4
Bathrooms: 4½
Width: 65' - 9"
Depth: 77' - 2"
Foundation: Basement

SEARCH ONLINE @ EPLANS.COM

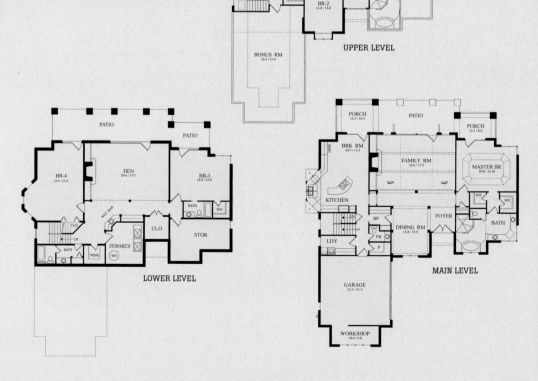

ORDER BLUEPRINTS 24 HOURS, 7 DAYS A WEEK, AT 1-800-521-6797

The columned foyer of this home welcomes you into a series of spaces that reach out in all directions. The living room has a spectacular view of the huge covered patio area that's perfect for summer entertaining. The dining room features a tray ceiling and French doors that lead to a covered porch. A secluded master suite affords great views through French doors and also has a tray ceiling. The family wing combines an island kitchen, nook, and family gathering space, with the built-in media/fireplace wall the center of attention. Two secondary bedrooms share a bath. A staircase overlooking the family room takes you up to the sunroom complete with a full bath.

plan# HPK0900033

Style: Mediterranean
First Floor: 2,365 sq. ft.
Second Floor: 364 sq. ft.
Total: 2,729 sq. ft.
Bedrooms: 3
Bathrooms: 3
Width: 69' - 0"
Depth: 70' - 0"
Foundation: Slab

SEARCH ONLINE @ EPLANS.COM

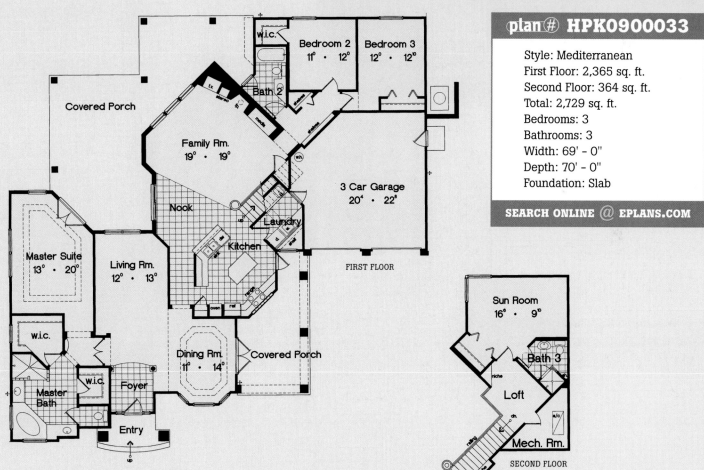

FIRST FLOOR

SECOND FLOOR

This charming country design puts its best foot forward by placing the two-car garage up front—thus protecting the living areas from most of the street noise. Inside, the living and dining areas flow together, defined by one simple column, letting the glow of the corner fireplace in the living area enhance any dinner party. The efficient kitchen has easy access to the garage and features a sink island and a pantry. The first-floor master suite offers a private bath and a walk-in closet, while a secondary bedroom accesses a hall bath. Upstairs, another spacious secondary bedroom provides a walk-in closet, private bath, and access to a large study area that over looks the living room below.

plan# HPK0900034

Style: Mediterranean
First Floor: 1,484 sq. ft.
Second Floor: 614 sq. ft.
Total: 2,098 sq. ft.
Bedrooms: 3
Bathrooms: 3
Width: 40' - 0"
Depth: 64' - 0"
Foundation: Slab

SEARCH ONLINE @ EPLANS.COM

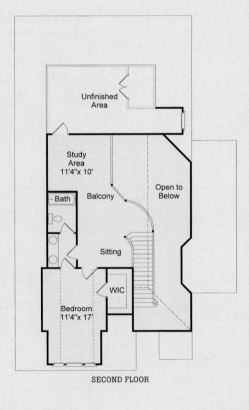

SECOND FLOOR

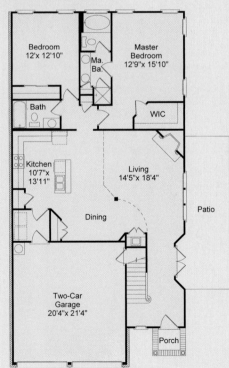

FIRST FLOOR

This charming home, well-suited to a narrow lot, features two unique dormer windows and a distinctive hipped roof. Inside, the expansive living room provides a corner fireplace as well as two sets of French doors that open to a side patio. Elegant columns introduce the dining area, which sits next to the efficient kitchen. The master bedroom boasts a walk-in closet and a private bath with a corner shower and whirlpool tub; a second bedroom, with access to a nearby bath, rounds out the first floor. Upstairs, one more bedroom opens to a balcony that overlooks the living room.

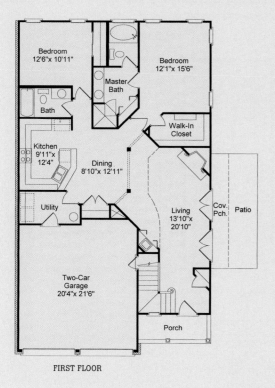

FIRST FLOOR

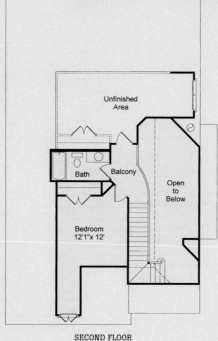

SECOND FLOOR

plan# HPK0900035

Style: Mediterranean
First Floor: 1,400 sq. ft.
Second Floor: 365 sq. ft.
Total: 1,765 sq. ft.
Bedrooms: 3
Bathrooms: 3
Width: 42' - 0"
Depth: 58' - 0"
Foundation: Slab

SEARCH ONLINE @ EPLANS.COM

This two-level cottage will be a grand place to spend as much of your free time as possible. Rustic, but elegant, it includes first- and second-level porches. The lower level comprises a workshop and two garages with combined space for three vehicles. The upper level is especially designed for relaxed entertaining. A spacious living room with a fireplace and vaulted ceiling flows into the dining area lighted by a bay window. Both are separated from the kitchen by a long, curved snack bar. The master bedroom soars 16 feet to the top of its vaulted ceiling and has its own entry to the home's bathroom. The bath can also be entered from the dining area through a hallway that also opens to a convenient utility room, linen closet, and laundry area.

plan# HPK0900036

Style: Lakefront
Main Level: 1,029 sq. ft.
Lower Level: 40 sq. ft.
Total: 1,069 sq. ft.
Bedrooms: 1
Bathrooms: 1
Width: 39' - 2"
Depth: 33' - 0"
Foundation: Slab

SEARCH ONLINE @ EPLANS.COM

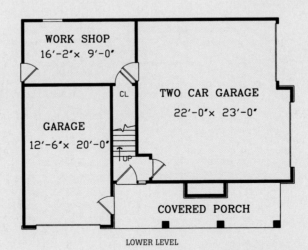

MAIN LEVEL

LOWER LEVEL

With the Craftsman stylings of a mountain lodge, this rustic four-bedroom home is full of surprises. The foyer opens to the right to the great room, warmed by a stone hearth. A corner media center is convenient for entertaining. The dining room, with a furniture alcove, opens to the side terrace, inviting meals alfresco. An angled kitchen provides lots of room to move. The master suite is expansive, with French doors, a private bath, and spa tub. On the lower level, two bedrooms share a bath; a third enjoys a private suite. The games room includes a fireplace, media center, wet bar, and wine cellar. Don't miss the storage capacity and work area in the garage.

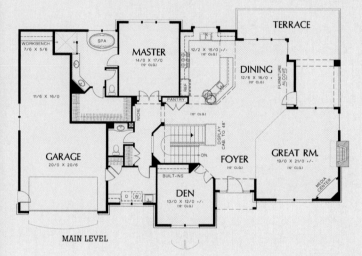

MAIN LEVEL

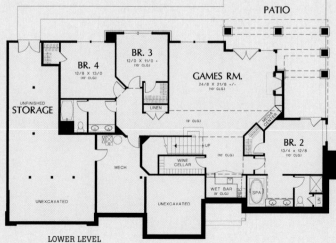

LOWER LEVEL

plan# HPK0900037

Style: Craftsman
Main Level: 2,172 sq. ft.
Lower Level: 1,813 sq. ft.
Total: 3,985 sq. ft.
Bedrooms: 4
Bathrooms: 3½
Width: 75' - 0"
Depth: 49' - 0"
Foundation: Basement

SEARCH ONLINE @ EPLANS.COM

plan# HPK0900038

Style: Seaside
Square Footage: 2,430
Bedrooms: 3
Bathrooms: 3
Width: 70' - 2"
Depth: 53' - 0"
Foundation: Basement

SEARCH ONLINE @ EPLANS.COM

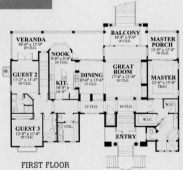

FIRST FLOOR

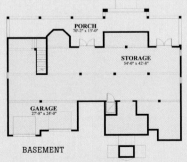

BASEMENT

plan# HPK0900039

Style: Italianate
First Floor: 1,266 sq. ft.
Second Floor: 1,324 sq. ft.
Total: 2,590 sq. ft.
Bedrooms: 3
Bathrooms: 2½
Width: 34' - 0"
Depth: 63' - 2"
Foundation: Slab

SEARCH ONLINE @ EPLANS.COM

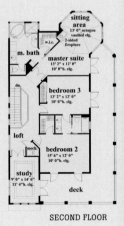

SECOND FLOOR

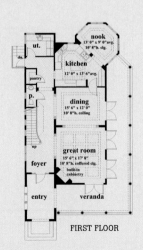

FIRST FLOOR

plan# HPK0900040

Style: Bungalow
First Floor: 1,342 sq. ft.
Second Floor: 511 sq. ft.
Total: 1,853 sq. ft.
Bedrooms: 3
Bathrooms: 2
Width: 44' - 0"
Depth: 40' - 0"
Foundation: Basement

SEARCH ONLINE @ EPLANS.COM

plan# HPK0900041

Style: Bungalow
First Floor: 1,798 sq. ft.
Second Floor: 900 sq. ft.
Total: 2,698 sq. ft.
Bedrooms: 3
Bathrooms: 3
Width: 54' - 0"
Depth: 57' - 0"
Foundation: Crawlspace

SEARCH ONLINE @ EPLANS.COM

SECOND FLOOR

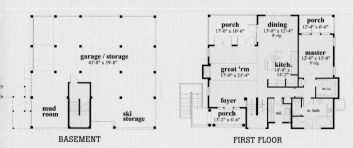

BASEMENT

FIRST FLOOR

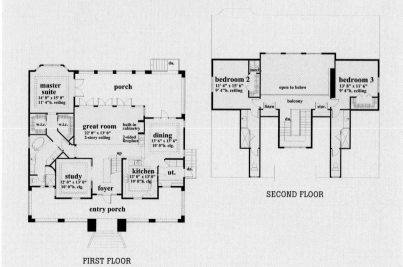

FIRST FLOOR

SECOND FLOOR

Though this home gives the impression of the Northwest, it will be the winner of any neighborhood. From the foyer, the two-story living room is just a couple of steps up and features a through-fireplace. The U-shaped kitchen has a cooktop work island, an adjacent nook, and easy access to the formal dining room. A spacious family room shares the fireplace with the living room, is enhanced by built-ins, and also offers a quiet deck for stargazing. The upstairs consists of two family bedrooms sharing a full bath and a vaulted master suite complete with a walk-in closet and sumptuous bath. A two-car, drive-under garage has plenty of room for storage.

plan # HPK0900042

Style: Craftsman
First Floor: 872 sq. ft.
Second Floor: 1,106 sq. ft.
Total: 1,978 sq. ft.
Bedrooms: 3
Bathrooms: 2½
Width: 38' - 0"
Depth: 35' - 0"
Foundation: Slab, Basement

SEARCH ONLINE @ EPLANS.COM

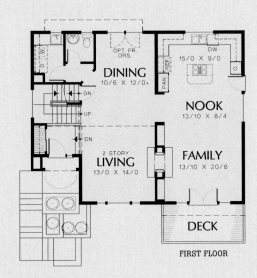

SECOND FLOOR

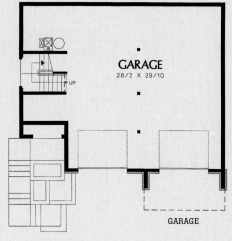

GARAGE

FIRST FLOOR

Shingles, stone, and gables are all elements of fine Craftsman styling, beautifully demonstrated on this three-bedroom home. The foyer is flanked by a formal dining room and a cozy den. A galley kitchen is open to the spacious gathering room and sunny, bayed nook. Upstairs, the secondary bedrooms share a hall bath. The master suite is full of amenities, including a sitting area with a private balcony, and a luxurious bath. A bonus room is located above the garage, perfect for a playroom, home office, or guest room.

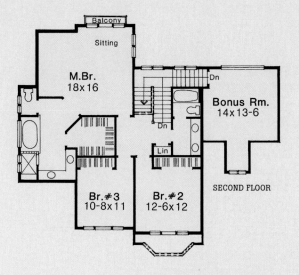

SECOND FLOOR

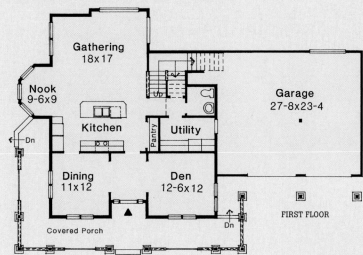

FIRST FLOOR

plan# HPK0900043

Style: NW Contemporary
First Floor: 1,170 sq. ft.
Second Floor: 1,091 sq. ft.
Total: 2,261 sq. ft.
Bonus Space: 240 sq. ft.
Bedrooms: 3
Bathrooms: 2½
Width: 66' - 0"
Depth: 46' - 0"
Foundation: Crawlspace

SEARCH ONLINE @ EPLANS.COM

plan# HPK0900044

Style: Craftsman
First Floor: 1,072 sq. ft.
Second Floor: 1,101 sq. ft.
Total: 2,173 sq. ft.
Bedrooms: 4
Bathrooms: 2½
Width: 40' – 0"
Depth: 48' – 0"
Foundation: Crawlspace

SEARCH ONLINE @ EPLANS.COM

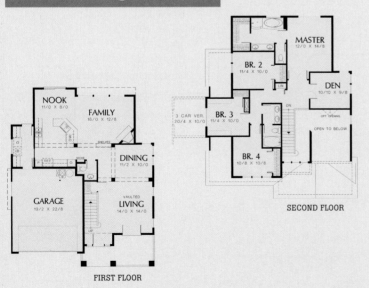

FIRST FLOOR

SECOND FLOOR

plan# HPK0900045

Style: Country Cottage
First Floor: 737 sq. ft.
Second Floor: 840 sq. ft.
Total: 1,577 sq. ft.
Bedrooms: 3
Bathrooms: 2½
Width: 36' – 0"
Depth: 42' – 0"
Foundation: Basement, Slab

SEARCH ONLINE @ EPLANS.COM

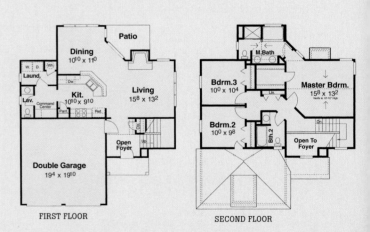

FIRST FLOOR

SECOND FLOOR

The contemporary look of this modern country design is both impressive and unique. Enormous windows brighten and enliven every interior space. The vaulted family room features a fireplace, and a two-sided fireplace warms the formal living and dining rooms. The gourmet island kitchen is open to a nook. Double doors open to a den that accesses a front deck. Upstairs, the master bedroom features a private bath with linen storage and a walk-in closet. Two family bedrooms share a Jack-and-Jill bath. The two-car garage features a storage area on the lower level.

BR. 2
10/0 X 12/6

BR. 3
10/8 X 12/6

LINEN

LINEN

DN

WINDOW SEAT

VAULTED
MASTER
13/8 X 14/6

OPEN TO LIVING RM BELOW

SECOND FLOOR

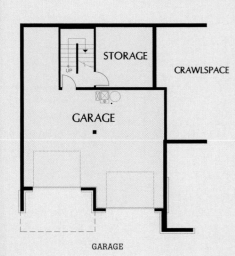

STORAGE

CRAWLSPACE

UP

GARAGE

GARAGE

DINING
10/10 X 13/6 +/-
(9' CLG)

KIT.
13/10 X 13/6 +/-

NOOK
10/0 X 10/0
(9' CLG)

UP DN

REF.

O.

PAN.

DN

VAULTED
FAMILY
13/4 X 14/8

WET BAR

DN

DEN
13/6 X 12/2
(9' CLG)

VAULTED
LIVING RM
13/0 X 17/10

DECK

FIRST FLOOR

plan# HPK0900046

Style: Craftsman
First Floor: 1,501 sq. ft.
Second Floor: 921 sq. ft.
Total: 2,422 sq. ft.
Bedrooms: 3
Bathrooms: 2½
Width: 52' - 0"
Depth: 36' - 0"
Foundation: Basement, Crawlspace

SEARCH ONLINE @ EPLANS.COM

This vacation home is certain to be a family favorite. The two-story great room boasts a built-in media center, access to a front deck, and a two-sided fireplace, shared by the adjacent den. The spacious island kitchen is ideal for entertaining. The second floor houses the master suite, two additional family bedrooms, and a full bath. A workshop and extra storage space in the garage are added bonuses.

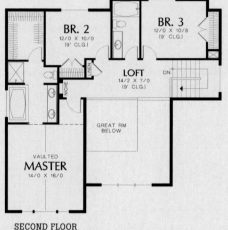

SECOND FLOOR

plan # HPK0900047

Style: Craftsman
First Floor: 1,302 sq. ft.
Second Floor: 960 sq. ft.
Total: 2,262 sq. ft.
Bedrooms: 3
Bathrooms: 2½
Width: 40' - 0"
Depth: 40' - 0"
Foundation: Crawlspace

SEARCH ONLINE @ EPLANS.COM

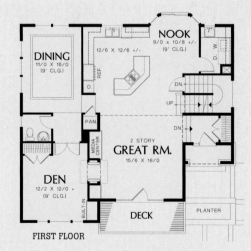

FIRST FLOOR

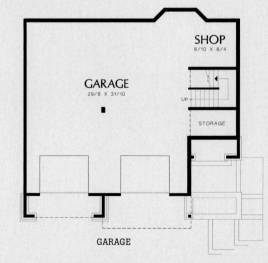

GARAGE

plan# HPK0900048

Style: Craftsman
First Floor: 897 sq. ft.
Second Floor: 740 sq. ft.
Total: 1,637 sq. ft.
Bedrooms: 3
Bathrooms: 2½
Width: 30' – 0"
Depth: 42' – 6"
Foundation: Basement

SEARCH ONLINE @ EPLANS.COM

BR. 2
10/0 X 12/0

BR. 3
10/0 X 12/0

LINEN

DN.

LINEN
W/D

OPEN TO BELOW

(VAULTED)
MASTER
14/10 X 12/2

SECOND FLOOR

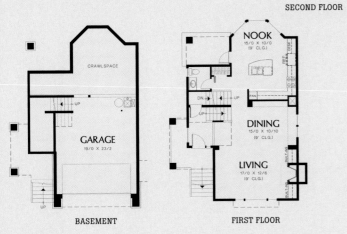

CRAWLSPACE

UP

GARAGE
19/0 X 23/2

UP

BASEMENT

NOOK
15/0 X 10/0
(9' CLG.)

DN.
UP
UP
PAN.

DINING
15/0 X 10/10
(9' CLG.)

LIVING
17/0 X 12/6
(9' CLG.)

FIRST FLOOR

plan# HPK0900049

Style: Country Cottage
First Floor: 576 sq. ft.
Second Floor: 576 sq. ft.
Total: 1,152 sq. ft.
Bedrooms: 1
Bathrooms: 1½
Width: 24' – 0"
Depth: 24' – 0"
Foundation: Crawlspace

SEARCH ONLINE @ EPLANS.COM

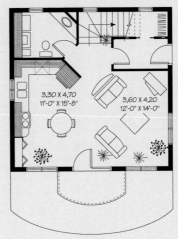

3,30 X 4,70
11'-0" X 15'-8"

3,60 X 4,20
12'-0" X 14'-0"

4,00 X 3,80
13'-4" X 12'-8"

4,50 X 3,60
15'-0" X 12'-0"

FIRST FLOOR

SECOND FLOOR

Combine a shingled exterior and an upstairs deck, and you can recall the joy of seaside vacations. Let breezes ruffle your hair and ocean spray settle on your skin in this comfortable two-story home. Unique window treatments provide views from every room. The lifestyle is casual, including meals prepared in a kitchen separated from the living room by a snack-bar counter. A powder room and a wet bar complete the upstairs. The first floor houses two bedrooms, a full bath and a laundry room. A walk-in closet enhances one of the bedrooms that could serve as the master suite. Built-ins make the most of compact space.

plan # HPK0900050

Style: Bungalow
First Floor: 507 sq. ft.
Second Floor: 438 sq. ft.
Total: 945 sq. ft.
Bedrooms: 2
Bathrooms: 1½
Width: 20' – 0"
Depth: 26' – 0"
Foundation: Crawlspace

SEARCH ONLINE @ EPLANS.COM

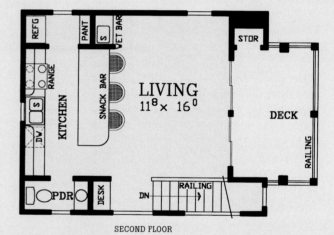

SECOND FLOOR

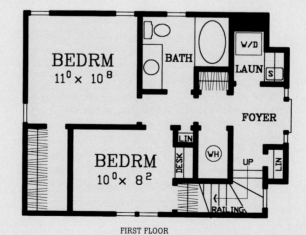

FIRST FLOOR

PHOTO COURTESY OF: ARTHUR MANNS HARDEN ARCHITECTS

This vacation home enjoys a screened porch and sits on stilts to avoid any water damage. Truly a free-flowing plan, the dining room, living room, and kitchen share a common space, with no walls separating them. An island snack counter in the kitchen provides plenty of space for food preparation. A family bedroom and full bath complete the first level. Upstairs, two additional bedrooms—with ample closet space—share a lavish bath, which includes a whirlpool tub and separate shower.

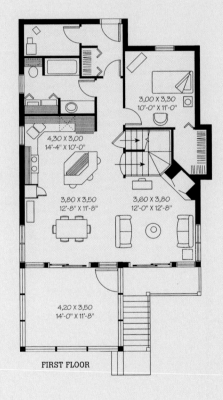

3,00 X 3,30
10'-0" X 11'-0"

4,30 X 3,00
14'-4" X 10'-0"

3,80 X 3,50
12'-8" X 11'-8"

3,60 X 3,80
12'-0" X 12'-8"

4,20 X 3,50
14'-0" X 11'-8"

FIRST FLOOR

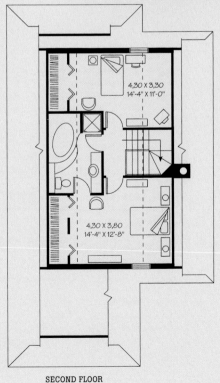

4,30 X 3,30
14'-4" X 11'-0"

4,30 X 3,80
14'-4" X 12'-8"

SECOND FLOOR

plan# HPK0900051

Style: Resort Lifestyles
First Floor: 908 sq. ft.
Second Floor: 576 sq. ft.
Total: 1,484 sq. ft.
Bedrooms: 3
Bathrooms: 2
Width: 26' - 0"
Depth: 36' - 0"
Foundation: Basement

SEARCH ONLINE @ EPLANS.COM

Run up a flight of stairs to an attractive four-bedroom home! The living room features a fireplace and easy access to the L-shaped kitchen. Here, a work island makes meal preparation a breeze. Two family bedrooms share a full bath and access to the laundry facilities. Upstairs, a third bedroom offers a private bath and two walk-in closets. The master suite is complete with a pampering bath, two walk-in closets, and a large private balcony.

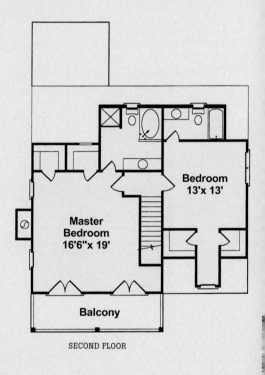

SECOND FLOOR

plan # HPK0900052

Style: Seaside
First Floor: 1,056 sq. ft.
Second Floor: 807 sq. ft.
Total: 1,863 sq. ft.
Bedrooms: 4
Bathrooms: 3
Width: 33' - 0"
Depth: 54' - 0"
Foundation: Crawlspace, Pier (same as Piling)

SEARCH ONLINE @ EPLANS.COM

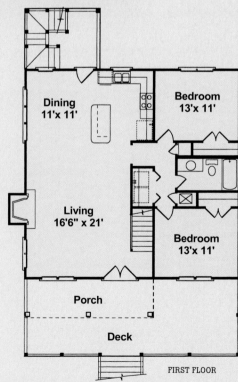

FIRST FLOOR

PHOTO COURTESY OF CHATHAM HOME PLANNING, INC.

ORDER BLUEPRINTS 24 HOURS, 7 DAYS A WEEK, AT 1-800-521-6797

Comforts of Home:
Homes with Multiple Bedroom Suites

Getaway homes can be magnetic attractions for visitors from far and near. After all, one of the reasons for building a vacation place is to find time to relax with family and friends. What better way to welcome them than with their own private suite where they can retreat by themselves? Inviting overnight guests to share your getaway with you and making them feel welcome is a snap when you plan ahead. Give your guests ample space for sleeping, reading, storing their personal items, and if at all possible, a bathroom of their own. Create a private haven that is as welcoming as the rest of your vacation house and guests will be sure to come. But be forewarned—they might never want to leave.

Cheerful paint and access to the outdoors characterize this gorgeous room (page 116).

Double columns grace the front porch of this shingled home, which showcases a turret, a balcony, and a variety of window treatments.

Special Effects

Filled with today's most-wanted amenities, this four-bedroom home is fit for royalty

Everyone wants a wonderful master suite where they can kick back, relax, and forget their cares. Nowhere is that more true than a getaway home, but this plan takes it a step further—that feeling of luxury prevails throughout every room, including a comfortable first-floor guest suite.

It begins from the facade, where the shapes and angles that come

Wicker chairs and a weathered bookcase create country style in the kitchen, but the stainless-steel appliances and hanging lamps are purely modern.

together on this home's shingle-and-stone exterior will captivate you. The second-floor balcony, an eyebrow dormer, a turret, and a large bay window show the tremendous attention to detail that you will enjoy inside.

The home's layout embraces natural light and open living spaces, with distinctive ceilings and hidden surprises that mirror the intricate details you see on the exterior.

The great room, complete with a media center, boasts a coffered ceiling, a fireplace, and an alcove overlooking the front yard. The

A rustic country feel and high-tech appliances aren't mutually exclusive in today's kitchens.

The entire master suite shows attention to detail, beginning with the wood built-ins.

kitchen and breakfast area conveniently opens to a side porch.

The dining room is just steps from the kitchen, and its bay window enjoys a view of the backyard. A spacious laundry room has a convenient location as well, including access to the three-car garage.

The guest suite, which includes a private bath and walk-in closet, is on the right side of the plan. With a large study between the guest room and the rest of the first floor, your visitors will enjoy privacy and comfort.

Upstairs, a vaulted bonus room joins three bedrooms, each of which contain special amenities. Bedroom 2 offers a window seat flanked by built-in shelves, and a barrel-vaulted ceiling graces Bedroom 3. The

Above: A linen closet, a corner shower, and a spa tub are highlights in the relaxing master bath, which receives natural light from a triple window near the tub. **Right:** This view of the master bedroom showcases the fireplace, built-in shelves and cabinetry, and a tall triple window.

comforts of home

The master bedroom serves as a soothing sanctuary, with a gently sloped ceiling and a wall niche that sets the bed back slightly; double doors open to the lush master bath.

master suite stands apart as truly exceptional, however. It includes a fireplace in the bedroom and a master bath that rivals a spa.

Bonus space and attic storage offer additional options—consider the possibilities of adding a media room, exercise room, or children's play room in the bonus room. ■

plan⊕ HPK0900053

Style: Craftsman
First Floor: 2,572 sq. ft.
Second Floor: 1,578 sq. ft.
Total: 4,150 sq. ft.
Bonus Space: 315 sq. ft.
Bedrooms: 4
Bathrooms: 4½
Width: 78' - 2"
Depth: 68' - 0"
Foundation: Crawlspace

SEARCH ONLINE @ EPLANS.COM

SECOND FLOOR

FIRST FLOOR

Filled with specialty rooms and abundant amenities, this countryside house is the perfect dream home. Double doors open into an angled foyer, flanked by a music room and a formal great room warmed by a fireplace. The music room leads to the master wing of the home, which includes a spacious bath with a dressing area and double walk-in closet. The great room is the heart of the home—its central position allows access to the island kitchen, formal dining room, and library. Stairs behind the kitchen lead upstairs to a balcony accessing three family bedrooms. The lower level features a billiard room, hobby room, media room, and future possibilities.

plan# HPK0900054

Style: Craftsman
First Floor: 2,782 sq. ft.
Second Floor: 1,027 sq. ft.
Total: 3,809 sq. ft.
Basement: 1,316 sq. ft.
Bedrooms: 4
Bathrooms: 4½
Width: 78' - 2"
Depth: 74' - 6"
Foundation: Basement

SEARCH ONLINE @ EPLANS.COM

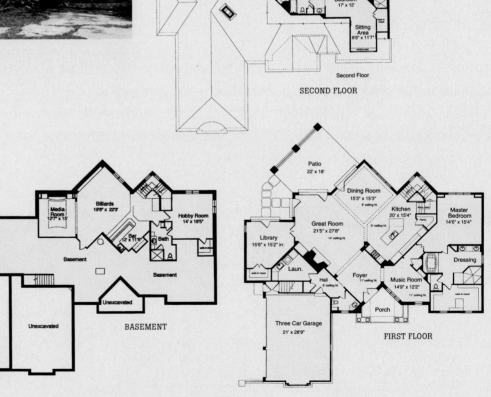

rear exterior

EXPOSURES UNLIMITED-RON & DONNA KOLB

plan# HPK0900055

Style: Traditional
Main Level: 1,572 sq. ft.
Basement: 1,916 sq. ft.
Total: 3,488 sq. ft.
Bedrooms: 4
Bathrooms: 3½
Width: 68' - 6"
Depth: 53' - 2"

SEARCH ONLINE @ EPLANS.COM

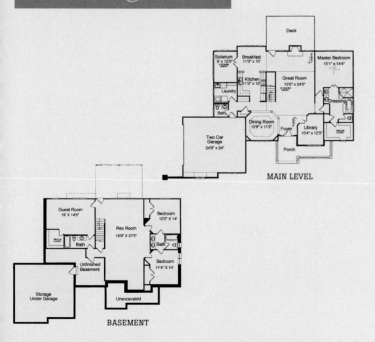

MAIN LEVEL

BASEMENT

plan# HPK0900056

Style: Craftsman
Main Level: 1,997 sq. ft.
Lower Level: 1,356 sq. ft.
Total: 3,353 sq. ft.
Bedrooms: 3
Bathrooms: 3
Width: 57' - 0"
Depth: 47' - 4"
Foundation: Basement

SEARCH ONLINE @ EPLANS.COM

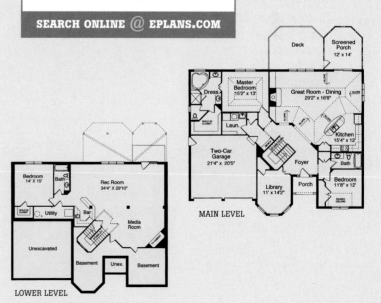

MAIN LEVEL

LOWER LEVEL

comforts of home

An eye-catching exterior and well-designed interior make this home worthy of a second look. An attractive stone entryway leads into the casual foyer which immediately opens to the rest of the home. A built-in entertainment center and central fireplace make this room ideal for family gatherings. The open design is perfect for entertaining. A guest suite is a comfortable retreat for visitors. Upstairs houses a third bedroom complete with full bath and a game room with wet bar.

plan # HPK0900057

Style: Craftsman
First Floor: 2,117 sq. ft.
Second Floor: 620 sq. ft.
Total: 2,737 sq. ft.
Bedrooms: 3
Bathrooms: 3½
Width: 56' - 0"
Depth: 60' - 0"
Foundation: Crawlspace

SEARCH ONLINE @ EPLANS.COM

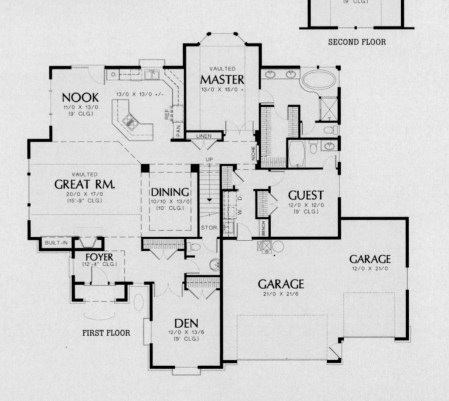

This splendid Craftsman home will look good in any neighborhood. Inside, the foyer offers a beautiful wooden bench to the right, flanked by built-in curio cabinets. On the left, double French doors lead to a cozy study. The formal dining room is complete with beamed ceilings, a built-in hutch, and cabinets. The large L-shaped kitchen includes a work island/snack bar, plenty of storage, and an adjacent sunny nook. The two-story great room surely lives up to its name, with a massive stone fireplace and a two-story wall of windows. Upstairs, two family bedrooms share a full bath, while the guest suite features its own bath. The lavish master bedroom suite pampers the homeowner with two walk-in closets, a fireplace, and a private deck.

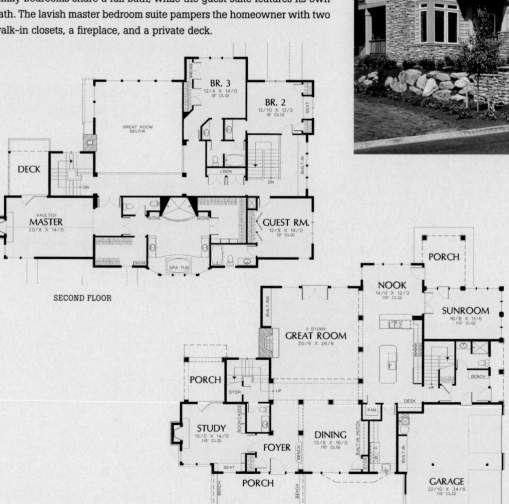

SECOND FLOOR

FIRST FLOOR

plan# HPK0900058

Style: Craftsman
First Floor: 2,597 sq. ft.
Second Floor: 2,171 sq. ft.
Total: 4,768 sq. ft.
Bedrooms: 4
Bathrooms: 4½
Width: 76' - 6"
Depth: 68' - 6"
Foundation: Crawlspace

SEARCH ONLINE @ EPLANS.COM

FOR MORE DETAILED INFORMATION, PLEASE CHECK THE FLOOR PLANS CAREFULLY.

An open courtyard takes center stage in this home, providing a happy marriage of indoor/outdoor relationships. Art collectors will appreciate the gallery that enhances the entry and showcases their favorite works. The centrally located great room supplies the nucleus for formal and informal entertaining. A raised-hearth fireplace flanked by built-in media centers adds a special touch. The master suite provides a private retreat where you may relax—try the sitting room or retire to the private bath for a pampering soak in the corner whirlpool tub.

plan# HPK0900059

Style: SW Contemporary
Square Footage: 3,163
Bedrooms: 4
Bathrooms: 3½
Width: 75' - 2"
Depth: 68' - 8"
Foundation: Slab

SEARCH ONLINE @ EPLANS.COM

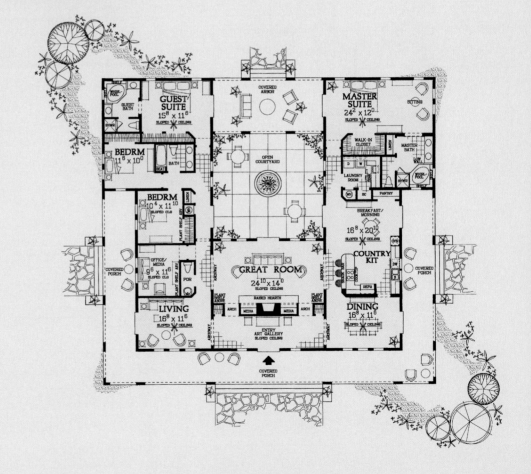

Though seemingly compact from the exterior, this home gives a definite feeling of spaciousness inside. The two-story entry connects directly to a formal living/dining area, a fitting complement to the more casual family room and cozy, bayed breakfast room. Located on the first floor for privacy, the master suite is luxury defined. A bayed sitting area, His and Hers walk-in closets, a whirlpool tub, and twin vanities all combine to provide a lavish retreat. Upstairs, three family bedrooms share a full hall bath, while a large guest room awaits to pamper with its private bath and access to its own deck. A three-car garage will protect both the family fleet and visitors' vehicles.

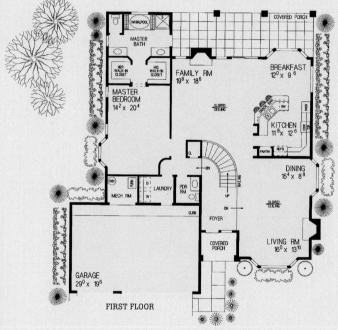

FIRST FLOOR

SECOND FLOOR

FOR MORE DETAILED INFORMATION, PLEASE CHECK THE FLOOR PLANS CAREFULLY.

plan # HPK0900060

Style: Contemporary
First Floor: 2,024 sq. ft.
Second Floor: 1,144 sq. ft.
Total: 3,168 sq. ft.
Bedrooms: 5
Bathrooms: 3½
Width: 57' - 0"
Depth: 64' - 0"
Foundation: Slab

SEARCH ONLINE @ EPLANS.COM

Sturdy pillars, stone accents, and gable detailing announce this design's Craftsman influences. Inside, the vaulted great room boasts a fireplace and built-in media center, and opens to the rear property through two sets of doors. Nearby, the breakfast nook—with access to a covered porch—adjoins a spacious island kitchen. The first-floor master suite provides a bay window, two walk-in closets, and a private bath with a compartmented toilet. Upstairs, a second master suite—also with a private bath—joins two additional bedrooms, one of which can double as a study.

plan # HPK0900061

Style: Craftsman
First Floor: 2,222 sq. ft.
Second Floor: 1,235 sq. ft.
Total: 3,457 sq. ft.
Bedrooms: 4
Bathrooms: 3½
Width: 70' - 0"
Depth: 100' - 6"
Foundation: Crawlspace

SEARCH ONLINE @ EPLANS.COM

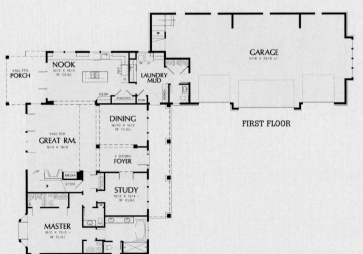

SECOND FLOOR

FIRST FLOOR

This airy bungalow belongs on the coastline among palm trees. The smoothly glazed, elongated windows and intricately ornamented openings give the exterior a modern but classy flair. Inside exists a maze of brightly lit, uniquely patterned rooms for entertaining or relaxing. Stunning details include arched and alcove entrances, His and Hers closets, and a wet bar.

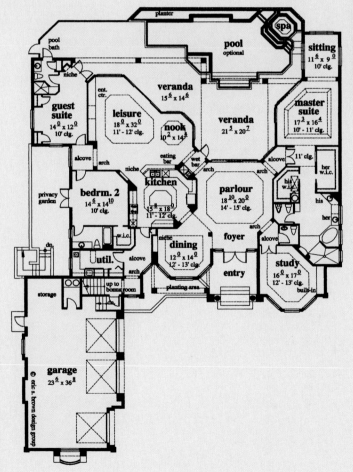

plan# HPK0900062

Style: Mediterranean
Square Footage: 3,725
Bonus Space: 595 sq. ft.
Bedrooms: 3
Bathrooms: 3½
Width: 84' - 3"
Depth: 115' - 2"
Foundation: Slab

SEARCH ONLINE @ EPLANS.COM

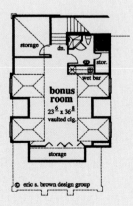

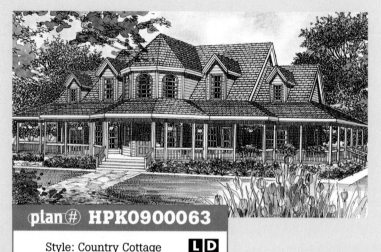

plan# **HPK0900063**

Style: Country Cottage **LD**
First Floor: 1,752 sq. ft.
Second Floor: 906 sq. ft.
Total: 2,658 sq. ft.
Bedrooms: 4
Bathrooms: 3½
Width: 74' – 0"
Depth: 51' – 7"
Foundation: Basement

SEARCH ONLINE @ EPLANS.COM

QUOTE ONE®

plan# **HPK0900064**

Style: Farmhouse
First Floor: 1,530 sq. ft.
Second Floor: 777 sq. ft.
Total: 2,307 sq. ft.
Bonus Space: 361 sq. ft.
Bedrooms: 3
Bathrooms: 3½
Width: 61' – 4"
Depth: 78' – 0"
Foundation: Slab

SEARCH ONLINE @ EPLANS.COM

SECOND FLOOR

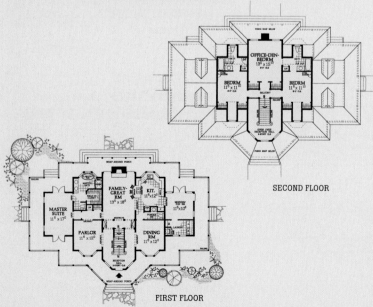

FIRST FLOOR

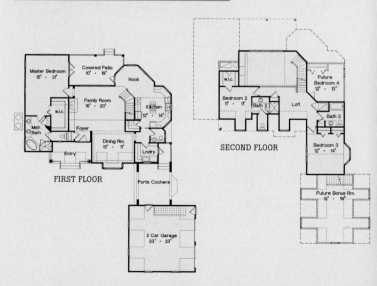

FIRST FLOOR

SECOND FLOOR

rear exterior

Gently curved arches and dormers contrast with the straight lines of gables and wooden columns on this French-style stone exterior. Small-pane windows are enhanced by shutters; tall chimneys and a cupola add height. Inside, a spacious gathering room with an impressive fireplace opens to a cheery morning room. The kitchen is a delight, with a beam ceiling, triangular work island, walk-in pantry, and angular counter with a snack bar. The nearby laundry room includes a sink, a work area, and plenty of room for storage. The first-floor master suite boasts a bay-windowed sitting nook, a deluxe bath, and a handy study.

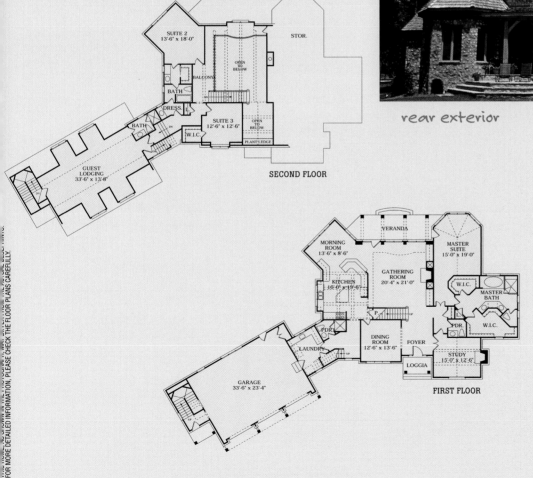

plan# HPK0900065

Style: Country Cottage
First Floor: 2,660 sq. ft.
Second Floor: 914 sq. ft.
Total: 3,574 sq. ft.
Bedrooms: 3
Bathrooms: 4½
Width: 114' - 8"
Depth: 75' - 10"
Foundation: Crawlspace

SEARCH ONLINE @ EPLANS.COM

© Copyright 2003, Garrell Associates, Inc.

Textures—rugged and weathered—and natural materials such as cedar shingles, exposed wood trusses, and stone create a cottage design perfectly suited to a coastal forest. From the foyer, take in the well-balanced combination of private, casual, and formal spaces defined by decorative square columns and a sense of function. The study—or guest room—offers seclusion and retreat with a full bath, walk-in closet, fireplace, and built-in shelves. A series of windows invites light and landscape into the grand room. A central fireplace is a great place to gather friends and family. An adjoining dining room offers a graceful presentation and features a china or serving alcove. Take a few steps to the right and meet the open C-shaped kitchen. A center island is simply a must have. A private porch opens to the bedroom and the bath. A second family bedroom enjoys a private bath and walk-in closet.

plan # HPK0900066

Style: Craftsman
First Floor: 2,075 sq. ft.
Second Floor: 1,204 sq. ft.
Total: 3,279 sq. ft.
Bedrooms: 3
Bathrooms: 3½
Width: 63' - 1"
Depth: 58' - 6"
Foundation: Basement

SEARCH ONLINE @ EPLANS.COM

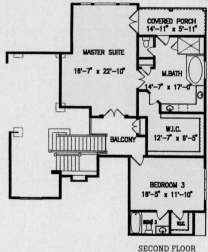

SECOND FLOOR

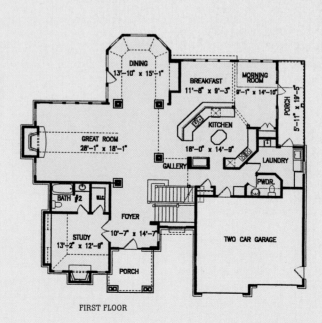

FIRST FLOOR

If you're looking for a spacious vacation home, big enough for the entire family and guests, this plan is worth taking a close look at. You will be astounded by the kitchen...easy to work in and miles of counter space. One counter serves both as a divider and a connecter to the dining room, and double French doors open to the rear porch. The two-story grand room warmed by a fireplace opens to another porch. A downstairs bedroom enjoys a private bath, and two more bedrooms on the upper level, one of them a resplendent master suite, also include private baths. Also, you get a bonus upstairs...extra space that can be turned into a fourth bedroom or a hobby area. Don't overlook the laundry room that opens to the three-car garage.

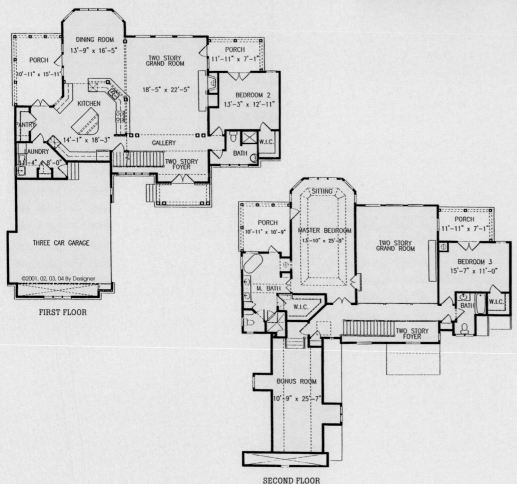

FIRST FLOOR

SECOND FLOOR

plan# HPK0900067

Style: Vacation
First Floor: 1,640 sq. ft.
Second Floor: 1,083 sq. ft.
Total: 2,723 sq. ft.
Bonus Space: 350 sq. ft.
Bedrooms: 3
Bathrooms: 3
Width: 62' - 0"
Depth: 65' - 6"
Foundation: Basement

SEARCH ONLINE @ EPLANS.COM

This contemporary French Country home features an exterior of a hipped roof, wood and brick siding, and an inviting covered porch. A handy den can serve as a guest suite with an adjacent access to a full bath. An open floor plan is featured in the vaulted living and dining rooms; the living and family rooms enjoy a warming fireplace. An island kitchen with a walk-in pantry and a built-in desk is open to a breakfast nook which accesses the rear deck. Two family bedrooms share the second floor with a private master suite; the two full bathrooms on this floor boast dual vanities and skylights. Included in this floor plan is an oversized garage that fits three cars and also includes a shop area.

plan # HPK0900068

Style: NW Contemporary
First Floor: 1,601 sq. ft.
Second Floor: 1,316 sq. ft.
Total: 2,917 sq. ft.
Bonus Space: 320 sq. ft.
Bedrooms: 4
Bathrooms: 3
Width: 70' - 0"
Depth: 49' - 0"
Foundation: Crawlspace

SEARCH ONLINE @ EPLANS.COM

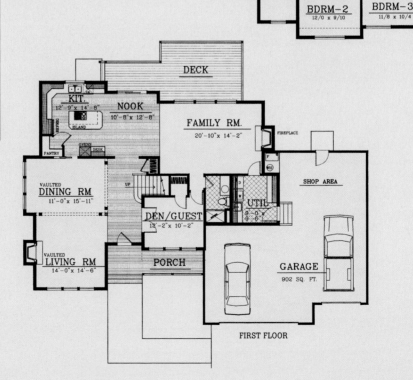

The rustic chic of Craftsman details makes this an unusual example of estate architecture. But, extravagant floor planning leaves no doubt that luxury is what this home is about. The first floor has open spaces for living: a reading room and dining room flanking the foyer, a huge family room with built-ins and fireplace plus covered deck access, and an island kitchen and nook with built-in table. The first-floor master suite is graced with a beamed ceiling. Its attached bath is well appointed and spacious. On the second floor are four bedrooms and three baths. Third-floor attic space can be used for whatever suits you best. Don't miss the home theater that can be developed in the basement and home-office space over the garage.

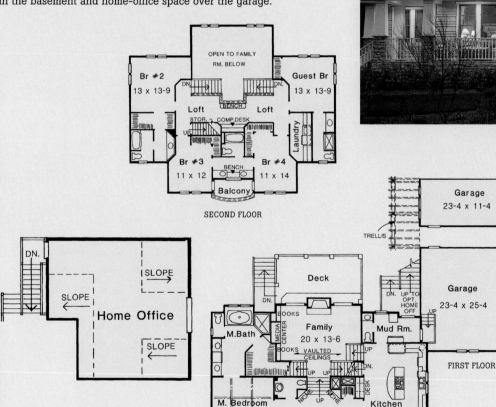

SECOND FLOOR

THIRD FLOOR

FIRST FLOOR

plan# HPK0900069

Style: NW Contemporary
First Floor: 2,120 sq. ft.
Second Floor: 1,520 sq. ft.
Third Floor: 183 sq. ft.
Total: 3,823 sq. ft.
Bedrooms: 5
Bathrooms: 4½ + ½
Width: 76' - 0"
Depth: 81' - 0"
Foundation: Basement, Slab, Crawlspace

SEARCH ONLINE @ EPLANS.COM

This stunning Mediterranean-influenced design features a spacious first-floor media room that doubles as a convenient home office. The formal living room adjoins the dining room, creating a fine area for entertaining. Nearby, the kitchen offers space for a dining table and access to the family room, which opens to the backyard. A luxurious master suite with a walk-in closet, dual vanities, and a soothing tub completes the first floor. A gently curved staircase leads up to five additional bedrooms, one of them a roomy guest suite with a private dual-vanity bath. The remaining four bedrooms access two full baths.

plan# HPK0900070

Style: Mediterranean
First Floor: 1,700 sq. ft.
Second Floor: 1,300 sq. ft.
Total: 3,000 sq. ft.
Bedrooms: 6
Bathrooms: 4½
Width: 60' - 0"
Depth: 43' - 4"
Foundation: Crawlspace, Slab, Basement

SEARCH ONLINE @ EPLANS.COM

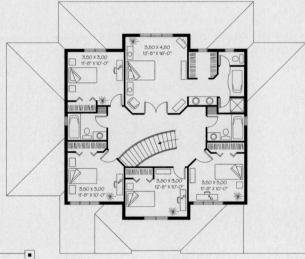

SECOND FLOOR

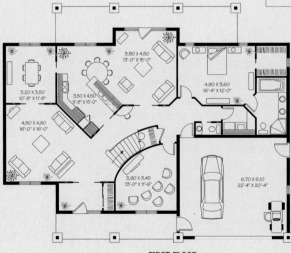

FIRST FLOOR

The variety in the rooflines of this striking waterfront home will certainly make it the envy of the neighborhood. The two-story great room, with its fireplace and built-ins, is a short flight down from the foyer. The three sets of French doors give access to the covered lanai. The huge, well equipped kitchen will easily serve the gourmet who loves to entertain. The stepped ceiling and bay window in the dining room will add style to every meal. The master suite completes the first level. Two bedrooms and two full baths, along with an expansive loft, constitute the second level. Bedroom 3 has an attached sundeck.

SECOND FLOOR

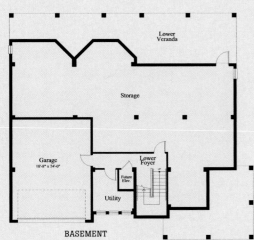

BASEMENT

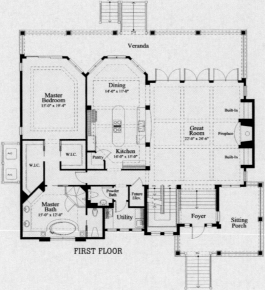

FIRST FLOOR

plan# HPK0900071

Style: Seaside
First Floor: 2,096 sq. ft.
Second Floor: 892 sq. ft.
Total: 2,988 sq. ft.
Bedrooms: 3
Bathrooms: 3½
Width: 58'- 0"
Depth: 54' - 0"
Foundation: Basement

SEARCH ONLINE @ EPLANS.COM

Italian Country elegance graces the exterior of this casa bellisima, swept in Mediterranean enchantment. The covered entryway extends into the foyer, where straight ahead, the two-story great room spaciously enhances the interior. This room features a warming fireplace and offers built-in cabinetry. The open dining room extends through double doors to the veranda on the left side of the plan. The adjacent kitchen features efficient pantry space. A family bedroom with a bath, a powder room, and a utility room also reside on this main floor. Upstairs, a vaulted master suite with a vaulted private bath and deck share the floor with a loft area, which overlooks the great room. Downstairs, the basement-level bonus room and storage area share space with the two-car garage. Two lanais open on either side of the bonus room for additional outdoor patio space.

plan# HPK0900072

Style: Italianate
First Floor: 1,143 sq. ft.
Second Floor: 651 sq. ft.
Total: 1,794 sq. ft.
Bonus Space: 476 sq. ft.
Bedrooms: 2
Bathrooms: 2½
Width: 32' - 0"
Depth: 57' - 0"
Foundation: Slab

SEARCH ONLINE @ EPLANS.COM

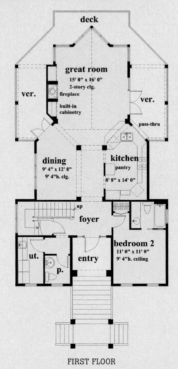

FIRST FLOOR

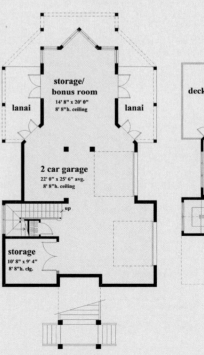

BASEMENT

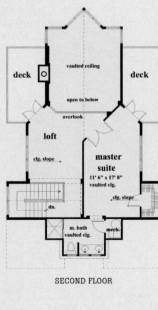

SECOND FLOOR

ORDER BLUEPRINTS 24 HOURS, 7 DAYS A WEEK, AT 1-800-521-6797

Whether an extravagant waterfront vacation home or an everyday residence, this luxury villa will delight at every turn. Almost 900 square feet of outdoor living areas surround the plan; inside, generous room sizes allow space for family and friends—there is even a "friends" entry! At the heart of the home, the great room offers a coffered ceiling, warming fireplace, built-in entertainment center, and French-door access to the veranda. On the right, the country kitchen features a walk-in pantry and convenient utility area and mudroom. An art niche announces the master suite, a treasure with a large bay window, ample walk-in closets, and a lovely bath with a corner tub. Upstairs, each bedroom enjoys a private bath and an added feature: Bedroom 1 is in a charming turret, Bedroom 2 opens to the sunporch, and the guest suite has a private deck.

© The Sater Design Collection, Inc.

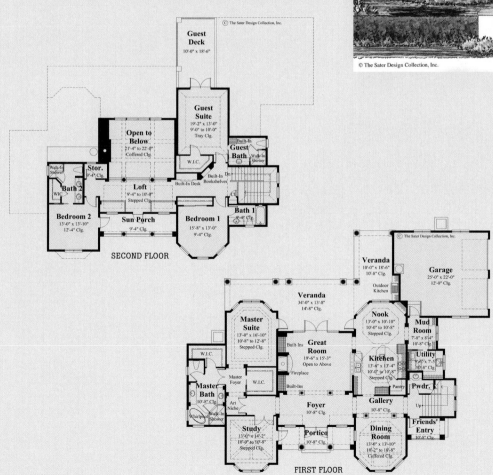

SECOND FLOOR

FIRST FLOOR

plan# HPK0900073

Style: Traditional
First Floor: 2,227 sq. ft.
Second Floor: 1,278 sq. ft.
Total: 3,505 sq. ft.
Bedrooms: 4
Bathrooms: 4½
Width: 63' - 9"
Depth: 80' - 0"
Foundation: Slab

SEARCH ONLINE @ EPLANS.COM

This elegant Old Charleston row design blends high vogue with a restful character that says shoes are optional. A flexible interior enjoys modern space that welcomes sunlight. Wraparound porticos on two levels offer views to the living areas, and a "sit-and-watch-the-stars" observation deck opens from the master suite. Four sets of French doors bring the outside into the great room. The second-floor master suite features a spacious bath and three sets of doors that open to the observation deck. A guest bedroom on this level leads to a gallery hall with its own access to the deck. Bonus space awaits development on the lower level, which—true to its Old Charleston roots—opens gloriously to a garden courtyard.

plan# HPK0900074

Style: Vacation
First Floor: 1,305 sq. ft.
Second Floor: 1,215 sq. ft.
Total: 2,520 sq. ft.
Bonus Space: 935 sq. ft.
Bedrooms: 3
Bathrooms: 3
Width: 30' - 6"
Depth: 72' - 2"
Foundation: Slab

SEARCH ONLINE @ EPLANS.COM

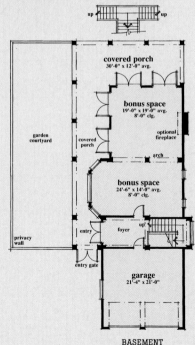

BASEMENT

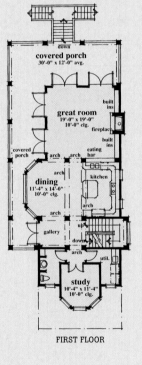

FIRST FLOOR

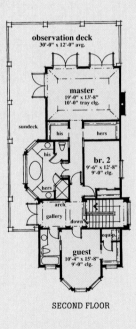

SECOND FLOOR

Tall windows wrap this noble exterior with dazzling details and allow plenty of natural light inside. A wraparound porch sets a casual but elegant pace for the home, with space for rockers and swings. Well-defined formal rooms are placed just off the foyer. A host of French doors opens the great room to an entertainment porch and, of course, inspiring views. Even formal meals take on the ease and comfort of a mountain region in the stunning open dining room. Nearby, a gourmet kitchen packed with amenities serves any occasion.

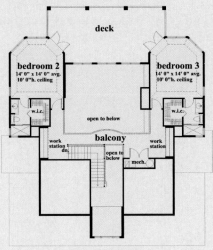

SECOND FLOOR

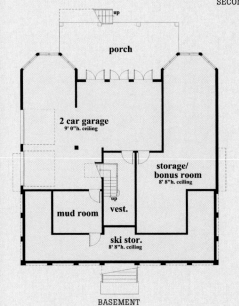

BASEMENT

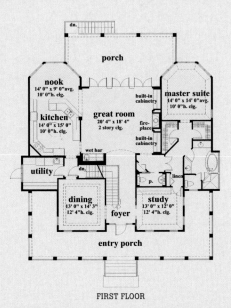

FIRST FLOOR

plan# HPK0900075

Style: Bungalow
First Floor: 2,146 sq. ft.
Second Floor: 952 sq. ft.
Total: 3,098 sq. ft.
Bedrooms: 3
Bathrooms: 3½
Width: 52' - 0"
Depth: 65' - 4"
Foundation: Basement

SEARCH ONLINE @ EPLANS.COM

Stonework and elements of Craftsman style make a strong statement but are partnered here with a sweet disposition. Sidelights and transoms enrich the elevation and offer a warm welcome to a well-accoutered interior with up-to-the-minute amenities. A wealth of windows allows gentle breezes to flow through the living space, and French doors extend an invitation to enjoy the rear covered porch. Nearby, a well-organized kitchen offers a pass-through to the great room, and service to the formal dining room through a convenient butler's pantry. Upstairs, the master suite sports a private sitting area that opens to an upper deck through French doors. The upper-level gallery provides an overlook to the great room and connects the master retreat with a secondary bedroom that opens to the deck.

plan# HPK0900076

Style: Bungalow
First Floor: 1,542 sq. ft.
Second Floor: 971 sq. ft.
Total: 2,513 sq. ft.
Bedrooms: 3
Bathrooms: 3
Width: 46' - 0"
Depth: 51' - 0"
Foundation: Basement

SEARCH ONLINE @ EPLANS.COM

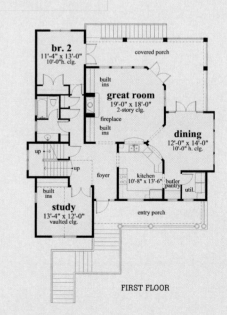

SECOND FLOOR

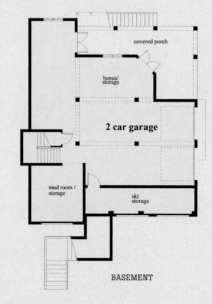

BASEMENT

FIRST FLOOR

ORDER BLUEPRINTS 24 HOURS, 7 DAYS A WEEK, AT 1-800-521-6797

Siding and shingles give this home a Craftsman look while columns and gables suggest a more traditional style. The foyer opens to a short flight of stairs that leads to the great room, which features a lovely coffered ceiling, a fireplace, built-ins, and French doors to the rear veranda. To the left, the open, island kitchen enjoys a pass-through to the great room and easy service to the dining bay. The secluded master suite has two walk-in closets, a luxurious bath, and veranda access. Upstairs, two family bedrooms enjoy their own full baths and share a loft area.

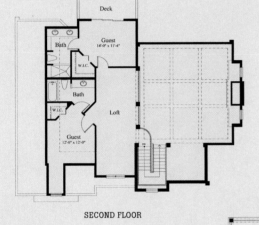

SECOND FLOOR

BASEMENT

FIRST FLOOR

plan# **HPK0900077**

Style: Bungalow
First Floor: 2,096 sq. ft.
Second Floor: 892 sq. ft.
Total: 2,988 sq. ft.
Bedrooms: 3
Bathrooms: 3½
Width: 56' - 0"
Depth: 54' - 0"
Foundation: Basement

SEARCH ONLINE @ EPLANS.COM

Key West Conch style blends Old World charm with New World comfort in this picturesque design. A glass-paneled entry lends a warm welcome and complements a captivating front balcony. Two sets of French doors open the great room to wide views and extend the living areas to the back covered porch. A gourmet kitchen is prepared for any occasion with a prep sink, plenty of counter space, an ample pantry, and an eating bar. The midlevel landing leads to two additional bedrooms, a full bath, and a windowed art niche. Double French doors open the upper-level master suite to a sundeck.

plan# HPK0900078

Style: Contemporary
First Floor: 876 sq. ft.
Second Floor: 1,245 sq. ft.
Total: 2,121 sq. ft.
Bedrooms: 4
Bathrooms: 2½
Width: 27' - 6"
Depth: 64' - 0"
Foundation: Crawlspace

SEARCH ONLINE @ EPLANS.COM

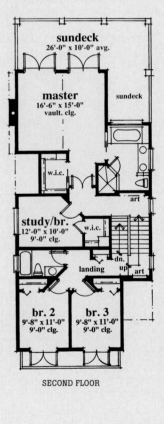

SECOND FLOOR

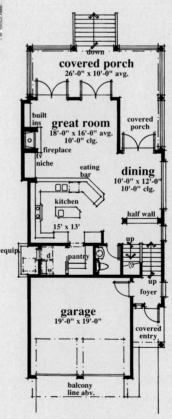

FIRST FLOOR

The individual charm and natural beauty of this sensational home reside in its pure symmetry and perfect blend of past and future. A steeply pitched roof caps a collection of Prairie-style windows and elegant columns. The portico leads to a midlevel foyer, which rises to the grand salon. A wide-open leisure room hosts a corner fireplace that's ultra cozy. The master wing sprawls from the front portico to the rear covered porch, rich with luxury amenities and plenty of secluded space.

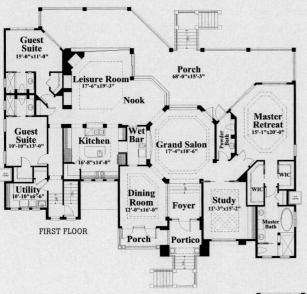

FIRST FLOOR

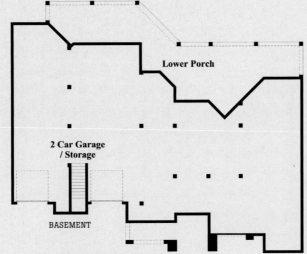

BASEMENT

plan# HPK0900079

Style: Seaside
Square Footage: 3,074
Bedrooms: 3
Bathrooms: 3½
Width: 77' - 0"
Depth: 66' - 8"
Foundation: Basement

SEARCH ONLINE @ EPLANS.COM

© 2003, Garrell Associates, Inc.

Beach living at its finest—this plan offers all of the amenities of a primary residence. Inside, front and rear porches on two levels mean you are never far from the view. The master bedroom, with private access to a rear porch, is warmed by a central fireplace. A convenient morning kitchen at the entrance of the master bedroom makes breakfast in bed an option everyday. A second bedroom on this level is complete with a full bath. The outdoor shower is an added bonus. The second level, warmed by a second fireplace, features an open floor plan perfect for entertaining. Flex space with a large walk-in closet and connected to a full bath could be used as a guest suite. The third level will surely be a family favorite. A cupola beach view, sleeping loft, morning kitchen, and private balcony make this area a relaxing retreat.

plan # HPK0900080

Style: Floridian
First Floor: 1,000 sq. ft.
Second Floor: 958 sq. ft.
Third Floor: 178 sq. ft.
Total: 2,136 sq. ft.
Bedrooms: 2
Bathrooms: 3½
Width: 31' - 4"
Depth: 52' - 0"
Foundation: Crawlspace

SEARCH ONLINE @ EPLANS.COM

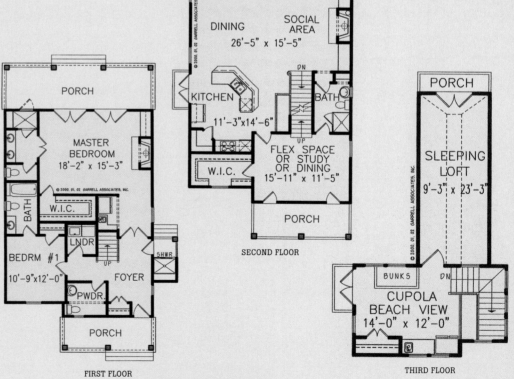

FIRST FLOOR

SECOND FLOOR

THIRD FLOOR

For families that enjoy lots of sun and ocean breezes, this dazzling Sun Country home is made for you. Rear and front covered porches and a rear screened porch extend the living space outdoors. A sunroom, perfect for your favorite plants, opens to the dining area and grand room. The kitchen and a half-bath are also located on the main floor. Two bedrooms, each with private baths, are found upstairs. The plan comes with an optional one-car garage with room for storage.

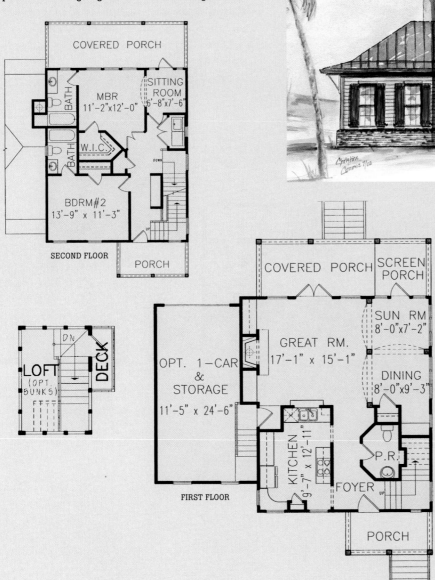

COVERED PORCH

SITTING ROOM
6'-8" x 7'-6"

MBR
11'-2" x 12'-0"

BATH

BATH

W.I.C.

DOWN

BDRM #2
13'-9" x 11'-3"

SECOND FLOOR

PORCH

LOFT
(OPT. BUNKS)

DN

DECK

COVERED PORCH

SCREEN PORCH

SUN RM
8'-0" x 7'-2"

GREAT RM.
17'-1" x 15'-1"

OPT. 1-CAR & STORAGE
11'-5" x 24'-6"

DINING
8'-0" x 9'-3"

KITCHEN
9'-7" x 12'-11"

P.R.

FOYER

FIRST FLOOR

PORCH

plan # HPK0900081

Style: Floridian
First Floor: 754 sq. ft.
Second Floor: 662 sq. ft.
Total: 1,416 sq. ft.
Bedrooms: 2
Bathrooms: 2½
Width: 38' - 0"
Depth: 44' - 0"
Foundation: Crawlspace

SEARCH ONLINE @ EPLANS.COM

Here's a favorite waterfront home with plenty of space to kick back and relax. A lovely sunroom opens from the dining room and allows great views. An angled hearth warms the living and dining areas. Three lovely windows brighten the dining space, which leads out to a stunning sunporch. The gourmet kitchen has an island counter with a snack bar. The first-floor master bedroom enjoys a walk-in closet and a nearby bath. Upstairs, a spacious bath with a whirlpool tub is thoughtfully placed between two bedrooms. A daylight basement allows a lower-level portico.

plan# HPK0900082

Style: Cape Cod
First Floor: 908 sq. ft.
Second Floor: 576 sq. ft.
Total: 1,484 sq. ft.
Bedrooms: 3
Bathrooms: 2
Width: 26' - 0"
Depth: 36' - 0"
Foundation: Basement

SEARCH ONLINE @ EPLANS.COM

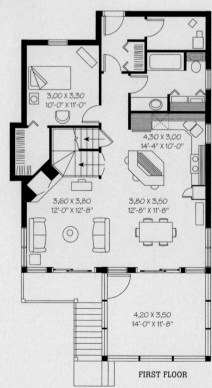

FIRST FLOOR

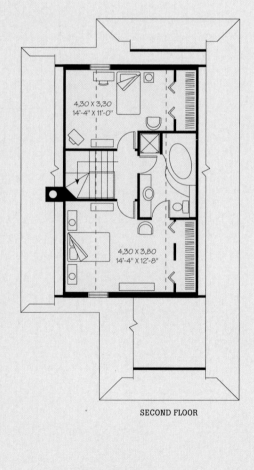

SECOND FLOOR

Situate this house by the sea and you've got yourself the ultimate waterfront retreat. Three levels of spacious living mean ample room for everyone, and extra storage provides a place to put seasonal equipment. Enter from the main level to find a grand family room. Nearby, a secluded sunroom makes an excellent den or home office. A snack-bar island in the open kitchen seats five, or enjoy meals in the bayed dining area. The master suite reigns on this level and boasts a private deck and palatial bath. Upstairs, a bedroom loft suite overlooks the family room. The lower level offers two bedrooms, a gathering room with a fireplace, and a large laundry room.

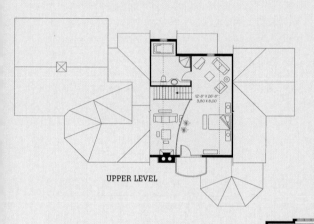

UPPER LEVEL

LOWER LEVEL

MAIN LEVEL

plan # HPK0900083

Style: Traditional
Main Level: 1,434 sq. ft.
Upper Level: 524 sq. ft.
Lower Level: 1,434 sq. ft.
Total: 3,392 sq. ft.
Bedrooms: 4
Bathrooms: 3½
Width: 72' - 0"
Depth: 42' - 0"
Foundation: Basement

SEARCH ONLINE @ EPLANS.COM

With a rugged stone-and-siding facade, this neighborhood-friendly home sets the pace in ultra-chic places with timeless character. A stately portico presents a warm welcome, while a mid-level foyer eases the transition to the elevated grand salon. Interior vistas extend throughout the living area, made even more inviting by rows of graceful arches and stunningly wide views. A wet bar and pantry serve planned events, and the formal dining room is spacious enough for the most elegant occasions. In the gourmet kitchen, wide counters and a walk-in pantry surround a food-preparation island that sports a vegetable sink. A rambling master suite includes a spacious bath with a whirlpool tub and oversized shower. A private hall leads through a pocket door to a quiet study with built-in cabinetry.

plan# HPK0900084

Style: Bungalow
Square Footage: 3,074
Bedrooms: 3
Bathrooms: 3½
Width: 77' - 0"
Depth: 66' - 8"
Foundation: Basement

SEARCH ONLINE @ EPLANS.COM

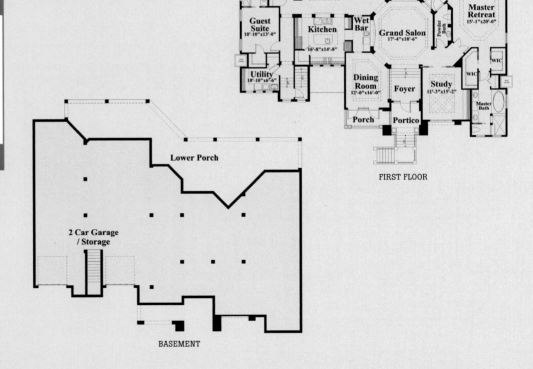

FIRST FLOOR

BASEMENT

Multiple windows bring natural light to this beautiful home, which offers a floor plan filled with special amenities. Arches provide a grand entry to the beam-ceilinged great room, where built-ins flank the fireplace and three sets of French doors open to a veranda. Step ceilings grace the master suite and the dining room. The master suite provides two walk-in closets and a resplendent bath; dazzling windows in the dining room allow enjoyment of the outdoors. Two second-floor bedrooms, one with a sundeck, feature walk-in closets and private baths.

SECOND FLOOR

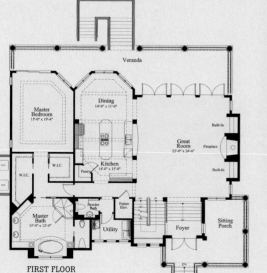

FIRST FLOOR

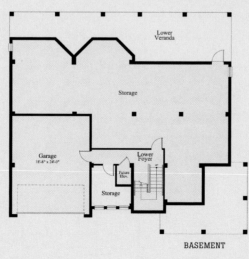

BASEMENT

plan# HPK0900085

Style: Italianate
First Floor: 2,096 sq. ft.
Second Floor: 892 sq. ft.
Total: 2,988 sq. ft.
Bedrooms: 3
Bathrooms: 3½
Width: 56' - 0"
Depth: 54' - 0"
Foundation: Basement

SEARCH ONLINE @ EPLANS.COM

With a rugged blend of stone and siding, an inviting mix of details creates the kind of comfortable beauty that every homeowner craves. Massive stone columns support a striking pediment entry. A spacious formal dining room complements a gourmet kitchen designed to serve any occasion and equipped with a walk-in pantry and a nearby powder room. The morning nook boasts a wall of glass that allows casual diners to kick back and be at one with nature. Separate sleeping quarters thoughtfully place the master suite to the right of the plan, in a wing of the home that includes a private porch. Guest suites on the opposite side of the plan share a hall and a staircase that leads to a lower-level mudroom, porch, and ski storage.

plan # HPK0900086

Style: Bungalow
Square Footage: 2,430
Bedrooms: 3
Bathrooms: 3
Width: 70' - 2"
Depth: 53' - 0"
Foundation: Basement

SEARCH ONLINE @ EPLANS.COM

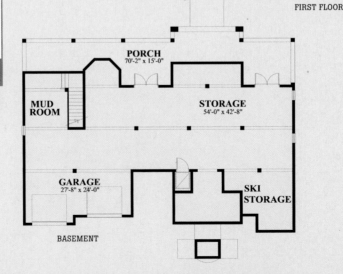

FIRST FLOOR

BASEMENT

This cabin is the ideal vacation home for a retreat to the mountains or the lake. Beyond the covered front porch, the foyer steps lead up to the formal living areas on the main floor. The study is enhanced by a vaulted ceiling and double doors, which open onto the front balcony. The vaulted central great room overlooks the rear deck. The island kitchen is open to an adjacent breakfast nook. The master suite is thoughtfully placed on the left side of the plan for privacy and offers two walk-in closets and a pampering master bath with a whirlpool tub.

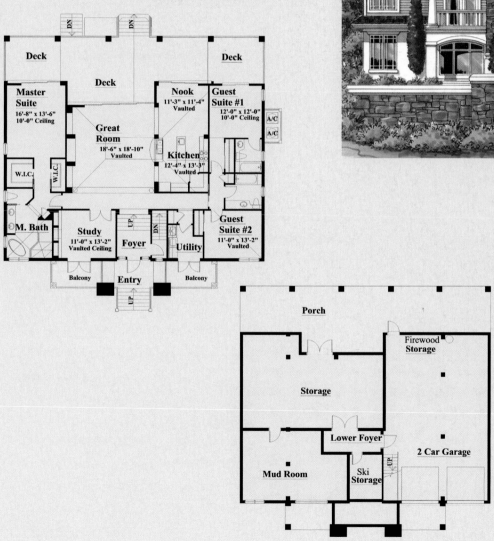

plan# HPK0900087

Style: Bungalow
Square Footage: 2,385
Bedrooms: 3
Bathrooms: 3
Width: 60' - 0"
Depth: 52' - 0"
Foundation: Basement

SEARCH ONLINE @ EPLANS.COM

A hipped roof, dormers, and plenty of muntin windows with keystones give this traditional home a welcome invitation. Located in the center of this home, the family room features a built-in entertainment center—note the sliding-door access to the rear screened porch and courtyard. A two-story dining room shows off elegance as it accesses the gourmet kitchen. The lavish master suite includes a private bath and a huge walk-in closet. Completing this plan are three additional family bedrooms, located to the far left of the home, and a full bath. All three family bedrooms include walk-in closets.

plan⊕ HPK0900088

Style: Traditional
Square Footage: 2,682
Bedrooms: 4
Bathrooms: 3½
Width: 74' - 6"
Depth: 75' - 0"
Foundation: Slab, Crawlspace

SEARCH ONLINE @ EPLANS.COM

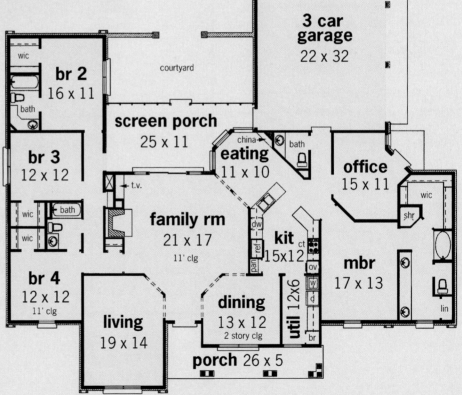

With a perfect balance of indoor and outdoor living spaces, this design is the consummate vacation home. A fireplace on the rear veranda makes outdoor entertaining and dining an option. The master suite sits at the rear of the first level along with a second family bedroom with full bath, and an office/guest suite. Upstairs houses a third family bedroom, enhanced by a sitting room and full bath. Bonus space complete with a wet bar could serve as a recreation room. Extra storage space, a powder room, and future expansion space complete this floor.

plan# HPK0900089

Style: Country Cottage
First Floor: 2,600 sq. ft.
Second Floor: 1,174 sq. ft.
Total: 3,774 sq. ft.
Bonus Space: 340 sq. ft.
Bedrooms: 4
Bathrooms: 4
Width: 58' - 1"
Depth: 125' - 4"
Foundation: Crawlspace

SEARCH ONLINE @ EPLANS.COM

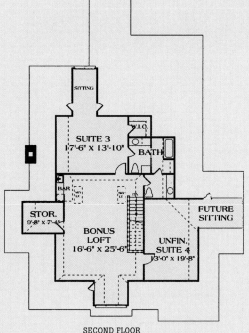

WORKSHOP
26'-0" x 13'-0"

GARAGE
26'-0" x 24'-0"

VERANDA

MASTER BATH

W.I.C.

MASTER SUITE
17'-0" x 14'-0"

GATHERING
23'-0" x 18'-0"

KITCHEN
15'-0" x 13'-6"

BRKFST
14'-0" x 13'-6"

LAUN.

OFFICE / SUITE 3
12'-0" x 13'-0"

BATH

DINING ROOM
14'-10" x 13'-0"

FOYER

BATH

SUITE 2
13'-10" x 13'-0"

LOGGIA

FIRST FLOOR

SITTING

SUITE 3
17'-6" x 13'-10"

W.I.C.

BATH

BAR

STOR.
9'-8" x 7'-4"

BONUS LOFT
16'-6" x 25'-6"

UNFIN. SUITE 4
13'-0" x 19'-8"

FUTURE SITTING

SECOND FLOOR

French style embellishes this dormered country home. Stepping through French doors to the foyer, the dining area is immediately to the left. To the right is a set of double doors leading to a study or secondary bedroom. A lavish master bedroom provides privacy and plenty of storage space. The living room sports three doors to the rear porch and a lovely fireplace with built-ins. A secluded breakfast nook adjoins an efficient kitchen. Upstairs, two of the three family bedrooms boast dormer windows. Plans include a basement-level garage that adjoins a game room and two handy storage areas.

plan# HPK0900090

Style: Country Cottage
First Floor: 2,129 sq. ft.
Second Floor: 1,206 sq. ft.
Total: 3,335 sq. ft.
Bonus Space: 422 sq. ft.
Bedrooms: 4
Bathrooms: 4
Width: 59' - 4"
Depth: 64' - 0"
Foundation: Basement

SEARCH ONLINE @ EPLANS.COM

Rear Exterior

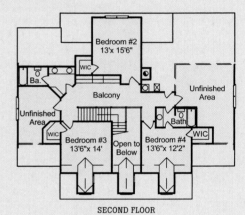

SECOND FLOOR

Bedroom #2 13'x 15'6"
Ba.
WIC
Balcony
Unfinished Area
Unfinished Area
WIC
Bath
WIC
Bedroom #3 13'6"x 14'
Open to Below
Bedroom #4 13'6"x 12'2"

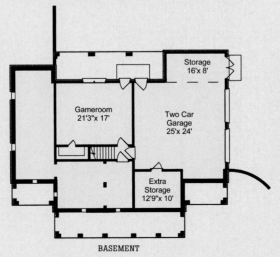

BASEMENT

Storage 16'x 8'
Gameroom 21'3"x 17'
Two Car Garage 25'x 24'
Extra Storage 12'9"x 10'

FIRST FLOOR

Wood Deck 30'10"x 13'
Porch 30'5"x 8'
Master Bedroom 16'4"x 16'4"
Breakfast 11'4"x 13'
Living 21'6"x 17'2"
Util.
WIC
WIC
Kitchen 11'4"x 18'4"
Bath
WIC
Ma. Bath
Dining 13'6"x 13'10"
Foyer
Study 13'8"x 12'
Porch
Porch
Porch 36'x 7'

This charming Craftsman design offers a second-story master bedroom with four windows under the gabled dormer. The covered front porch displays column and pier supports. The hearth-warmed gathering room opens to the dining room on the right, where the adjoining kitchen offers enough space for an optional breakfast booth. A home office/guest suite is found in the rear. The second floor holds the lavish master suite and a second bedroom suite with its own private bath.

GARAGE
20'-0" x 22'-0"

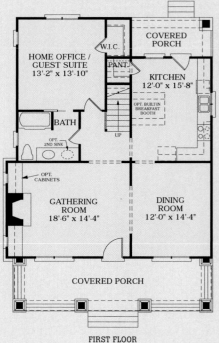

FIRST FLOOR

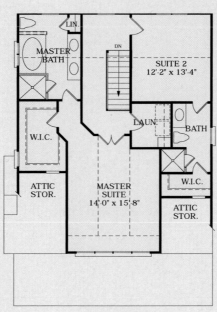

SECOND FLOOR

plan# HPK0900091

Style: Craftsman
First Floor: 1,060 sq. ft.
Second Floor: 914 sq. ft.
Total: 1,974 sq. ft.
Bedrooms: 3
Bathrooms: 3
Width: 32' - 0"
Depth: 35' - 0"
Foundation: Crawlspace

SEARCH ONLINE @ EPLANS.COM

A bright arched window and two dormers add country charm to this midsize home. Enter to a foyer with a columned dining room on the right. An angled kitchen follows, easily serving the breakfast nook. The vaulted family room features a fireplace and sundeck access, making this area a family favorite. Three bedrooms are nearby, one of which boasts a private bath—all three have walk-in closets. The master suite is hidden to the right and furnished with a tray ceiling, doors to the sundeck, and a lavish bath. Optional space may be built at any time to offer a fifth bedroom, study/home office, or play area.

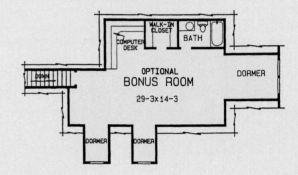

plan # HPK0900092

Style: Farmhouse
Square Footage: 2,186
Bonus Space: 704 sq. ft.
Bedrooms: 4
Bathrooms: 3½
Width: 65' - 2"
Depth: 52' - 0"
Foundation: Basement

SEARCH ONLINE @ EPLANS.COM

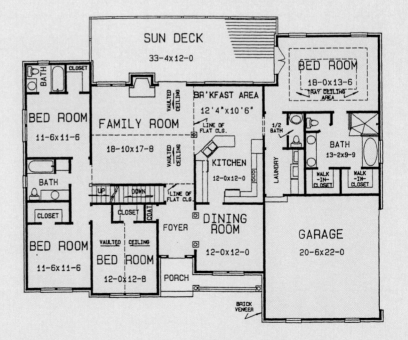

ORDER BLUEPRINTS 24 HOURS, 7 DAYS A WEEK, AT 1-800-521-6797

This breathtaking Mediterranean manor looks great from the curb, but it is the interior that will steal your heart. The entry is lit by twin two-story Palladian windows for subtle drama. On the right, the dining room is defined by columns. The living room makes an elegant impression with a vaulted ceiling and French doors to the rear porch. The kitchen is nearby and sports a "boomerang" counter and a central island. A breakfast bay creates a cheerful place for casual meals. The family room is warmed by a fireplace, and brightened by a rear wall of windows. The master suite is in the left wing, decadent with a bayed sitting area, porch access, and an indulgent spa bath. A nearby bedroom makes a great guest suite or home office. Upstairs, two lovely bedrooms share a full bath and a game room.

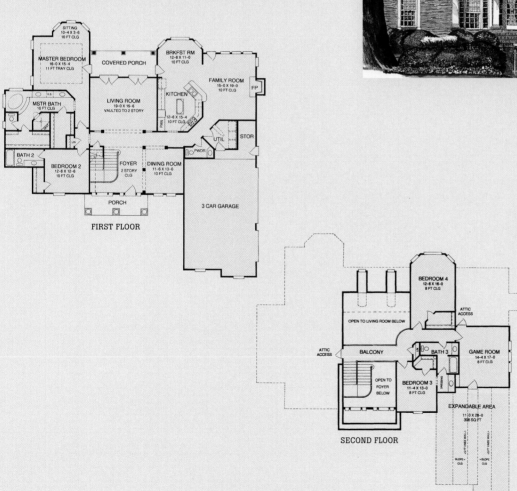

FIRST FLOOR

SECOND FLOOR

plan# HPK0900093

Style: European Cottage
First Floor: 2,657 sq. ft.
Second Floor: 1,026 sq. ft.
Total: 3,683 sq. ft.
Bonus Space: 308 sq. ft.
Bedrooms: 4
Bathrooms: 3½
Width: 75' - 8"
Depth: 74' - 2"
Foundation: Basement, Crawlspace, Slab

SEARCH ONLINE @ EPLANS.COM

Charming Colonial and European accents grace the exterior of this quaint design. Inside, the foyer is flanked on either side by a formal dining room and a study that easily converts to a guest bedroom. Straight ahead, the family room, warmed by a fireplace, accesses the rear screened porch. The snack-bar kitchen overlooks the casual morning room and family room. The first-floor master suite features a private bath and a walk-in closet. This floor is completed by a three-car garage and a laundry room. Upstairs, an additional bedroom provides a walk-in closet and a hall bath is conveniently close. The recreation room is great for entertaining family or friends. A second-floor laundry is placed just across from the office, which accesses the attic space.

plan # HPK0900094

Style: NE Colonial
First Floor: 1,758 sq. ft.
Second Floor: 1,087 sq. ft.
Total: 2,845 sq. ft.
Bonus Space: 307 sq. ft.
Bedrooms: 4
Bathrooms: 3
Width: 65' - 0"
Depth: 49' - 9"
Foundation: Slab

SEARCH ONLINE @ EPLANS.COM

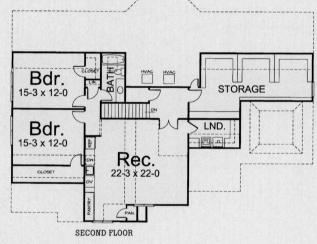

SECOND FLOOR

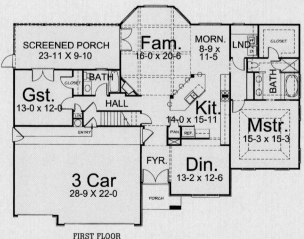

FIRST FLOOR

Tall dormer windows and matching pediments bring a Colonial tone to the design. The columned portico is high enough to showcase the large transom lights and brings even more character to the facade. The layout is efficient: a brief foyer leads to the large two-story living room, with a fireplace and deck access. The master suite and bath reside at the left, along with the study. The right side houses the kitchen, nook, and formal dining room. A guest room occupies the far right side of the plan. Two bedrooms share a full bath upstairs. There's also room for a library or loft, and an exciting bonus space

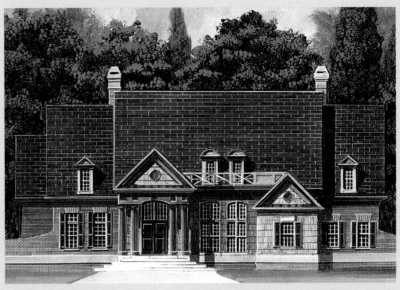

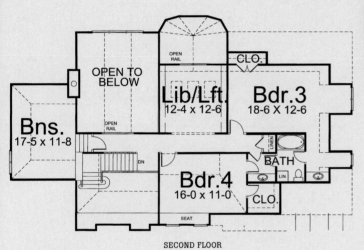

SECOND FLOOR

plan# **HPK0900095**

Style: Colonial
First Floor: 1,920 sq. ft.
Second Floor: 912 sq. ft.
Total: 2,832 sq. ft.
Bonus Space: 228 sq. ft.
Bedrooms: 4
Bathrooms: 3½
Width: 70' - 0"
Depth: 40' - 0"
Foundation: Basement

SEARCH ONLINE @ EPLANS.COM

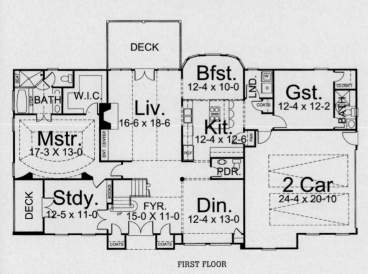

FIRST FLOOR

This handsome bungalow offers many splendid features. A cozy fireplace in the family room, a rear covered porch, and a plant shelf in the laundry are some of the highlights. The plan includes two bedrooms, both with private baths, and a spacious dining room, off the well-equipped kitchen. A front-loading, two-car garage also comes with the plan.

plan# HPK0900096

Style: Cape Cod
Square Footage: 1,093
Bedrooms: 2
Bathrooms: 2
Width: 35' - 0"
Depth: 56' - 0"
Foundation: Slab

SEARCH ONLINE @ EPLANS.COM

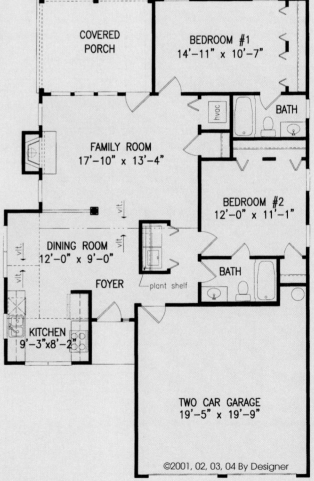

COVERED PORCH

BEDROOM #1
14'-11" x 10'-7"

BATH

hvac

FAMILY ROOM
17'-10" x 13'-4"

BEDROOM #2
12'-0" x 11'-1"

vlt.

DINING ROOM
12'-0" x 9'-0"

BATH

plant shelf

FOYER

KITCHEN
9'-3"x8'-2"

TWO CAR GARAGE
19'-5" x 19'-9"

©2001, 02, 03, 04 By Designer

Petite and modern, this Craftsman home fits comfortably in narrow lots and still has plenty of room for the family. Flanking the foyer is the dining room—or make it a study—and a secondary bedroom. The convenient kitchen offers a serving bar and a roomy breakfast area. An open and vaulted family room is cozy with a fireplace and smart with a built-in TV niche. A private side patio is a great spot for outdoor dining. The master suite sits to the rear and enjoys a full bath and walk-in closet.

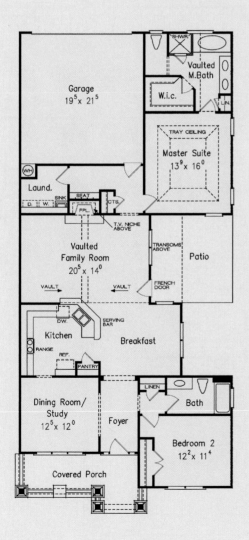

plan# HPK0900097

Style: Craftsman
Square Footage: 1,670
Bedrooms: 2
Bathrooms: 2
Width: 34' - 0"
Depth: 77' - 0"
Foundation: Crawlspace, Basement

SEARCH ONLINE @ EPLANS.COM

This narrow-lot plan still manages to feel balanced and coordinated by incorporating great height and flow-through. The vaulted ceilings in the master bedroom and bath and in the family room keep spaces bright and airy. The functional kitchen, dining room, and patio span the width of the plan for ease of use. A full bath attends the second bedroom, located near the foyer for use also as a powder room. The separate laundry room and pantry near the garage is a welcome accomodation that shows sensible planning.

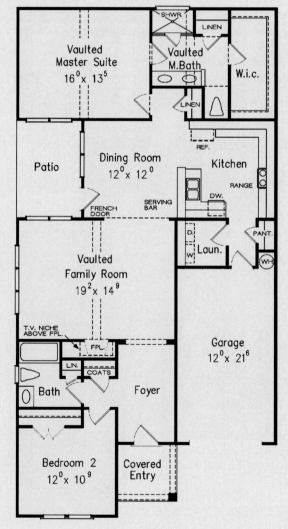

plan # HPK0900098

Style: Craftsman

Square Footage: 1,472

Bedrooms: 2

Bathrooms: 2

Width: 32' - 0"

Depth: 63' - 0"

Foundation:
Crawlspace, Basement

SEARCH ONLINE @ EPLANS.COM

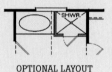

OPTIONAL LAYOUT

At just under 1,700 square feet, this traditonal home offers amenities often found in larger homes. Decorative columns distinguish the space between the foyer, dining, and family rooms. Vaulted ceilings outfit the living spaces. The master suite faces the front of the home where it receives abundant natural light. A serving bar in the kitchen is easily accessible by the dining and family rooms. Enhanced by a fireplace and built-in TV niche, the family room offers access to a side patio. A short hallway reveals two additional family bedrooms sharing a full bath, a coat closet, and laundry room.

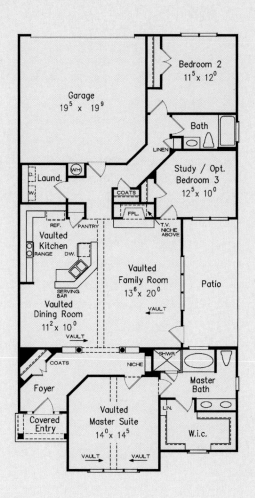

plan # HPK0900099

Style: Craftsman
Square Footage: 1,644
Bedrooms: 3
Bathrooms: 2
Width: 34' - 0"
Depth: 68' - 0"
Foundation: Crawlspace, Basement

SEARCH ONLINE @ EPLANS.COM

The asymmetrical facade brings together a two-tiered porch, gables, and an array of windows for an interesting pastiche of Early American styles. The layout takes full advantage of the design's height: the two-story foyer and family room provide a dramatic entrance. Even more open space can be found at the left of the plan, where the large island kitchen opens easily into the breakfast nook and keeping room. The second floor comprises the bedrooms. The master suite and bath at the left are well appointed, with vaulted ceilings and plenty of windows. The remaining three bedrooms share two full baths. One of the bedrooms enjoys access to the second-floor porch.

plan# HPK0900100

Style: Cape Cod
First Floor: 1,935 sq. ft.
Second Floor: 1,753 sq. ft.
Total: 3,688 sq. ft.
Bedrooms: 5
Bathrooms: 4½
Width: 65' - 6"
Depth: 59' - 0"
Foundation: Basement, Crawlspace

SEARCH ONLINE @ EPLANS.COM

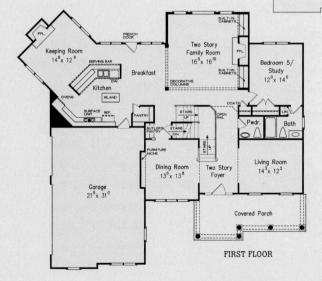

SECOND FLOOR

FIRST FLOOR

Charming gables with Victorian-inspired trusses and a combination of exterior materials bring European Country flavor to the design. The interior features a thoughtful layout anchored by a large family room and breakfast nook at the center of the plan. Privacy spaces are at the right of the plan: a grand master suite including a sitting area and gorgeous bath, and a guest room of generous proportions. Upstairs reside the remaining two bedrooms and a shared bath, as well as a common area.

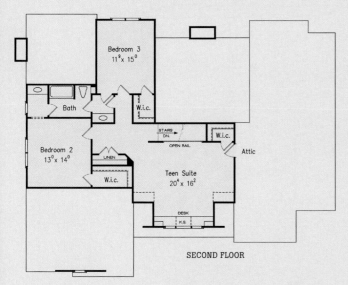

SECOND FLOOR

plan# HPK0900101

Style: Country Cottage
First Floor: 2,224 sq. ft.
Second Floor: 1,030 sq. ft.
Total: 3,254 sq. ft.
Bedrooms: 4
Bathrooms: 3
Width: 65' - 4"
Depth: 53' - 8"
Foundation:
Crawlspace, Basement

SEARCH ONLINE @ EPLANS.COM

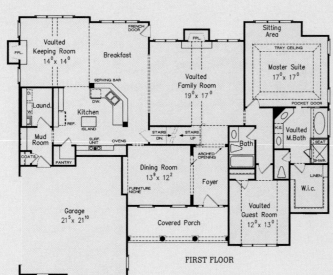

FIRST FLOOR

Shingles and a covered front porch dress up this traditional family design. Inside, a study and dining room flank the two-story foyer. The island kitchen, breakfast room, and two-story family room cluster together as one large gathering area. Upstairs, the master suite is a dream with a sitting area, vaulted bath, and His and Hers walk-in closets.

plan# HPK0900102

Style: Cape Cod
First Floor: 1,692 sq. ft.
Second Floor: 1,620 sq. ft.
Total: 3,312 sq. ft.
Bedrooms: 5
Bathrooms: 4½
Width: 60' - 0"
Depth: 56' - 0"
Foundation:
Crawlspace, Basement

SEARCH ONLINE @ EPLANS.COM

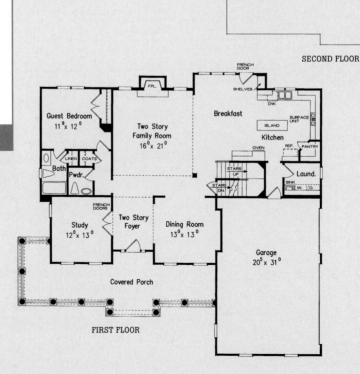

SECOND FLOOR

FIRST FLOOR

Outdoor Living:
Homes with Outdoor Rooms

Outdoor living rooms extend the usable boundaries of a house. They are a natural continuation of a getaway place, expanding its exterior architecture, interior style, and overall purpose to a private outdoor oasis. Designed and furnished much like indoor rooms, outside living areas help create a leisurely transition from a home's interior to its surrounding natural environment. Patios, porches, courtyards, and atriums are some of the most popular forms of outdoor living rooms.

Sometimes these spaces are delineated only by perimeter walls or corner columns, sometimes with ceilings or vine-covered arbors, or living fences of foliage. Other times the outdoor room is really a glass-enclosed extension of the house, but with numerous doors or movable walls that open with the season. Some of the best incorporate complete outdoor kitchens or outdoor fireplaces as centerpieces of the space. From simple to complex, these areas are designed for relaxation, cooking, and entertaining—all perfect activities for a getaway house.

With an outdoor kitchen and fireplace located next to each other, you'll never want to go inside.

House Blend

A covered deck with a fireplace and built-in grill allows easy enjoyment of the outdoors

Craftsman styling calls for an appreciation of natural materials, so perhaps it's not surprising that this Craftsman design shows such an affinity for its natural surroundings. Its deck beckons as an outdoor family room and dining space, perfectly situated off the kitchen and in place to enjoy the backyard views.

The interior of the home celebrates those views as well, with large

Above: A close-up of the entry highlights this home's shingle and stone accents. **Left:** Craftsman styling fits comfortably on a well-landscaped lot.

windows stretching across the back of the house. An open, flowing floor plan and 12-foot-high ceilings make for spacious living areas.

The kitchen serves as the hub of the home, with an angled serving bar that also houses the sink, providing a perfect vantage point into the great room. A work island offers even more preparation and storage space.

The great room has a large hearth as the centerpiece of one wall,

You can have a great outdoor living space and still enjoy beautiful interiors.

Left: Elegant columns define the entry to the great room, visible from the foyer. **Below:** Double ovens and a central island make the kitchen an efficient workspace.

This master suite is the perfect place to start and end your day.

with a corner media center next to it. The room's impressive space—at more than 19 by 23 feet—is accentuated by the high ceilings and large windows.

Two bedroom suites lie to the right of the first floor. The largest, the master, includes a luxurious whirlpool tub, a walk-in shower, and a closet big enough to double as a dressing room. Guests will feel right at home in the second bedroom suite as well.

Right: A bay window and coffered ceiling enhance the master suite. **Above:** Stunning stained-glass windows surround the tub in the master bath.

With a fireplace and built-in grill, the deck provides a great spot for outdoor entertaining.

MAIN LEVEL

If the weather ever turns wet on the deck, family and friends can relax in the lower level. A large party room will keep bringing people back, with its wet bar, rec room, media room, and space for a pool table.

Two more bedrooms complete the lower level, which opens to a patio in back. ▪

plan⊕ HPK0900103

Style: Craftsman
Main Level: 3,171 sq. ft.
Lower Level: 1,897 sq. ft.
Total: 5,068 sq. ft.
Bedrooms: 5
Bathrooms: 3½
Width: 86' - 2"
Depth: 63' - 8"
Foundation: Basement

SEARCH ONLINE @ EPLANS.COM

LOWER LEVEL

The warmth of brick facade treatments, intricate molding detailing, and classic Palladian windows set this home apart from the rest. The wood detailing continues inside this magnificent home. The floor plan is a play on octagonal shapes, which create angular vistas throughout the home. Columns and pediments greet you in the formal living and dining rooms, bathed in natural light. The master suite enjoys all the latest amenities, including a sitting room, trayed ceilings, His and Hers bath appointments, doorless shower, and huge closets. The family side of this home enjoys tile-lined traffic areas, large bedrooms, an island kitchen, and a bonus room, which can overlook the golf course or lake, with balcony. Details like a window in the laundry room and direct access to the three car garage make this the perfect house.

plan# HPK0900104

Style: French
Square Footage: 3,723
Bonus Space: 390 sq. ft.
Bedrooms: 5
Bathrooms: 4
Width: 82' - 4"
Depth: 89' - 0"
Foundation: Slab

SEARCH ONLINE @ EPLANS.COM

Rear Exterior

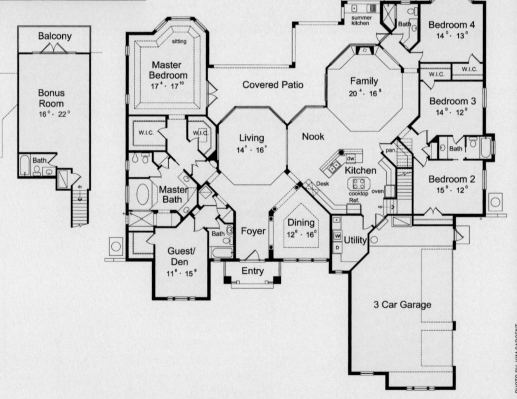

plan # HPK0900105

Style: Craftsman
Main Level: 1,268 sq. ft.
Second Level: 931 sq. ft.
Lower Level: 949 sq. ft.
Total: 3,148 sq. ft.
Bedrooms: 4
Bathrooms: 3½
Width: 53' - 6"
Depth: 73' - 0"
Foundation: Basement

SEARCH ONLINE @ EPLANS.COM

plan # HPK0900106

Style: NW Contemporary
Square Footage: 2,468
Bedrooms: 3
Bathrooms: 3½
Width: 79' - 0"
Depth: 86' - 0"
Foundation: Crawlspace

SEARCH ONLINE @ EPLANS.COM

SECOND LEVEL

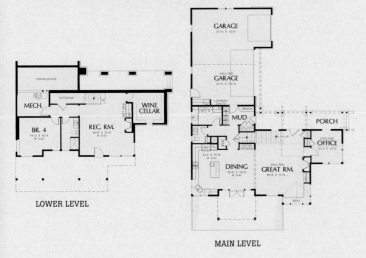

LOWER LEVEL

MAIN LEVEL

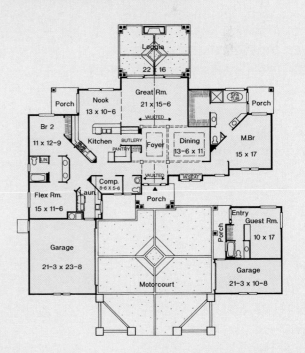

This Parade of Homes award winner has striking curb appeal with its well-balanced and detailed Mediterranean facade. The floor plan offers open, formal, and casual living areas. Plenty of natural light and views to spacious outdoor areas are provided by the use of pocketing sliding-glass doors, French doors, windows, and mitered glass. This design offers four full bedrooms with four full baths. The family room features a built-in entertainment center with fireplace and is easily furnished. The functional and spacious kitchen is open to the family room and dinette.

plan # HPK0900107

Style: Mediterranean
Square Footage: 3,490
Bedrooms: 4
Bathrooms: 4
Width: 69' – 8"
Depth: 115' – 0"
Foundation: Slab

SEARCH ONLINE @ EPLANS.COM

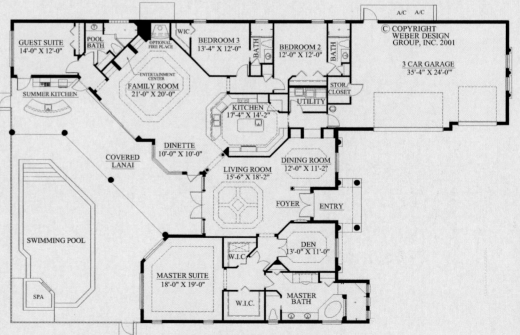

Classic columns, a tiled roof, and beautiful arched windows herald a gracious interior for this fine home. Arched windows also mark the entrance into the vaulted living room with a tiled fireplace. The dining room opens off the vaulted foyer. Filled with light from a wall of sliding glass doors, the family room leads to the covered patio—note the wet bar and range that enhance outdoor living. The kitchen features a vaulted ceiling and unfolds into the roomy nook, which boasts French doors to the patio. The master bedroom also has patio access and shares a dual fireplace with the master bath—a solarium lights this space. A vaulted study/den sits between two additional bedrooms.

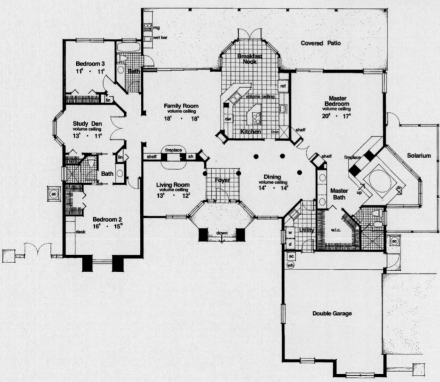

plan# HPK0900108

Style: SW Contemporary
Square Footage: 2,987
Bedrooms: 3
Bathrooms: 3
Width: 74' - 4"
Depth: 82' - 4"
Foundation: Slab

SEARCH ONLINE @ EPLANS.COM

This comely exterior reveals an intricate design packed with amenities. The master suite dominates the right side of the plan, enhanced by tray-ceilings, private access to the veranda, His and Hers walk-in closets and vanities, a garden tub, a separate shower, and a compartmented toilet with bidet. An adjacent study is ideal for late nights. A central parlour opens to a rear covered veranda, a nook leading to a leisure room, a formal dining room, and a seated art niche. The U-shaped kitchen offers practical convenience. Two family bedrooms boast full baths. An outdoor kitchen extends the living space.

plan# HPK0900109

Style: Italianate
Square Footage: 3,230
Bedrooms: 3
Bathrooms: 3½
Width: 65' - 0"
Depth: 94' - 10"
Foundation: Slab

SEARCH ONLINE @ EPLANS.COM

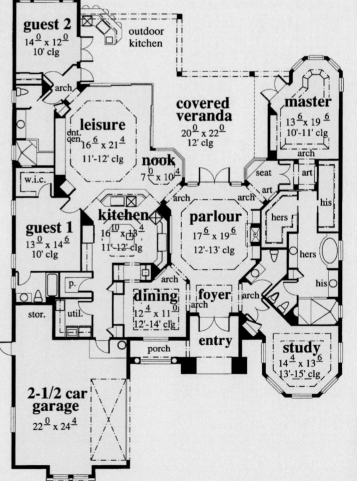

If entertaining is your passion, then this is the design for you. With a large, open floor plan and an array of amenities, every gathering will be a success. The foyer embraces living areas accented by a glass fireplace and a wet bar. The grand room and dining room each access a screened veranda for outside enjoyments. The gourmet kitchen delights with its openness to the rest of the house. A morning nook here also adds a nice touch. Two bedrooms and a study radiate from the first-floor living areas. Upstairs is a masterful master suite. It contains a huge walk-in closet, a whirlpool tub, and a private sundeck with a spa.

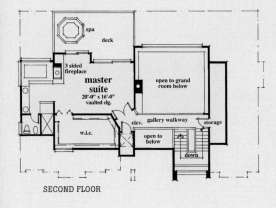

SECOND FLOOR

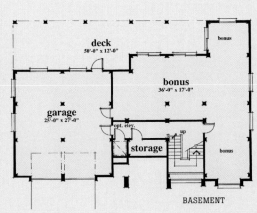

BASEMENT

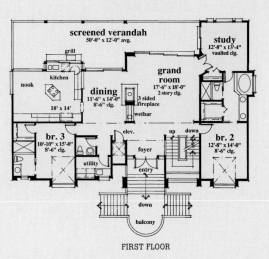

FIRST FLOOR

plan# HPK0900110

Style: Floridian
First Floor: 2,066 sq. ft.
Second Floor: 809 sq. ft.
Total: 2,875 sq. ft.
Bonus Space: 1,260 sq. ft.
Bedrooms: 3
Bathrooms: 3½
Width: 64' - 0"
Depth: 45' - 0"
Foundation: Pier (same as Piling)

SEARCH ONLINE @ EPLANS.COM

Rear Exterior

Looking a bit like a French Country manor, this alluring home maintains privacy with a stucco wall that encloses a splendid courtyard. Inside, 14-foot ceilings grace the family living areas. The foyer opens to the dining room on the left or to the brightly lit living room straight ahead. Thoughtful amenities in the living room include French doors to the rear porch, a fireplace, and a built-in entertainment center. The U-shaped kitchen is accentuated by an island and hosts bookshelves and a phone niche. Sleeping quarters begin with a guest room (with a semi-private bath) and two secondary bedrooms, one of which also makes a perfect study. The master suite is separated for privacy, enhanced by a private bath with a garden tub and dual walk-in closets.

plan# HPK0900111

Style: Traditional
Square Footage: 2,366
Bedrooms: 4
Bathrooms: 3
Width: 50' - 0"
Depth: 86' - 0"
Foundation: Slab

SEARCH ONLINE @ EPLANS.COM

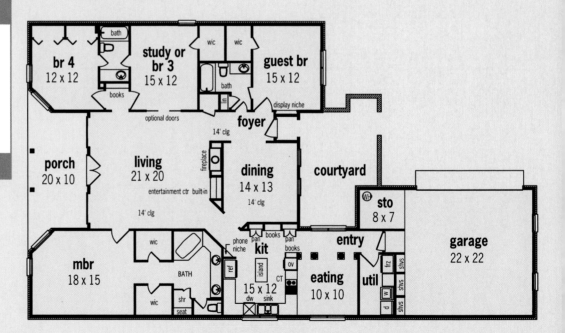

The elegance and grace of this split-level plan are apparent at first sight. Impressive arches open into the foyer, with the wide-open great room beyond, opening to a covered porch through French doors. Enter both the master suite and the adjacent den/study through French doors. A private courtyard keeps the master bath shielded from the front yard. From the nook, near two good-sized bedrooms with a shared bathroom, stairs lead up to a bonus room, which includes a large balcony to take advantage of your lot with a view.

plan # HPK0900112

Style: Contemporary
Square Footage: 2,237
Bonus Space: 397 sq. ft.
Bedrooms: 3
Bathrooms: 2
Width: 60' - 0"
Depth: 70' - 0"
Foundation: Slab

SEARCH ONLINE @ EPLANS.COM

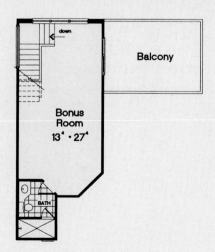

This exquisite European cottage offers all the charm of the Old World. A beautiful courtyard announces your entry. The foyer is flanked by a dining room and study. The kitchen features a snack counter, while the nook extends double-door access to the three-season porch. The master suite includes a pampering private bath and walk-in closet. A three-car garage completes the first floor. Three family bedrooms reside upstairs.

plan# HPK0900113

Style: Country Cottage
First Floor: 2,079 sq. ft.
Second Floor: 796 sq. ft.
Total: 2,875 sq. ft.
Bedrooms: 4
Bathrooms: 2½
Width: 63' - 0"
Depth: 68' - 0"
Foundation: Basement

SEARCH ONLINE @ EPLANS.COM

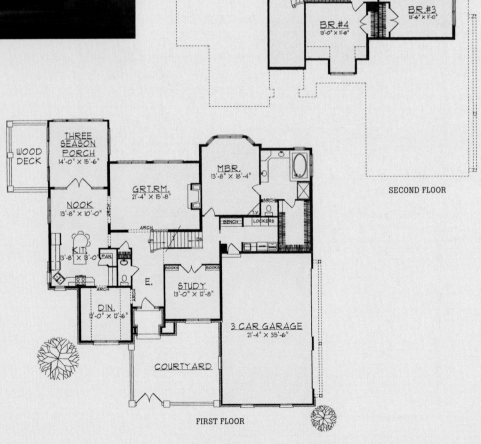

SECOND FLOOR

FIRST FLOOR

The impressive entry into this Mediterranean-style home leads directly into a spacious gathering room, with unique angles and a mitered glass window. This is the perfect home for the family that entertains! The large gathering room and covered porch with summer kitchen are ready for a pool party! Elegance and style grace this split floor plan, with large bedrooms and a very spacious kitchen/breakfast nook area. The kitchen includes a center island and a walk-in pantry. The master suite showcases a fireplace next to French doors which lead onto the covered porch at the rear, sweetly arranged for romantic evenings.

plan# **HPK0900114**

Style: Mediterranean
Square Footage: 2,367
Bedrooms: 3
Bathrooms: 2
Width: 76' - 0"
Depth: 71' - 4"
Foundation: Slab

SEARCH ONLINE @ EPLANS.COM

Master Bedroom
13⁰ · 18⁰

Master Bath

W.I.C.

Foyer

Entry

Dining
13⁰ · 11⁰

Gathering Room
19⁸ · 23⁰

opt. Summer Kitchen

Kitchen

island

desk oven

Covered Porch

Nook

Pan.

Utility

2 Car Garage

Den / Bedroom 3
13⁰ · 11²

Bath

Bedroom 2
15¹⁰ · 11⁰

The use of stone and stucco has created a very pleasant exterior that would fit in well with a traditional environment. The double-door entry, which leads to the foyer, welcomes guests to a formal living and dining room area. Upon entering the master suite through double doors, the master bed wall becomes the focal point. A stepped ceiling treatment adds excitement, with floor-length windows framing the bed. The sitting area created by the bayed door wall further enhances the opulence of the suite. The master bath comes complete with His and Hers walk-in closets, dual vanities with a makeup area, and a soaking tub balanced by the large shower and private toilet chamber.

plan # HPK0900115

Style: Floridian
Square Footage: 2,755
Bonus Space: 440 sq. ft.
Bedrooms: 4
Bathrooms: 3
Width: 73' - 0"
Depth: 82' - 8"
Foundation: Slab

SEARCH ONLINE @ EPLANS.COM

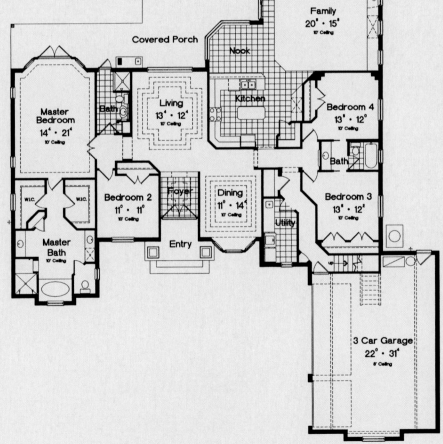

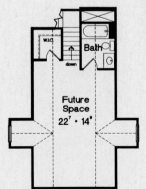

This attractive bungalow design separates the deluxe master suite from family bedrooms and puts casual living to the back in a family room. The formal living and dining areas are centrally located and have access to a rear terrace, as does the master suite. The kitchen sits between formal and informal living areas, sharing a snack bar with both. The two family bedrooms are found to the front of the plan, with a full bath nearby. A home office or study opens off the front foyer and the master suite.

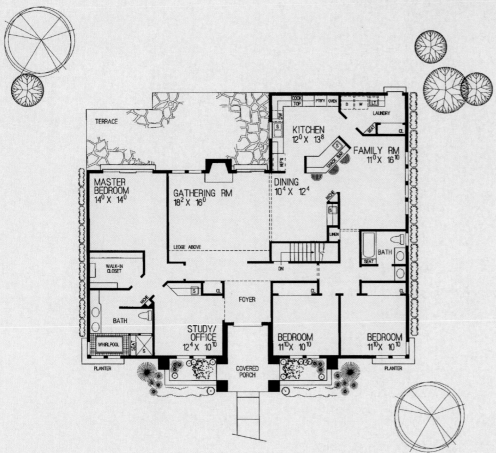

plan# **HPK0900116**

Style: NW Contemporary **LD**
Square Footage: 2,274
Bedrooms: 3
Bathrooms: 2
Width: 58' – 0"
Depth: 54' – 0"
Foundation: Basement

SEARCH ONLINE @ EPLANS.COM

QUOTE ONE®

A majestic facade makes this home pleasing to view. This home provides dual-use space in the wonderful sunken sitting room and media area. The kitchen has a breakfast bay and overlooks the snack bar to the sunken family area. A few steps from the kitchen is the formal dining room, which functions well with the upper patio. Two family bedrooms share a full bath. The private master suite includes a sitting area and French doors that open to a private covered patio.

plan # HPK0900117

Style: SW Contemporary
Square Footage: 2,086
Bedrooms: 3
Bathrooms: 2
Width: 82' - 0"
Depth: 58' - 4"
Foundation: Slab

SEARCH ONLINE @ EPLANS.COM

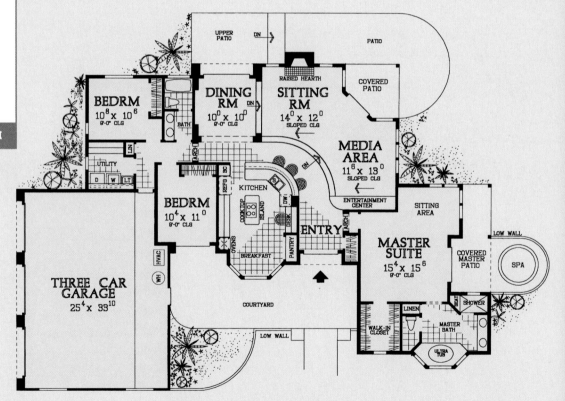

The wraparound front porch, the varying roof planes, and the paneled front door flanked by twin glass panels all blend to create the grand first impression of this family home. Inside, a popular floor plan caters to multiple living patterns. The central foyer, with its handy powder room, routes traffic efficiently to all areas. There are two living areas: the formal front living room and the informal rear family room. The kitchen and the breakfast room enjoy a multitude of conveniences. Four bedrooms and two baths highlight the second floor. In the master suite you'll find a walk-in closet in addition to a long wardrobe closet. The master bath is outstanding with its twin lavatories, whirlpool tub, stall shower, and compartmented toilet.

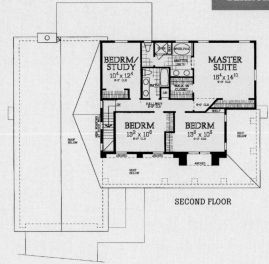

FIRST FLOOR

SECOND FLOOR

plan # HPK0900118

Style: Transitional
First Floor: 1,595 sq. ft.
Second Floor: 1,112 sq. ft.
Total: 2,707 sq. ft.
Bedrooms: 4
Bathrooms: 2½
Width: 63' - 6"
Depth: 51' - 6"
Foundation: Slab

SEARCH ONLINE @ EPLANS.COM

© The Sater Design Collection, Inc.

Come home to luxurious living—all on one level—with this striking Mediterranean plan. Unique ceiling treatments highlight the living areas—the living and dining rooms, as well as the study, feature stepped ceilings, and the leisure room soars with a vaulted ceiling. The gourmet kitchen includes a spacious center island; another kitchen, this one outdoors, can be accessed from the leisure room. The master suite boasts plenty of amenities: a large, skylit walk-in closet, a bath with a whirlpool tub and walk-in shower, and private access to a charming garden area. Two suites, both with private baths, sit to the right of the plan.

plan# HPK0900119

Style: European Cottage
Square Footage: 3,640
Bedrooms: 3
Bathrooms: 3½
Width: 106' - 4"
Depth: 102' - 4"
Foundation: Slab

SEARCH ONLINE @ EPLANS.COM

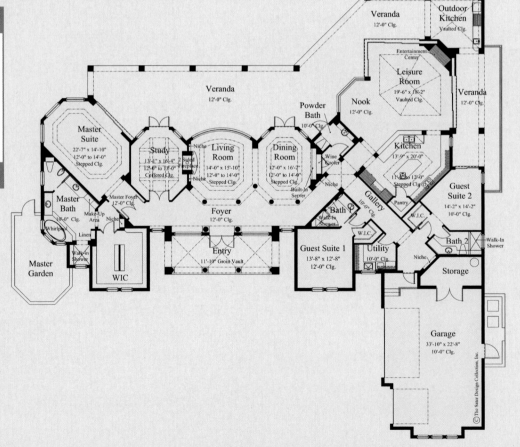

With striking Mediterranean affluence, this Renaissance estate invites family and guests with triplet arches and a dramatic vaulted portico. Upon entering, the bayed dining room is to the left; a study resides in the turret, bright with circumambient light courtesy of intricate full-length windows. The great room soars with a vintage exposed-beam ceiling and offers a fireplace and three sets of French doors to the veranda. Don't miss the country kitchen, a tribute to gourmet cooking. The master suite has an extended-bow window, access to the courtyard, and a luxurious bath with a Roman tub. An elegant staircase leads to two generous bedrooms; the vaulted bonus room is accessible from garage stairs or the outdoor deck off of Bedroom 3.

© The Sater Design Collection, Inc.

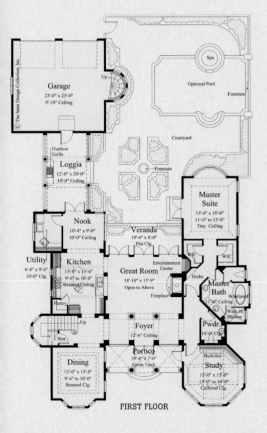

FIRST FLOOR

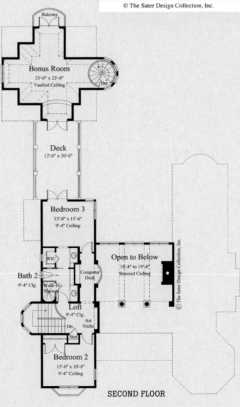

SECOND FLOOR

plan # HPK0900120

Style: Mediterranean
First Floor: 2,084 sq. ft.
Second Floor: 652 sq. ft.
Total: 2,736 sq. ft.
Bonus Space: 375 sq. ft.
Bedrooms: 3
Bathrooms: 2½
Width: 60' - 6"
Depth: 94' - 0"
Foundation: Slab

SEARCH ONLINE @ EPLANS.COM

Impressive pillars, keystone lintel arches, a covered carport, an abundance of windows, and an alluring fountain are just a few of the decorative touches of this elegant design. The two-story foyer leads to a two-story great room, which enjoys built-in cabinetry, a two-sided fireplace, and spectacular views to the rear property. To the left of the great room is the dining area, with a wet bar, island kitchen, and nearby bayed breakfast nook. Bedroom 2 boasts a semicircular wall of windows, a full bath, and a walk-in closet. The second-floor master suite is filled with amenities, including a two-sided fireplace.

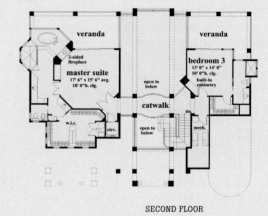

SECOND FLOOR

plan# HPK0900121

Style: Italianate
First Floor: 2,391 sq. ft.
Second Floor: 1,539 sq. ft.
Total: 3,930 sq. ft.
Bedrooms: 3
Bathrooms: 3½
Width: 71' - 0"
Depth: 69' - 0"
Foundation: Basement

SEARCH ONLINE @ EPLANS.COM

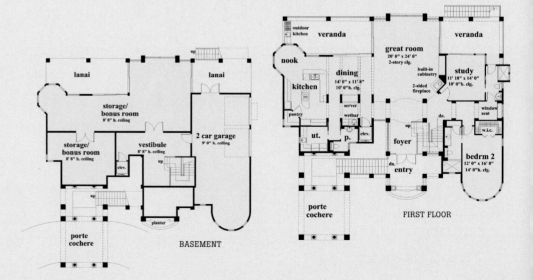

BASEMENT

FIRST FLOOR

Outside living spaces extend the interior of this sensational Bahamian-style home, bringing the outdoors in with three sets of sliding glass doors. The grand foyer leads to a winding staircase and opens to the great room. An open arrangement of the spacious living area and formal dining room is partially defined by a three-sided fireplace and a wet bar, and the entire space boasts a nine-foot ceiling. The wide veranda is home to an outdoor kitchen. A utility room and two bedrooms, each with a full bath, complete the main level. The upper level is dedicated to a lavish master suite. A three-sided fireplace warms the master bedroom and a sitting area, which open to an upper deck.

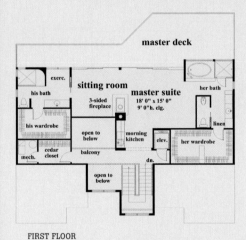

FIRST FLOOR

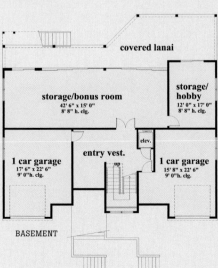

BASEMENT

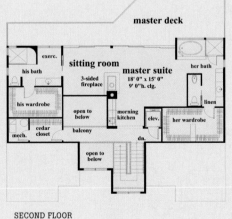

SECOND FLOOR

plan# HPK0900122

Style: Seaside
First Floor: 2,039 sq. ft.
Second Floor: 1,426 sq. ft.
Total: 3,465 sq. ft.
Bedrooms: 3
Bathrooms: 4
Width: 56' - 0"
Depth: 54' - 0"
Foundation: Basement

SEARCH ONLINE @ EPLANS.COM

This dream cabin captures the finest historic details in rooms furnished with comfort and style. A grand foyer features a radius staircase that decks out the entry hall and defines the wide-open interior. A formal dining room is served through a butler's pantry by a well-equipped kitchen. Casual space includes a leisure room that sports a corner fireplace, tray ceiling, and built-in media center. An outdoor kitchen makes it easy to enjoy life outside on the wraparound porch. The main-level master suite is suited with a spacious bedroom, two walk-in closets, and a lavish bath with separate vanities and a bumped-out whirlpool tub. Upstairs, two family bedrooms share a compartmented bath, and a guest suite boasts a roomy bath.

plan# HPK0900123

Style: Bungalow
First Floor: 2,083 sq. ft.
Second Floor: 1,013 sq. ft.
Total: 3,096 sq. ft.
Bedrooms: 4
Bathrooms: 3½
Width: 59' - 6"
Depth: 88' - 0"
Foundation: Slab

SEARCH ONLINE @ EPLANS.COM

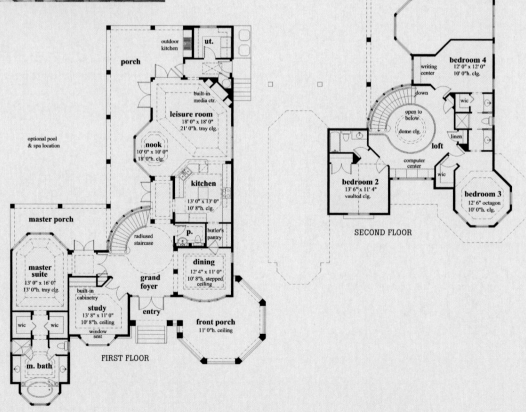

This country villa design is accented by a gazebo-style front porch and an abundance of arched windows. Most of the rooms in this house are graced with tray, stepped, or vaulted ceilings, enhancing the entire plan. The first-floor master suite boasts multiple amenities, including a private lanai, His and Hers walk-in closets, and a bayed whirlpool tub. Other highlights on this floor include a study with a window seat and built-in cabinetry, a bayed breakfast nook, a butler's pantry in the island kitchen, a utility room, and an outdoor kitchen on the lanai. Three secondary bedrooms reside upstairs, along with two full baths.

plan⊞ HPK0900124

Style: Italianate
First Floor: 2,083 sq. ft.
Second Floor: 1,013 sq. ft.
Total: 3,096 sq. ft.
Bedrooms: 4
Bathrooms: 3½
Width: 74' - 0"
Depth: 88' - 0"
Foundation: Slab

SEARCH ONLINE @ EPLANS.COM

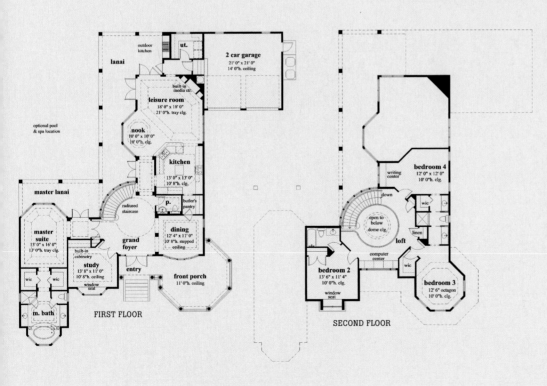

FIRST FLOOR

SECOND FLOOR

This beautiful design is accented by the circular front porch and the abundance of windows. The entry leads into a grand foyer, where a radius staircase presents itself. Most of the rooms in this house are graced with tray, stepped, or vaulted ceilings, adding a sense of spaciousness to the plan. The first-floor master suite boasts many amenities including a private lanai, His and Hers walk-in closets, a bayed tub area, and a separate shower. Other unique features on the first-floor include a study, with a window seat and built-in cabinetry, a breakfast nook, butler's pantry, utility room, and outdoor kitchen, among others. The upstairs houses three family bedrooms and two full baths. Bedroom 3 boasts an octagonal ceiling, and the ceiling of Bedroom 2 is vaulted. A computer center, linen area, and loft complete the second floor.

plan# HPK0900125

Style: Tidewater
First Floor: 2,083 sq. ft.
Second Floor: 1,013 sq. ft.
Total: 3,096 sq. ft.
Bedrooms: 4
Bathrooms: 3½
Width: 74' - 0"
Depth: 88' - 0"
Foundation: Slab

SEARCH ONLINE @ EPLANS.COM

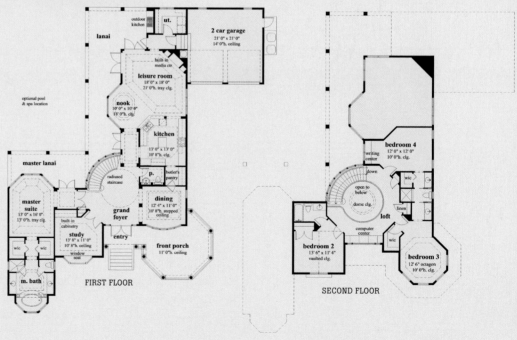

FIRST FLOOR

SECOND FLOOR

Chic and glamorous, this Mediterranean facade pairs ancient shapes, such as square columns, with a refined disposition set off by radius windows. A magnificent entry leads to an interior gallery and the great room. This extraordinary space is warmed by a two-sided fireplace and defined by extended views of the rear property. Sliding glass doors to a wraparound veranda create great indoor/outdoor flow. The gourmet kitchen easily serves any occasion and provides a pass-through to the outdoor kitchen. A powder room accommodates visitors, and an elevator leads to the sleeping quarters upstairs. Double doors open to the master suite, which features a walk-in closet, two-sided fireplace, and angled whirlpool bath. The master bedroom boasts a tray ceiling and doors to a spacious deck. The upper-level catwalk leads to a bedroom suite that can easily accommodate a guest or live-in relative. The basement level features future space and a two-car garage.

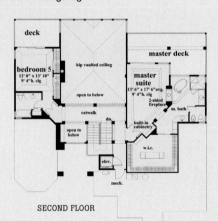

SECOND FLOOR

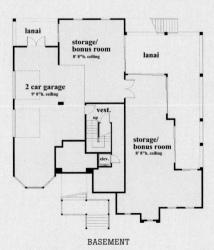

BASEMENT

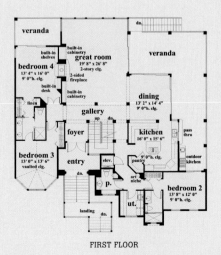

FIRST FLOOR

plan# HPK0900126

Style: Italianate
First Floor: 2,491 sq. ft.
Second Floor: 1,290 sq. ft.
Total: 3,781 sq. ft.
Bonus Space: 358 sq. ft.
Bedrooms: 5
Bathrooms: 4½
Width: 62' - 0"
Depth: 67' - 0"
Foundation: Basement

SEARCH ONLINE @ EPLANS.COM

An engaging blend of comfort and high architectural style creates a high-spirited home.

The foyer provides a magnificent view through the great room, where a two-story glass wall allows the vista to extend to the rear property. Amenities such as two-sided fireplaces, built-in shelves and cabinetry, wide decks, and verandas are perfectly suited to a casual yet elegant lifestyle. Bedroom 4 shares a fireplace with the great room, while Bedroom 3 provides a beautiful bay window. The wrap-around veranda includes an outdoor kitchen with a grill, rinsing sink, and pass-through to the main kitchen. The upper-level master suite offers its own observation deck and a private bath loaded with amenities.

plan# HPK0900127

Style: Bungalow
First Floor: 2,491 sq. ft.
Second Floor: 1,290 sq. ft.
Total: 3,781 sq. ft.
Bedrooms: 5
Bathrooms: 4½
Width: 62' - 0"
Depth: 67' - 0"
Foundation: Basement

SEARCH ONLINE @ EPLANS.COM

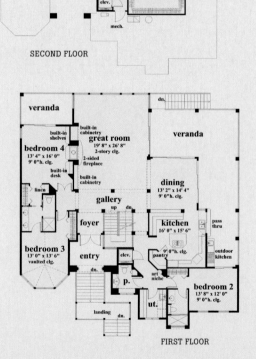

SECOND FLOOR

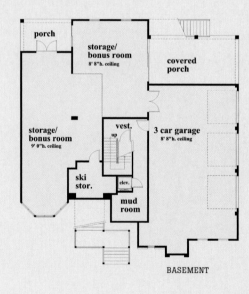

BASEMENT

FIRST FLOOR

The design of this French Country estate captures its ambiance with its verandas, grand entry, and unique balconies. A spectacular panorama of the formal living areas and the elegant curved stairway awaits just off the foyer. A large island kitchen, breakfast nook, and family room will impress, as will the wine cellar. Plenty of kitchen pantry space leads to the laundry and motor court featuring a two-car garage attached to the main house and a three-car garage attached by a breezeway. The master suite boasts a sunken sitting area with a see-through fireplace, His and Hers walk-in closets, island tub, and large separate shower. A study area, three additional bedrooms, a full bath, and a bonus area reside on the second floor.

plan# HPK0900128

Style: Chateau
First Floor: 3,517 sq. ft.
Second Floor: 1,254 sq. ft.
Total: 4,771 sq. ft.
Bedrooms: 5
Bathrooms: 4½ + ½
Width: 95' - 8"
Depth: 107' - 0"
Foundation: Slab

SEARCH ONLINE @ EPLANS.COM

FIRST FLOOR

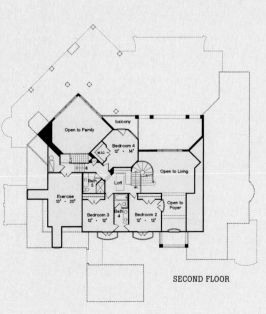

SECOND FLOOR

A stunning transom creates a picture-perfect entry and a glorious complement to the arch-top windows with this exquisite villa. Double stairs embraced by a classic balustrade lead to a mid-level landing, easing the transition from ground level to the front door. The foyer opens to a central gallery, which enjoys extensive views through the interior. Amenities in the great room create an inviting environment for crowd-size entertaining or cozy gatherings. A balcony overlook provides an elegant touch, while a wet bar and three-sided fireplace help define the space and add comfort and convenience. Secondary bedrooms reside to the front of the plan. The upper floor is dedicated to a rambling master suite, which provides a spacious sitting area, three-sided fireplace, and separate baths and wardrobes. An elevator connects three levels, including a basement-level storage and bonus area.

plan# HPK0900129

Style: Italianate
First Floor: 2,039 sq. ft.
Second Floor: 1,426 sq. ft.
Total: 3,465 sq. ft.
Bedrooms: 3
Bathrooms: 4
Width: 56' - 0"
Depth: 54' - 0"
Foundation: Basement

SEARCH ONLINE @ EPLANS.COM

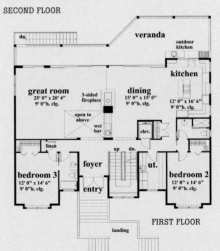

SECOND FLOOR

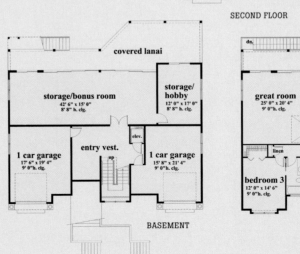

BASEMENT

FIRST FLOOR

This fabulous mountain home

begins with a stunning transom, which tops a classic paneled door and sets off a host of windows brightening the facade. Inside, a three-sided fireplace and wet bar invites entertaining on any scale, grand or cozy. The gourmet of the family will easily prepare meals in a well-equipped kitchen. A wide window overlooks the outdoor kitchen area of the patio, which includes a rinsing sink and outdoor grill. An upper level dedicated to the master retreat boasts a wide deck where, on a clear day, the beauty of natural light splashes this room with a sense of the outdoors and mingles with the crackle of the fireplace. Private baths for two provide separate amenities, including an exercise area and a knee-space vanity. Separate garages on the lower level lead to an entry vestibule with both an elevator and stairs.

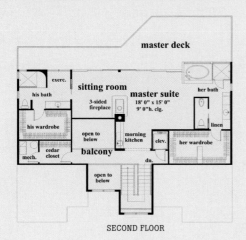

SECOND FLOOR

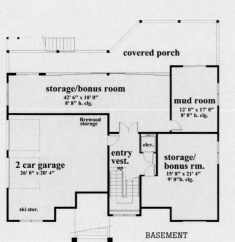

BASEMENT

FIRST FLOOR

plan# HPK0900130

Style: Bungalow
First Floor: 2,039 sq. ft.
Second Floor: 1,426 sq. ft.
Total: 3,465 sq. ft.
Bedrooms: 3
Bathrooms: 4
Width: 56' - 0"
Depth: 54' - 0"
Foundation: Basement

SEARCH ONLINE @ EPLANS.COM

plan # HPK0900131

Style: Bungalow
First Floor: 2,391 sq. ft.
Second Floor: 1,539 sq. ft.
Total: 3,930 sq. ft.
Bedrooms: 3
Bathrooms: 4½
Width: 71' - 0"
Depth: 69' - 0"
Foundation: Basement

SEARCH ONLINE @ EPLANS.COM

Climate is a key component of any mountain retreat, and outdoor living is an integral part of its design. This superior cabin features open and covered porches. A mix of matchstick details and rugged stone set off this lodge-house facade, concealing a well-defined interior. Windows line the breakfast bay and brighten the kitchen, which features a center cooktop island. A door leads out to a covered porch with a summer kitchen. The upper level features a secluded master suite with a spacious bath beginning with a double walk-in closet and ending with a garden view of the porch. A two-sided fireplace extends warmth to the whirlpool spa-style tub.

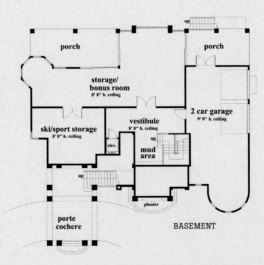

SECOND FLOOR

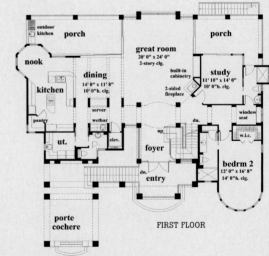

BASEMENT

FIRST FLOOR

ORDER BLUEPRINTS 24 HOURS, 7 DAYS A WEEK, AT 1-800-521-6797

plan# **HPK0900132**

Style: NW Contemporary
Square Footage: 1,484
Bedrooms: 3
Bathrooms: 2
Width: 38' - 0"
Depth: 70' - 0"
Foundation: Crawlspace

SEARCH ONLINE @ EPLANS.COM

plan# **HPK0900133**

Style: Craftsman
Square Footage: 1,502
Bedrooms: 2
Bathrooms: 2
Width: 32' - 0"
Depth: 67' - 8"
Foundation: Slab, Basement

SEARCH ONLINE @ EPLANS.COM

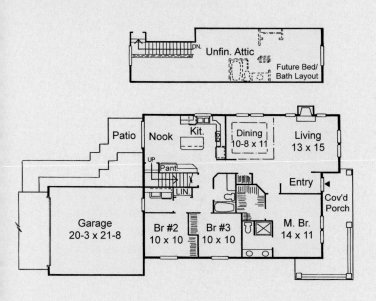

OPTIONAL LAYOUT

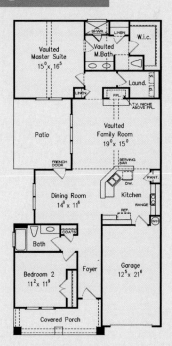

Perfect fit for a narrow lot, this home offers delicate details. A sweet front porch accents the country cottage facade and large gable roof. The foyer opens to optional French doors on the left for a grand dining room or study entry. Built-ins flank the fireplace and a stunning bumped-out bay adds character and beauty to the family room. A breakfast area connects to the spacious kitchen and a private side patio—a great spot for a garden. Two bedrooms sit to the rear; the master enjoys a private vaulted bath and walk-in closet.

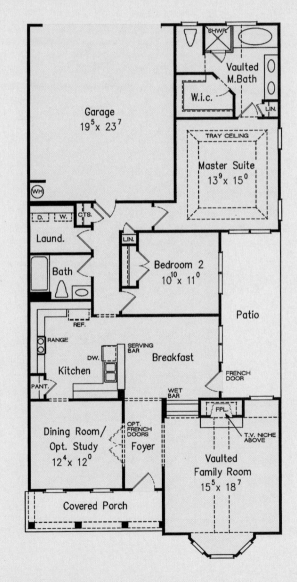

plan # HPK0900134

Style: Craftsman
Square Footage: 1,610
Bedrooms: 2
Bathrooms: 2
Width: 34' - 0"
Depth: 72' - 0"
Foundation: Crawlspace, Basement

SEARCH ONLINE @ EPLANS.COM

This narrow-lot plan offers a ton of amenities in a neat package. The family room features a vaulted ceiling and flows easily into the central dining area. The covered porch and patio at right can be customized easily into a large sunroom or formal dining room. The bedrooms are located at the rear of the plan and each is attended by a full bath. The master suite enjoys a vaulted ceiling and walk-in closet. Finally, a laundry room does its job away from the center of the home, near the garage.

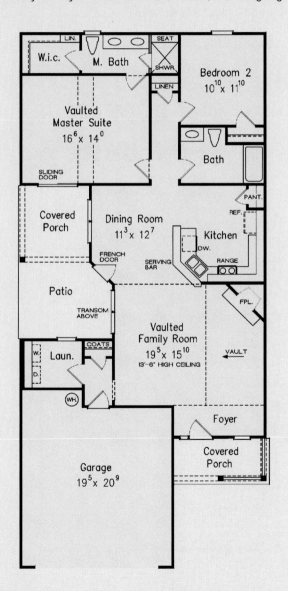

OPTIONAL LAYOUT

plan # HPK0900135

Style: Bungalow
Square Footage: 1,393
Bonus Space: 206 sq. ft.
Bedrooms: 2
Bathrooms: 2
Width: 32' - 0"
Depth: 70' - 0"
Foundation: Crawlspace, Basement

SEARCH ONLINE @ EPLANS.COM

This efficient yet feature-packed design offers a great solution to narrow lot dilemmas. Vaulted ceilings in the master bedroom and family room bring refreshing height and keep spaces feeling airy. The left exterior in-sets at the dining room to let windows bring more natural light into the center of the plan. Owners will also appreciate the home's many amenities, such as an oversized walk-in closet, furniture and media niches, a built-in pantry, and compartmented laundry area. The gabled exterior is a classic.

plan# HPK0900136

Style: Craftsman

Square Footage: 1,634

Bedrooms: 3

Bathrooms: 2

Width: 32' - 0"

Depth: 68' - 0"

Foundation: Crawlspace, Basement

SEARCH ONLINE @ EPLANS.COM

OPTIONAL LAYOUT

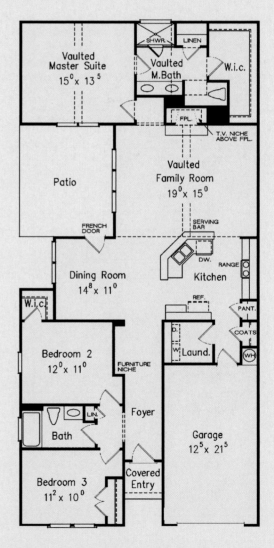

Compact yet contemporary, this Craftsman home fits comfortably in narrow lots while maintaining a modern feel using an open design. The foyer gives way to the spacious dining room with windows lining two walls, one with a view of the rear patio. A serving bar in the adjoining kitchen caters to both rooms. The vaulted family room is enhanced by a fireplace and a built-in TV niche. The master suite, adorned with a tray ceiling, features a dual-sink vanity, a separate shower and tub, and a large walk-in closet. The area outside the master suite serves as a mud room, complete with a built-in bench and a second coat closet.

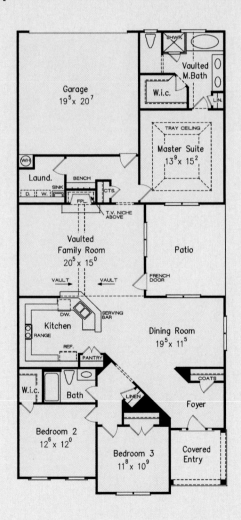

plan # HPK0900137

Style: Craftsman
Square Footage: 1,847
Bedrooms: 3
Bathrooms: 2
Width: 34' - 0"
Depth: 76' - 0"
Foundation: Crawlspace, Basement

SEARCH ONLINE @ EPLANS.COM

This easy-living design offers plenty of open spaces and height without sacrificing function. A laundry/utility room placed near the kitchen ensures quiet enjoyment for those in the bedroom, as well as easy entry to the kitchen. The continuous breakfast nook and family room forms the heart of the plan and allows privacy in the master suite. A tray ceiling, large walk-in closet, compartmented toilet, and whirlpool tub make this suite a quiet retreat. Two more bedrooms and a full bath complete the plan.

plan # HPK0900138

Style: Country Cottage
Square Footage: 1,627
Bedrooms: 3
Bathrooms: 2
Width: 37' - 0"
Depth: 66' - 0"
Foundation: Slab

SEARCH ONLINE @ EPLANS.COM

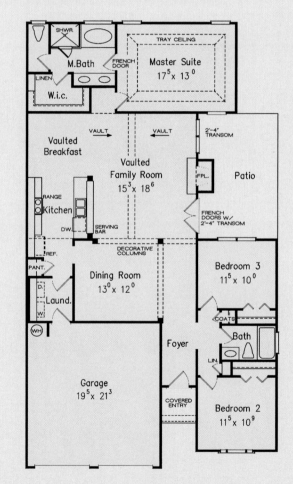

Petite in proportions and scaled for narrow lots—great first-home builders, city in-fill, and empty-nesters—this design considers modern comforts. A casual foyer connects with the vaulted family room adding warmth to the space with a fireplace. A series of windows face the large side patio, extending private living space to the outdoors. The dining room also enjoys the patio view and the convenience of the nearby C-shaped kitchen with walk-in pantry and serving bar. A short, wide hallway makes room for two family bedrooms and a full hall bath. The master suite, enhanced by a tray ceiling, is outfitted with a walk-in closet, roomy bath with dual-sink vanities, separate shower and tub, and a private toilet.

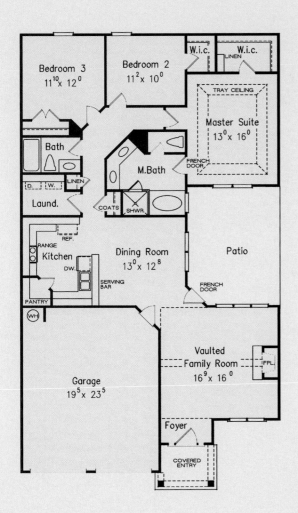

plan# HPK0900139

Style: Country Cottage
Square Footage: 1,546
Bedrooms: 3
Bathrooms: 2
Width: 37' - 0"
Depth: 65' - 5"
Foundation: Slab

SEARCH ONLINE @ EPLANS.COM

A two-car garage topped by twin dormers, and a covered and pillared front porch capture a timeless essence on the facade of this country home. In one story you get two bedrooms and two full baths, perfect for a small family, empty-nesters, or even as a vacation home. The long foyer leads directly into a great room filled with amenities such as a fireplace flanked by built-in shelves, decorative colums, French-door access to a vast side patio, and a vaulted ceiling. From there you can enter the dining room, wisely placed adjacent to the kitchen with convenient serving bar. The master suite leaves nothing to be desired; pass through the French doors into the master bath and discover the dual sink vanity and access to a spacious walk-in closet.

plan# HPK0900140

Style: Country Cottage
Square Footage: 1,437
Bedrooms: 2
Bathrooms: 2
Width: 37' - 0"
Depth: 64' - 5"
Foundation: Slab

SEARCH ONLINE @ EPLANS.COM

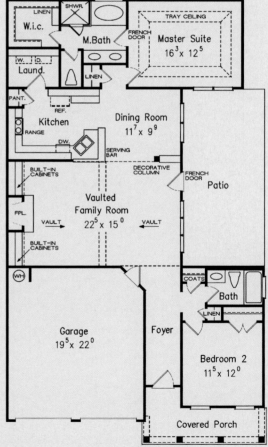

This compact home has a lot more packed inside its walls than it might appear from the outside. It enjoys three bedrooms, one of them an amenity-filled master suite; two baths; a well-equipped laundry; and a two-car garage. The grand room, with a warming fireplace, soars two stories high to a vaulted ceiling. It easily opens to the kitchen and a breakfast nook, which opens to a rear deck or patio.

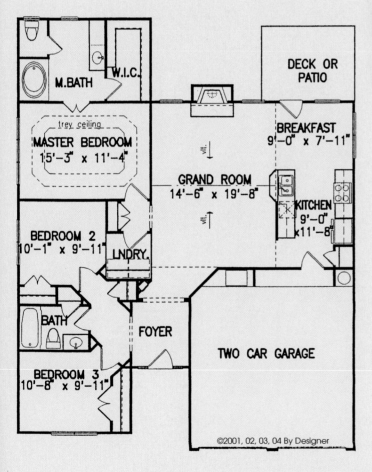

plan# HPK0900141

Style: Country Cottage
Square Footage: 1,328
Bedrooms: 3
Bathrooms: 2
Width: 40' - 0"
Depth: 52' - 0"
Foundation: Slab

SEARCH ONLINE @ EPLANS.COM

This snappy-looking home is roomier than it might

appear, and a front wraparound porch and rear patio extend usable space. A den and a parlor to either side of the entrance offer possibilities for both formal get-togethers and informal conversations. The family room and dining area mesh together under a vaulted ceiling; at one end, French doors open onto the patio. An angled snack bar—great for quick breakfasts and late-night munching—separates the kitchen from the dining room. A splendid master suite with a luxuriant private bath and a family bedroom are on the right side of the plan. Upstairs, another bedroom and bath open to a loft overlooking the family and dining rooms.

plan ⊕ **HPK0900142**

Style: NW Contemporary
First Floor: 1,508 sq. ft.
Second Floor: 446 sq. ft.
Total: 1,954 sq. ft.
Bonus Space: 651 sq. ft.
Bedrooms: 3
Bathrooms: 3
Width: 50' - 0"
Depth: 50' - 0"
Foundation: Crawlspace, Slab

SEARCH ONLINE @ EPLANS.COM

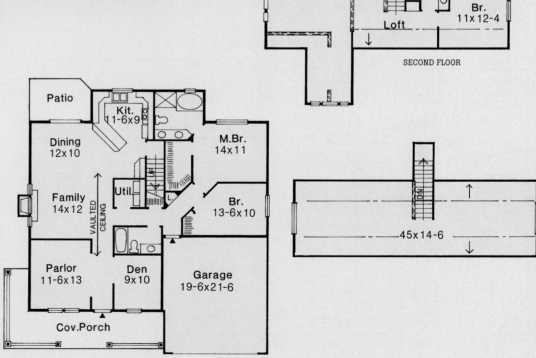

Contemporary Northwestern style lends a natural look to this modern home, allowing it to fit perfectly in any neighborhood. The entry presents a sunken living room, giving the space a more formal appeal. The family room opens up completely to the gourmet kitchen and breakfast nook, allowing them to view the family room's fireplace. Bedrooms are located upstairs, featuring a master suite with a spa tub set in a bay window. Three additional bedrooms share one-and-a-half baths and a generous playroom.

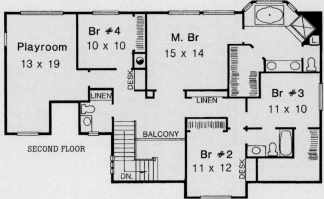

SECOND FLOOR

FIRST FLOOR

plan # HPK0900143

Style: NW Contemporary
First Floor: 1,200 sq. ft.
Second Floor: 1,323 sq. ft.
Total: 2,523 sq. ft.
Bonus Space: 247 sq. ft.
Bedrooms: 4
Bathrooms: 2 ½ + ½
Width: 71' - 6"
Depth: 40' - 0"
Foundation: Crawlspace

SEARCH ONLINE @ EPLANS.COM

Skylights illuminate the interior of this attractive contemporary design. A large wraparound porch welcomes outdoor activities for warm seasonal events. Inside, the living room, dining room, and island/snack-bar kitchen are open to each other. The living room is warmed by a fireplace. The first-floor master suite features ample closet space and is placed just across the hall from a spacious bath with a laundry closet. Upstairs, two family bedrooms share a full hall bath.

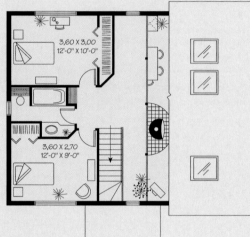

3,60 X 3,00
12'-0" X 10'-0"

3,60 X 2,70
12'-0" X 9'-0"

SECOND FLOOR

plan # HPK0900144

Style: Resort Lifestyles
First Floor: 984 sq. ft.
Second Floor: 560 sq. ft.
Total: 1,544 sq. ft.
Bedrooms: 3
Bathrooms: 2
Width: 34' - 0"
Depth: 28' - 0"
Foundation: Basement

SEARCH ONLINE @ EPLANS.COM

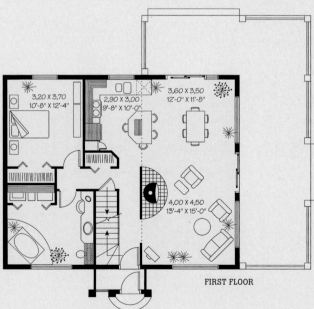

3,20 X 3,70
10'-8" X 12'-4"

2,90 X 3,00
9'-8" X 10'-0"

3,60 X 3,50
12'-0" X 11'-8"

4,00 X 4,50
13'-4" X 15'-0"

FIRST FLOOR

plan# HPK0900145

Style: Country Cottage
First Floor: 1,440 sq. ft.
Second Floor: 1,086 sq. ft.
Total: 2,526 sq. ft.
Bedrooms: 3
Bathrooms: 3½
Width: 48' - 0"
Depth: 60' - 0"
Foundation: Basement

SEARCH ONLINE @ EPLANS.COM

SECOND FLOOR

FIRST FLOOR

plan# HPK0900146

Style: Traditional
Main Level: 1,406 sq. ft.
Lower Level: 1,406 sq. ft.
Total: 2,812 sq. ft.
Bedrooms: 4
Bathrooms: 3
Width: 58' - 0"
Depth: 41' - 4"
Foundation: Basement

SEARCH ONLINE @ EPLANS.COM

MAIN LEVEL

LOWER LEVEL

plan# HPK0900147

Style: Country Cottage
First Floor: 1,373 sq. ft.
Second Floor: 777 sq. ft.
Total: 2,150 sq. ft.
Bedrooms: 3
Bathrooms: 2½
Width: 44' - 4"
Depth: 58' - 4"
Foundation: Crawlspace, Slab

SEARCH ONLINE @ EPLANS.COM

plan# HPK0900148

Style: Cape Cod
Main Level: 2,298 sq. ft.
Lower Level: 1,718 sq. ft.
Total: 4,016 sq. ft.
Bedrooms: 3
Bathrooms: 2½ + ½
Width: 60' - 0"
Depth: 71' - 0"
Foundation: Basement

SEARCH ONLINE @ EPLANS.COM

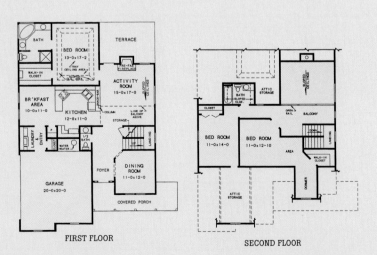

FIRST FLOOR

SECOND FLOOR

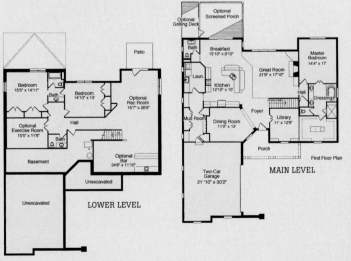

LOWER LEVEL

MAIN LEVEL

First Floor Plan

RON & DONNA KOLB, EXPOSURES UNLIMITED

Here's an expandable Colonial with a full measure of Cape Cod charm. Salt-box shapes and modular structures popular in Early America enjoyed a revival at the turn of the century and have come to life again—this time with added square footage and some very comfortable amenities. Upstairs, a spacious master suite shares a gallery hall which leads to two family bedrooms and sizable storage space. The expanded version of the basic plan adds a study wing to the left of the foyer as well as an attached garage with a service entrance to the kitchen.

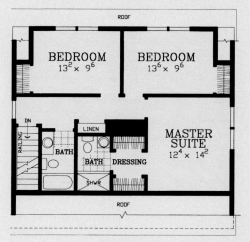

ROOF

BEDROOM
13² x 9⁶

BEDROOM
13⁶ x 9⁶

DN

RAILING

LINEN

BATH

BATH   DRESSING

SHWR

MASTER
SUITE
12⁴ x 14²

ROOF

SECOND FLOOR

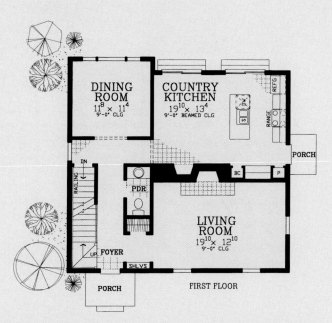

DINING
ROOM
11⁸ x 11⁴
9'-0" CLG

COUNTRY
KITCHEN
19¹⁰ x 13⁴
9'-0" BEAMED CLG

REFG

RANGE

DW
S

PORCH

DN

RAILING

PDR

BC

P

LIVING
ROOM
19¹⁰ x 12¹⁰
9'-0" CLG

UP   FOYER

SHLVS

PORCH

FIRST FLOOR

plan# HPK0900149

L D

Style: Cape Cod
First Floor: 1,016 sq. ft.
Second Floor: 766 sq. ft.
Total: 1,782 sq. ft.
Bedrooms: 3
Bathrooms: 2½
Width: 33' - 0"
Depth: 30' - 0"
Foundation: Basement

SEARCH ONLINE @ EPLANS.COM

This Early American design offers great livability with an expansive living room accented by a fireplace. Nearby, an efficient island kitchen serves the formal dining room and a cozy breakfast nook. A quiet study with built-in bookshelves sits to the left of the foyer. A convenient powder room rounds out the first floor. Upstairs, the master bedroom includes a walk-in closet and a private bath; two family bedrooms share a full dual-vanity bath just across the hall. The two-car, side-loading garage makes this plan perfect for a corner lot.

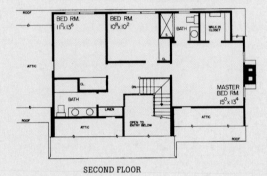

SECOND FLOOR

plan # HPK0900150

D

Style: European Cottage
First Floor: 1,388 sq. ft.
Second Floor: 809 sq. ft.
Total: 2,197 sq. ft.
Bedrooms: 3
Bathrooms: 2½
Width: 73' - 4"
Depth: 32' - 0"
Foundation: Basement

SEARCH ONLINE @ EPLANS.COM

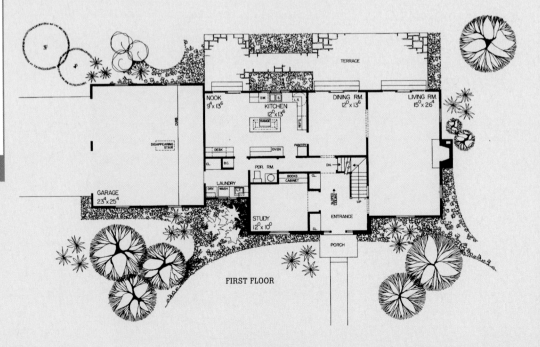

FIRST FLOOR

ORDER BLUEPRINTS 24 HOURS, 7 DAYS A WEEK, AT 1-800-521-6797

Arched windows and doorways and nested gables enhance this traditional home through symmetry in design to the delight of the neighborhood. The columns and arch of the covered porch are repeated in the entrance to the living/dining room and the foyer. The breakfast area adjoins the island kitchen and the family room where a warming fireplace is flanked by a built-in TV center and china cabinet. Two family bedrooms share a full bath while the master suite boasts a private bath. The covered patio gains access from the master bedroom and the family room.

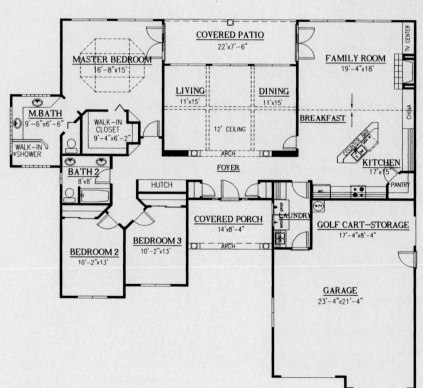

plan # HPK0900151

Style: Cape Cod
Square Footage: 2,138
Bedrooms: 3
Bathrooms: 2
Width: 67' - 8"
Depth: 62' - 6"
Foundation: Slab

SEARCH ONLINE @ EPLANS.COM

ORDER BLUEPRINTS 24 HOURS, 7 DAYS A WEEK, AT 1-800-521-6797

This charming vacation retreat will feel like home in the mountains as well as by a wooded lakefront. With a covered deck, screened porch, and spacious patio, this home is designed for outdoors lovers. Inside, a comfy, rustic aura dominates. On the main level, a lodge-like living area with an extended-hearth fireplace and snack bar dominates. A library, easy-to-use kitchen, and enchanting master suite are also located on this floor. Downstairs, there are two more bedrooms, a huge recreation room, a hobby room (or make it into another bedroom), and lots of storage space.

plan# HPK0900152

Style: Craftsman
Main Level: 1,984 sq. ft.
Lower Level: 1,451 sq. ft.
Total: 3,435 sq. ft.
Bedrooms: 4
Bathrooms: 3½
Width: 56' - 0"
Depth: 65' - 0"
Foundation: Basement

SEARCH ONLINE @ EPLANS.COM

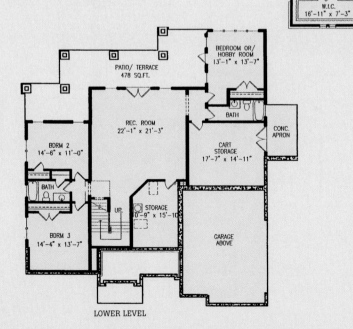

MAIN LEVEL

LOWER LEVEL

A brick and stone exterior and a courtyard garage adorn the facade of this delightful home. Designed for a narrow lot, the open floor plan offers views to the rear yard to enjoy a golf course or lake front setting. Gatherings will be a breeze in the great room, dining area, and kitchen combination. U-shaped stairs set at an angle and the sloped ceiling of the great room add luxurious detailing. The warmth of the fireplace radiates through the combined living area and an island with seating is set to an angle that mimics the stairs and sets the kitchen apart. A screened porch opens off of the dining area, offering outdoor dining in comfort. The master suite features a recessed ceiling, deck access, and a lavish bath. A library or second bedroom set to the front of the home offers a flexible room. Expanded living space is available in the optional finished basement.

plan # HPK0900153

Style: Transitional
Main Level: 2,068 sq. ft.
Lower Level: 1,357 sq. ft.
Total: 3,425 sq. ft.
Bedrooms: 4
Bathrooms: 3
Width: 48' - 0"
Depth: 78' - 4"
Foundation: Basement

SEARCH ONLINE @ EPLANS.COM

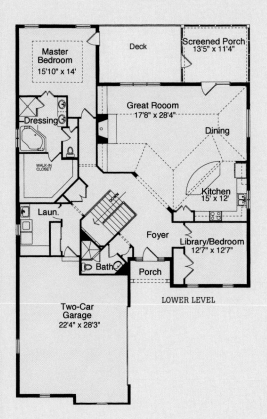

LOWER LEVEL

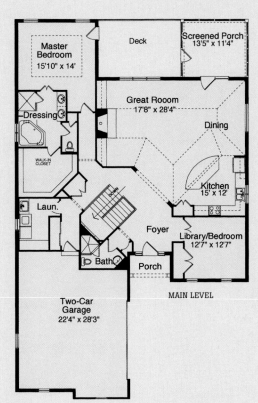

MAIN LEVEL

A **stone-and-brick exterior** presents a rich aura for this home. The foyer introduces a library to the left, accessed by French doors. A corner fireplace in the combined great room and dining area sets off the open feel of the area. A second fireplace warms the covered porch just beyond the great room. Gourmet cooks will fancy this island kitchen with its serving bar to the great room and dining area. The laundry and powder rooms are conveniently located between the kitchen and the garage. The master bedroom features private deck access and a luxurious private bath and walk-in closet. A family bedroom has access to a full bath to the front of the home. The option of a finished walkout basement is available with this home, adding a bedroom, bathroom, recreation room with a wet bar, media area, and exercise room to the plan.

plan# HPK0900154

Style: Craftsman
Square Footage: 2,716
Bedrooms: 2
Bathrooms: 2½
Width: 85' - 2"
Depth: 49' - 8"
Foundation: Basement

SEARCH ONLINE @ EPLANS.COM

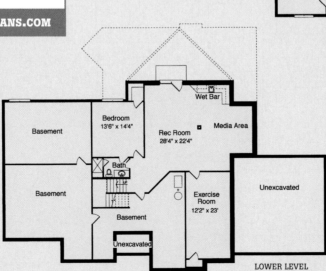

Room to Grow:
Homes with Storage + Bonus Spaces

This home boasts striking curb appeal, plus tremendous storage space in the basement (page 231).

When it would be nice to have more finished space than the construction budget for a second home allows, selecting house plans with bonus space could be the perfect solution. Bonus rooms are exactly what they sound like—extra space for future expansion. Such multifunctional spaces allow for unique designs that can be tailored to fit your lifestyle. There will be room to spread into, whether for additional family members or to indulge your getaway plans for everything from a multimedia room to an exercise place to a studio or office. Bonus space is also great for organization. A place for everything and everything in its place is a motto to live by, but where in the house will you put all the stuff you need to get away in comfort? Even small bonus rooms can be converted to walk-in closets and pantries, or lined with walls of storage for bulky sports equipment, extra linens, or clothing. Many of the following home plans come with unfinished rooms located above the main floor. So when finances allow and the need arises, bonus space in these designs can be finished to almost double the living area in a vacation home. If future getaway plans harbor a need for more rooms, choose a home plan with bonus space. Then let your getaway plans grow—the possibilities are almost endless.

White double columns outline the entry of this design, providing a striking contrast to its earth tones and stone accents.

Inside Outstanding

This luxury home is smart on space, big on windows, and has room to grow with a spacious bonus room

Enter this luxury villa through the statuesque front portico to the spacious foyer. An elegant dining room is on your left, largely open to the rest of the home as columns substitute obstructing walls. The dining room boasts a vaulted ceiling and also enjoys views of the front yard. To the right of the foyer is the study, more sheltered than the dining room, as it requires more privacy than entertaining.

The master wing begins just down the hall from the study, on the right side of the home. Designed for total indulgence, the master suite is accented by massive His and Hers closets. The lavish master bath comes equipped with a soaking tub and double vanity. Looking for a serene place to sit and talk? The master bedroom flows into a private sitting room, with direct access to the scenic lanai.

This home caters to views, as the rear of the home is lined with windows. The result is an illuminated first floor providing friends and family with extensive sweeping views of the backyard from almost every room. The foyer opens to the living room, which boasts direct access to the lanai—again blurring the distinction between the interior and the outdoors.

The second story of this home is relatively small, allowing for some dramatic ceiling treatments on the first floor.

Left: A charming art niche sits just outside the dining room. **Right:** The kitchen, breakfast nook, and family room feature a comfortable open design.

Left: Family and friends will delight in the stunning views of the lanai via the room's wall of windows.
Right: A copper-basin sink lends rustic style in the master bath.

The spacious gourmet kitchen is designed for more than one family chef. This large kitchen includes a center island for added counter space and an additional sink, fully equipped for serving large parties or preparing family meals. A breakfast room, with access to the lanai, is adjacent to the kitchen, ideal for preparing meals without the concern of immediate cleanup.

The sprawling family room will certainly be the hub of activity. It has a view of the backyard as well as a storage closet for family board games. Both of the guest bedrooms share a full bath and are located off the family room. One enjoys a private lanai; the other has a walk-in closet. An added bonus to the layout of the home is that both guests and homeowners will enjoy privacy.

The gorgeous first floor is completed with a three-car garage and a utility room.

Planning sitting areas outdoors will dramatically expand the living space in a getaway home.

The second floor offers all the extra rooms a homeowner could ask for. A sizable activity space, measuring more than 18 by 15 feet, can be converted into virtually anything the homeowner desires. The large room can easily be transformed into a game/recreation room, art studio, gym, or even a spare bedroom. This versatile space also boasts a closet for added storage. A study niche is located off the activity space and includes a closet. This secluded area offers a quiet place for the kids to do homework, or for the grownups to sit and read or enjoy a relaxing coffee with company. A second-floor bath is across from the study niche, and a home office completes the second floor. ■

The expansive rear lanai, dramatically lit and with plenty of space for lawn chairs and a patio set, overlooks a uniquely shaped swimming pool.

plan # HPK0900155

Style: Prairie
First Floor: 3,097 sq. ft.
Second Floor: 873 sq. ft.
Total: 3,970 sq. ft.
Bedrooms: 3
Bathrooms: 4
Width: 78' - 0"
Depth: 75' - 4"
Foundation: Slab

SEARCH ONLINE @ EPLANS.COM

SECOND FLOOR

FIRST FLOOR

This "little jewel" of a home emanates a warmth and joy not soon forgotten. The two-story foyer leads to the formal living room, defined by graceful columns. A formal dining room opens off from the living room, making entertaining a breeze. A family room at the back features a fireplace and works well with the kitchen and breakfast areas. A lavish master suite is secluded on the first floor; three family bedrooms reside upstairs.

plan # HPK0900156

Style: Country Cottage
First Floor: 1,627 sq. ft.
Second Floor: 783 sq. ft.
Total: 2,410 sq. ft.
Bonus Space: 418 sq. ft.
Bedrooms: 4
Bathrooms: 2½
Width: 46' - 0"
Depth: 58' - 6"
Foundation: Crawlspace

SEARCH ONLINE @ EPLANS.COM

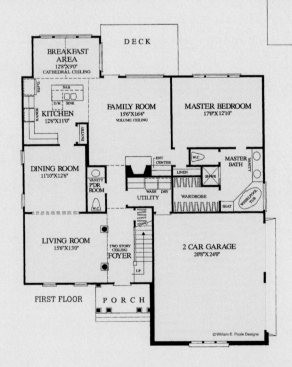

Stone and siding create a stunning exterior, especially when combined with a sloped roofline and a decorative wood bracket. A metal roof embellishes the garage's box-bay window, and arches are seen in and above windows as well as the front entrance. The great room is filled with light from its many windows and French doors, and a glimpse of the fireplace can be seen from every gathering room. The master bedroom is topped by a cathedral ceiling and has a large walk-in closet. The loft makes a perfect sitting or study area that receives a lot of light from the open, two-story great room. The second floor bathroom includes twin lavatories, and the versatile bonus room is easily accessible.

© 2001 Donald A. Gardner, Inc.

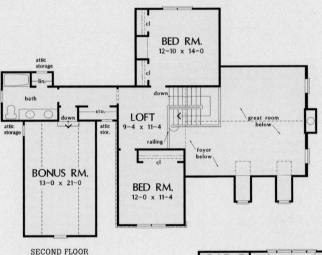

SECOND FLOOR

FIRST FLOOR

© 2001 DONALD A. GARDNER
All rights reserved

plan# HPK0900157

Style: European Cottage
First Floor: 1,547 sq. ft.
Second Floor: 684 sq. ft.
Total: 2,231 sq. ft.
Bonus Space: 300 sq. ft.
Bedrooms: 3
Bathrooms: 2½
Width: 59' - 2"
Depth: 44' - 4"

SEARCH ONLINE @ EPLANS.COM

Stone and siding combine to give this Craftsman design striking curb appeal. A portico sets the tone with a gentle arch and four stately columns. A clerestory above the front entrance floods the two-story foyer with natural light. Inside, Old World charm gives way to an open, family-efficient floorplan. The kitchen partitions the dining room and breakfast area and easily accesses a screen porch for outdoor entertaining. The great room features a two-story fireplace and French doors that lead to the rear porch. A family room also sports a fireplace and patio access. The master bedroom is crowned by a tray ceiling, and a balcony with a curved alcove separates two additional bedrooms upstairs.

plan # HPK0900158

Style: Contemporary
Main Level: 1,682 sq. ft.
Second Level: 577 sq. ft.
Lower Level: 690 sq. ft.
Total: 2,949 sq. ft.
Bonus Space: 459 sq. ft.
Bedrooms: 4
Bathrooms: 3½
Width: 79' - 0"
Depth: 68' - 2"

SEARCH ONLINE @ EPLANS.COM

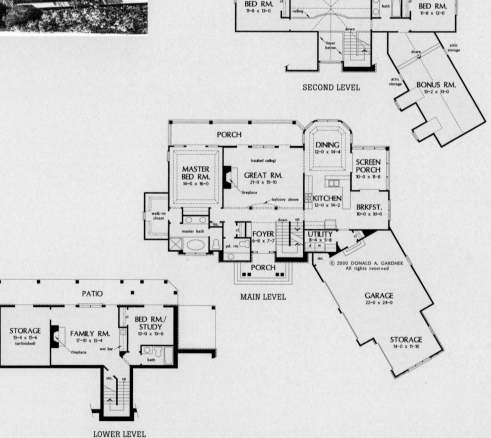

© 1999 Donald A. Gardner, Inc.

A stunning center dormer with an arched window embellishes the exterior of this Craftsman-style home. The dormer's arched window allows light into the foyer and built-in niche. The second-floor hall is a balcony that overlooks both the foyer and great room. A generous back porch extends the great room, which features an impressive vaulted ceiling and fireplace; a tray ceiling adorns the formal dining room. The master suite, which includes a tray ceiling as well, enjoys back-porch access, a built-in cabinet, generous walk-in closet, and private bath. Two more bedrooms are located upstairs; a fourth can be found in the basement along with a family room.

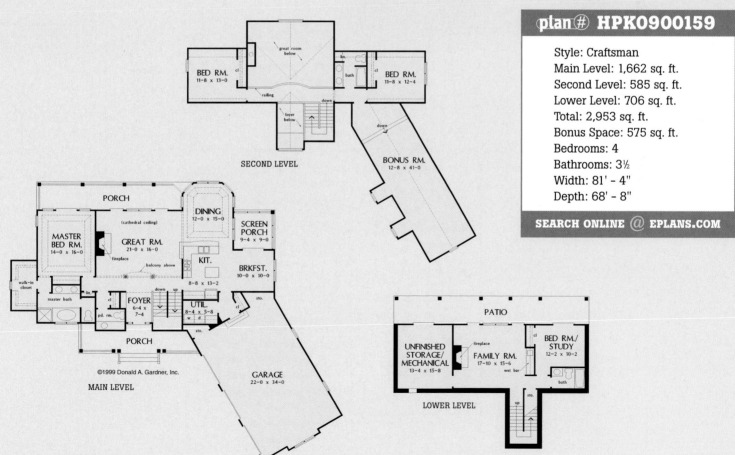

plan# **HPK0900159**

Style: Craftsman
Main Level: 1,662 sq. ft.
Second Level: 585 sq. ft.
Lower Level: 706 sq. ft.
Total: 2,953 sq. ft.
Bonus Space: 575 sq. ft.
Bedrooms: 4
Bathrooms: 3½
Width: 81' - 4"
Depth: 68' - 8"

SEARCH ONLINE @ EPLANS.COM

SECOND LEVEL

MAIN LEVEL

LOWER LEVEL

©1999 Donald A. Gardner, Inc.

The curve of the Palladian window softens the strong stone wall and gable, and a prominent dormer towers above the front entrance with its pilasters, sidelights, and arched transom that lead eyes inside. Stone creates a powerful impression on the exterior. All of the common rooms, along with the master bedroom, are positioned to take advantage of rear views through numerous windows and French doors. A cathedral ceiling and fireplace highlight the great room. The kitchen is placed to easily serve the connecting dining room, but also accesses the convenient utility room. A coat closet and pantry create storage. The bedrooms are grouped together to form the quiet zone. The master bedroom features a large walk-in closet and private bath. One of the family bedrooms features a vaulted ceiling, and they share a full hall bath.

plan# HPK0900160

Style: Craftsman
Square Footage: 1,676
Bonus Space: 376 sq. ft.
Bedrooms: 3
Bathrooms: 2
Width: 56' - 8"
Depth: 48' - 4"

SEARCH ONLINE @ EPLANS.COM

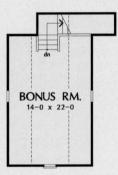

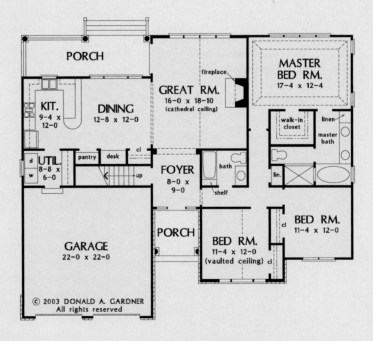

This rustic French Country exterior opens up to a plan full of modern amenities. The foyer, preceded by a petite porch, leads into a gallery hall that opens to a sunny, vaulted great room. With its fireplace and porch access, this will be the most popular room in the house. As an added convenience, the great room flows into the breakfast room, with its box-bay window and built-ins. The island kitchen features a pantry and plenty of counter space. A formal dining room is adjacent. The deluxe master suite awaits on the left of the plan, enjoying a pampering bath and double walk-in closets. Upstairs, two bedrooms boast ample closet space and a private bath. Bonus space awaits expansion over the garage.

© 2002 Donald A. Gardner, Inc.

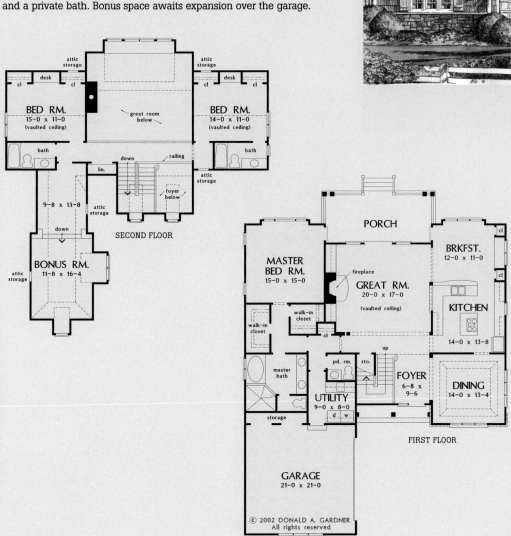

plan# **HPK0900161**

Style: French Country
First Floor: 1,834 sq. ft.
Second Floor: 681 sq. ft.
Total: 2,515 sq. ft.
Bonus Space: 365 sq. ft.
Bedrooms: 3
Bathrooms: 3½
Width: 50' - 8"
Depth: 66' - 8"

SEARCH ONLINE @ EPLANS.COM

© 2001 Donald A. Gardner, Inc.

Stone and horizontal siding give a definite country flavor to this two-story home. The front study makes an ideal guest room with the adjoining powder room. The formal dining room is accented with decorative columns that define its perimeter. The great room boasts a fireplace, built-ins, and a magnificent view of the backyard beyond one of two rear porches. The master suite boasts two walk-in closets and a private bath. Two bedrooms share a full bath on the second floor.

plan# HPK0900162

Style: Craftsman
First Floor: 1,707 sq. ft.
Second Floor: 514 sq. ft.
Total: 2,221 sq. ft.
Bonus Space: 211 sq. ft.
Bedrooms: 4
Bathrooms: 2½
Width: 50' - 0"
Depth: 71' - 8"

SEARCH ONLINE @ EPLANS.COM

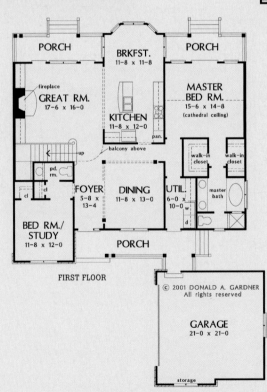

SECOND FLOOR

FIRST FLOOR

© 2001 DONALD A. GARDNER
All rights reserved

Graceful arches contrast with high gables for a stunning exterior on this Craftsman home. Windows with decorative transoms and several French doors flood the open floor plan with natural light. Tray ceilings in the dining room and master bedroom as well as cathedral ceilings in the bedroom/study, great room, kitchen, and breakfast area create architectural interest and visual space. Built-ins in the great room and additional space in the garage offer convenient storage. A screened porch allows for comfortable outdoor entertaining; a bonus room, near two additional bedrooms, offers flexibility. Positioned for privacy, the master suite features access to the screened porch, dual walk-in closets, and a well-appointed bath, including a private toilet, garden tub, double vanity, and spacious shower.

© 2002 Donald A. Gardner, Inc.

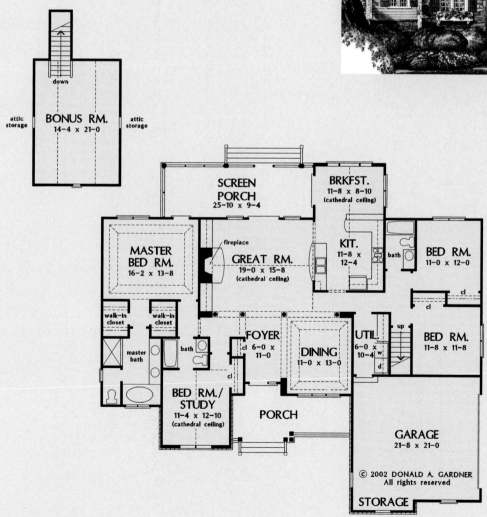

plan # HPK0900163

Style: Craftsman
Square Footage: 2,097
Bonus Space: 352 sq. ft.
Bedrooms: 4
Bathrooms: 3
Width: 64' - 10"
Depth: 59' - 6"

SEARCH ONLINE @ EPLANS.COM

Traditional with a country flair, this lovely plan is full

of the personal touches that make it a truly comfortable place to call home. The vaulted foyer presents a dining room on the left, lit by a box-bay window. The family room is ahead, with a graceful vaulted ceiling and a cozy fireplace. The kitchen, breakfast nook, and keeping room are grouped for convenience and provide a pleasing layout. The right wing is devoted to the master suite, resplendent with an indulgent bath. Two bedrooms and ample bonus space are located on the second floor and all share a full bath.

plan # HPK0900164

Style: Cape Cod
First Floor: 1,397 sq. ft.
Second Floor: 482 sq. ft.
Total: 1,879 sq. ft.
Bonus Space: 267 sq. ft.
Bedrooms: 3
Bathrooms: 2½
Width: 51' - 0"
Depth: 46' - 4"
Foundation: Crawlspace, Basement

SEARCH ONLINE @ EPLANS.COM

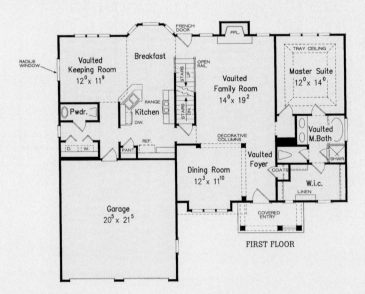

This charming cottage is much more than just a pretty face! Inside, a wealth of amenities, spacious rooms, and expansion options make this home a joy to own. A vaulted foyer creates a dramatic impression and opens on the right to a formal dining room. The great room lies ahead, lit by windows topped with transom accents. The bayed breakfast nook and country kitchen offer plenty of room to prepare and enjoy gourmet meals. Just beyond, two bedrooms share a full bath. The master suite is located on the far right with a vaulted luxury bath. A fourth bedroom, or study, completes the floor plan. An optional bonus room may be built above the garage.

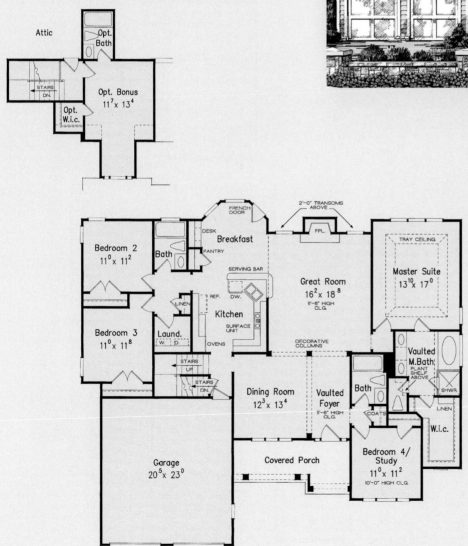

plan # HPK0900165

Style: Country Cottage
Square Footage: 2,054
Bonus Space: 306 sq. ft.
Bedrooms: 4
Bathrooms: 3
Width: 60' - 0"
Depth: 54' - 6"
Foundation: Crawlspace, Basement

SEARCH ONLINE @ EPLANS.COM

© 2002 Donald A. Gardner, Inc.

Blending stone with siding, this cottage has many wonderful architectural features: an arch and column porch, metal roof on a box-bay window, decorative vents, and striking shed dormer. Built-in cabinetry in the great room, tray ceilings in the dining room and master bedroom, and a cooktop island are just a few of the lush amenities. A pass-through connects the great room and kitchen—visually and conveniently. The master suite includes dual walk-in closets, a double vanity, private toilet, garden tub, and separate shower. The study/bedroom and bonus room allow for versatility and expansion to meet the family's changing needs.

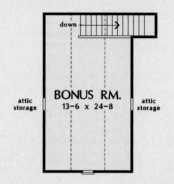

plan ⊕ HPK0900166

Style: Craftsman
Square Footage: 1,904
Bonus Space: 366 sq. ft.
Bedrooms: 3
Bathrooms: 2
Width: 53' - 10"
Depth: 57' - 8"

SEARCH ONLINE @ EPLANS.COM

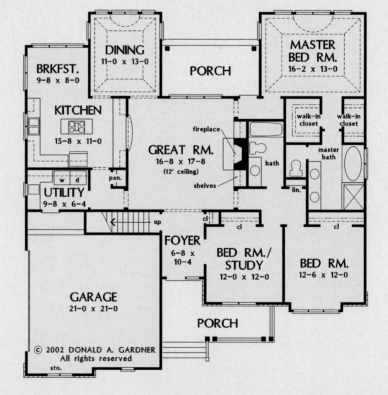

Twin dormers, multiple gables, and bold columns create a lovely exterior; inside, the floor plan provides a natural traffic flow. A tray ceiling and column distinguish the dining room, and double doors grace the flexible study/bedroom and master suite. A pass-through with a breakfast bar connects the kitchen to the great room, and built-ins flank the fireplace. The master suite also features a bay window, which provides a sitting area. Perfect for outdoor entertaining and relaxation, the rear porch includes a wet bar, skylights, and French doors that lead into the great room. The bonus room could also provide additional recreation space.

© 2003 Donald A. Gardner, Inc.

plan # HPK0900167

Style: Bungalow
Square Footage: 2,243
Bonus Space: 332 sq. ft.
Bedrooms: 4
Bathrooms: 2
Width: 62' - 0"
Depth: 67' - 2"

SEARCH ONLINE @ EPLANS.COM

MASTER BED RM.
14-8 x 17-0

BRKFST.
10-0 x 9-0

skylights

PORCH

wet bar

BED RM.
11-0 x 13-0

cl

walk-in closet

lin.

walk-in closet

shelves

(cathedral ceiling)

master bath

KIT.
11-4 x 13-4

GREAT RM.
19-0 x 17-0

fireplace

BED RM.
13-0 x 11-0

cl

UTIL.
7-4 x 7-0

d w

up

DINING
13-0 x 11-0

FOYER
6-4 x 11-0

bath

cl

GARAGE
22-0 x 22-0

PORCH

BED RM./ STUDY
11-0 x 13-0

cl

storage

down

attic storage

BONUS RM.
14-10 x 22-0

(cathedral ceiling)

attic storage

This delightful vacation home, designed for relaxation, will fit as well on a lakefront as in the mountains. Rear and front covered porches help to extend the living space outdoors. Three upstairs bedrooms, with an option for a fourth, offer plenty of room to put up family members and guests. A possible media room or office on the same level allows space to get some work done at home. On the main level, a luxurious master suite, informal living room, formal dining room, and a grand room with an extended hearth fireplace are located. The hub of family activity will be the area that includes the keeping room with a cozy fireplace, breakfast nook, and magnificent kitchen where an island counter will make food preparation a breeze.

plan # HPK0900168

Style: Craftsman
First Floor: 2,160 sq. ft.
Second Floor: 828 sq. ft.
Total: 2,988 sq. ft.
Bonus Space: 541 sq. ft.
Bedrooms: 4
Bathrooms: 3½
Width: 68' - 3"
Depth: 60' - 11"
Foundation: Basement

SEARCH ONLINE @ EPLANS.COM

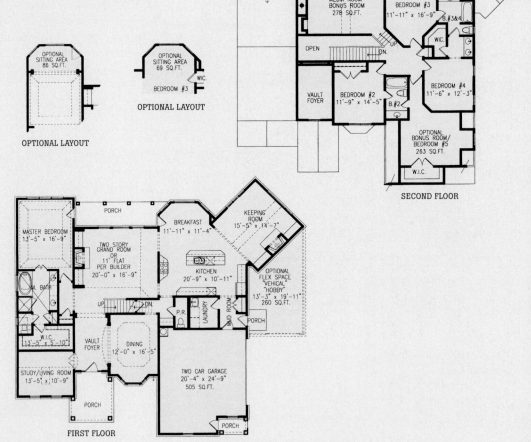

OPTIONAL SITTING AREA 86 SQ.FT.

OPTIONAL LAYOUT

OPTIONAL SITTING AREA 69 SQ.FT.

BEDROOM #3

OPTIONAL LAYOUT

SECOND FLOOR

FIRST FLOOR

A charming country cottage adds curb appeal to any neighborhood. The island kitchen easily serves the adjoining lodge room and the breakfast room offers a bayed view of the backyard and access to a rear porch. The master bathroom is equipped with a dual-sink vanity, garden tub, walk-in closet, private toilet, and shower. Two additional bedrooms each have a full bath. The basement is available for future expansion

© Copyright 2004, Garrell Associates, Inc.

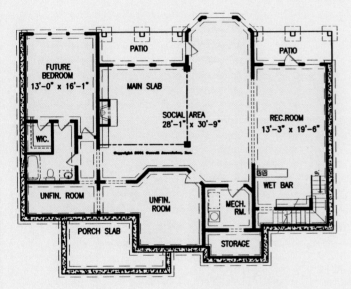

plan# HPK0900169

Style: Country Cottage
Square Footage: 2,086
Bedrooms: 3
Bathrooms: 3
Width: 57' - 6"
Depth: 46' - 6"
Foundation: Basement

SEARCH ONLINE @ EPLANS.COM

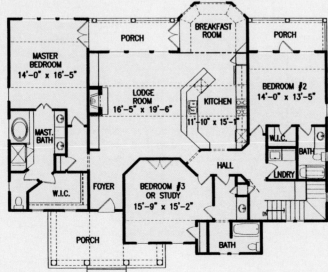

© 1997 Donald A. Gardner Architects, Inc.

The open floor plan of this delightful design combines the great room, kitchen, and dining room for today's family. With light drawn through two rear dormers, the great room boasts a cathedral ceiling and a fireplace with flanking built-ins. Impress guests with this breathtaking dining room with an octagonal tray ceiling and light-filled bay windows. Tray ceilings also adorn the master bedroom and one of two secondary bedrooms. Escape to the relaxing master suite with a private bath oasis featuring a garden tub and two vanity sinks set in a bay window. An optional bonus room gives flexibility to this amazing home.

plan# HPK0900170

Style: Country Cottage
Square Footage: 1,770
Bonus Space: 401 sq. ft.
Bedrooms: 3
Bathrooms: 2
Width: 54' - 0"
Depth: 57' - 8"

SEARCH ONLINE @ EPLANS.COM

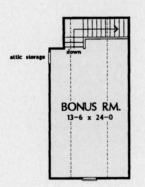

BONUS RM.
13-6 x 24-0

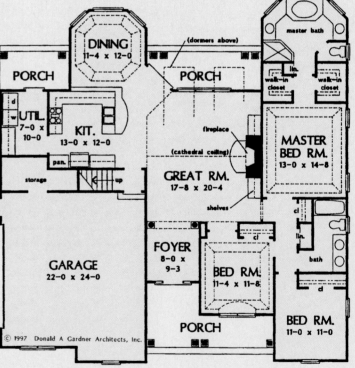

© 1997 Donald A Gardner Architects, Inc.

Decorative columns can be found throughout, beginning with the covered front porch. Once inside, the foyer opens to the dining room on the right, and the family room straight ahead. Enhanced by a coffered ceiling and built-in cabinets, a fireplace warms the space. A bay window view of the backyard extends private living space to the outdoors. Entry to the vaulted master suite reveals a walk-in closet, roomy bath with dual-sink vanities, separate shower and tub, and a private toilet. A serving bar in the kitchen allows for casual meals and easy interaction between the breakfast area and family room. Two additional family bedrooms share a full bath. Upstairs, a fourth bedroom and full bath, possible guest quarters, and a bonus room complete the plan.

plan# HPK0900171

Style: Country Cottage
Square Footage: 2,400
Bonus Space: 845 sq. ft.
Bedrooms: 3
Bathrooms: 2½
Width: 61' - 0"
Depth: 70' - 6"
Foundation: Basement, Crawlspace

SEARCH ONLINE @ EPLANS.COM

SECOND FLOOR

FIRST FLOOR

Mixed materials and a front covered porch highlight the exterior of this lovely home. The two-story foyer is flanked on either side by the study and dining room. The vaulted family room features a fireplace and built-ins. The master suite is located on the first floor for privacy and includes a vaulted bath and a roomy walk-in closet. Three additional bedrooms and an optional bonus room are located on the second floor.

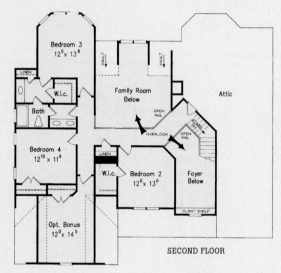

SECOND FLOOR

plan# HPK0900172

Style: Country Cottage
First Floor: 1,969 sq. ft.
Second Floor: 894 sq. ft.
Total: 2,863 sq. ft.
Bonus Space: 213 sq. ft.
Bedrooms: 4
Bathrooms: 2½
Width: 55' - 0"
Depth: 54' - 0"
Foundation: Crawlspace, Basement

SEARCH ONLINE @ EPLANS.COM

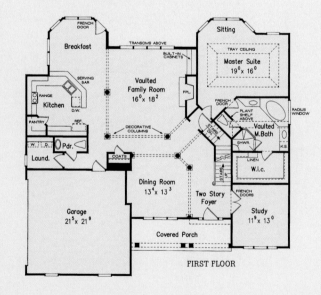

FIRST FLOOR

Craftsman-style pillars lend a country look to this Cape Cod-style home. An elegant entry opens to the vaulted family room, where a fireplace warms and bright windows illuminate. The kitchen is designed for the true chef, with step-saving orientation and a serving bar to the vaulted breakfast nook. A bedroom nearby is ideal for a home office or live-in help. The master suite is on the left, pampering with a vaulted bath and enormous walk-in closet. Two bedrooms upstairs share a full bath and an optional bonus room.

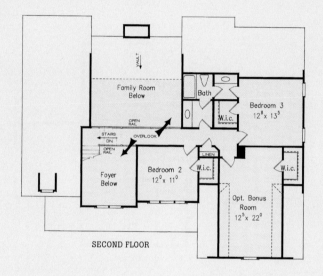

SECOND FLOOR

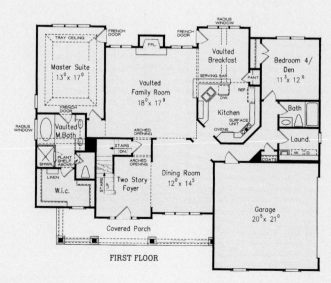

FIRST FLOOR

plan# HPK0900173

Style: Craftsman
First Floor: 1,761 sq. ft.
Second Floor: 577 sq. ft.
Total: 2,338 sq. ft.
Bonus Space: 305 sq. ft.
Bedrooms: 4
Bathrooms: 3
Width: 56' - 0"
Depth: 48' - 0"
Foundation: Crawlspace, Basement

SEARCH ONLINE @ EPLANS.COM

Three bedrooms, spacious family living areas, and plenty of amenities make this Craftsman design a pleasure to come home to. Vaulted ceilings enhance the den and living room, and built-in bookshelves, a media center, and a fireplace highlight the family room. The kitchen, with a built-in desk and island cooktop, serves the breakfast nook and dining room with ease. Sleeping quarters—the vaulted master suite and two family bedrooms—are upstairs, along with a bonus room and the utility area.

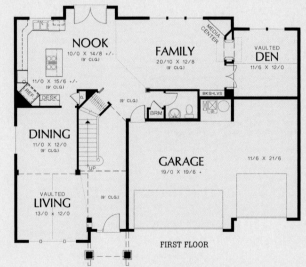

SECOND FLOOR

FIRST FLOOR

plan# HPK0900174

Style: Craftsman
First Floor: 1,360 sq. ft.
Second Floor: 1,154 sq. ft.
Total: 2,514 sq. ft.
Bonus Space: 202 sq. ft.
Bedrooms: 3
Bathrooms: 2½
Width: 52' - 0"
Depth: 45' - 6"
Foundation: Crawlspace

SEARCH ONLINE @ EPLANS.COM

Mixed exterior textures—shingles, siding, and stone—create a distinctive look for this traditional plan. An efficient home office, brightened by two sets of windows, sits to the right of the foyer; the dining room, defined by columns, sits to the left. Directly ahead, the two-story great room offers a built-in media center and a fireplace. Nearby, the kitchen boasts an island snack bar and adjoins a nook that opens to a covered patio. Sleeping quarters consist of a first-floor master suite and two second-floor bedrooms.

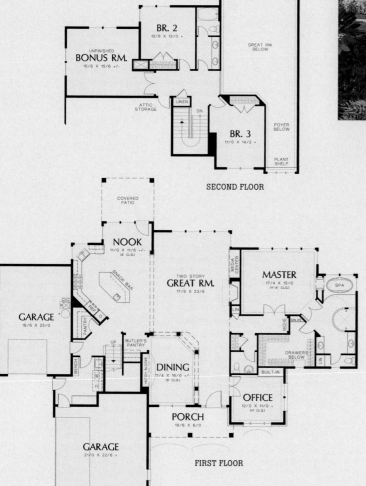

SECOND FLOOR

FIRST FLOOR

plan# HPK0900175

Style: Farmhouse
First Floor: 2,440 sq. ft.
Second Floor: 626 sq. ft.
Total: 3,066 sq. ft.
Bonus Space: 302 sq. ft.
Bedrooms: 3
Bathrooms: 2½
Width: 83' - 0"
Depth: 77' - 0"
Foundation: Crawlspace

SEARCH ONLINE @ EPLANS.COM

room to grow

This Craftsman cottage combines stone, siding, and cedar shake to create striking curb appeal. The interior features an open floor plan with high ceilings, columns, and bay windows to visually expand space. Built-in cabinetry, a fireplace, and a kitchen pass-through highlight and add convenience to the great room. The master suite features a tray ceiling in the bedroom and a bath with garden tub, separate shower, dual vanities, and a walk-in closet. On the opposite side of the home is another bedroom that could be used as a second master suite. Above the garage, a bonus room provides ample storage and space to grow.

plan # HPK0900176

Style: Traditional
Square Footage: 1,971
Bonus Space: 358 sq. ft.
Bedrooms: 3
Bathrooms: 3
Width: 62' - 6"
Depth: 57' - 2"

SEARCH ONLINE @ EPLANS.COM

Rear Exterior

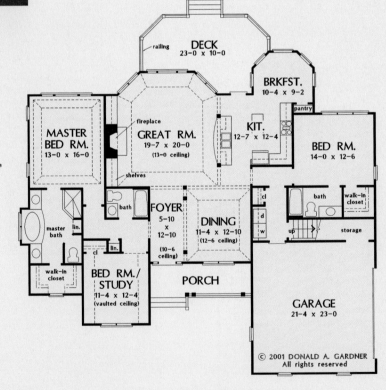

ORDER BLUEPRINTS 24 HOURS, 7 DAYS A WEEK, AT 1-800-521-6797

Arched windows and triple gables provide a touch of elegance to this traditional home. An entrance supported by columns welcomes family and guests inside. On the main level, the dining room offers round columns at the entrance. The great room boasts a cathedral ceiling, a fireplace, and an arched window over the doors to the deck. The kitchen features an island cooktop and an adjoining breakfast nook for informal dining. The master suite offers twin walk-in closets and a lavish bath that includes a whirlpool tub and a double-basin vanity.

Rear Exterior

plan# HPK0900177

Style: Bungalow
First Floor: 1,416 sq. ft.
Second Floor: 445 sq. ft.
Total: 1,861 sq. ft.
Bonus Space: 284 sq. ft.
Bedrooms: 3
Bathrooms: 2½
Width: 58' - 3"
Depth: 68' - 6"

SEARCH ONLINE @ EPLANS.COM

FIRST FLOOR

- seat
- DECK
- spa
- arched window above door
- GREAT RM. 15-4 × 18-0 (cathedral ceiling)
- fireplace
- KIT./BRKFST. 16-8 × 16-0
- master bath
- walk-in closet
- walk-in closet
- MASTER BED RM. 13-0 × 13-6
- pd. rm.
- up
- sto.
- cl
- FOYER 7-8 × 9-0
- DINING 12-4 × 12-4
- UTILITY 10-0 × 6-4
- w d
- PORCH
- up
- storage
- GARAGE 20-0 × 20-0

©1991 Donald A. Gardner Architects, Inc.

SECOND FLOOR

- BED RM. 10-4 × 11-9
- walk-in closet
- down
- bath
- cl
- BED RM. 12-4 × 13-6
- down
- BONUS RM. 11-0 × 20-0

FOR MORE DETAILED INFORMATION, PLEASE CHECK THE FLOOR PLANS CAREFULLY.

ORDER BLUEPRINTS 24 HOURS, 7 DAYS A WEEK, AT 1-800-521-6797

With rustic rafter tails, sturdy pillars, and a siding-and-shingle facade, this welcoming bungalow offers plenty of curb appeal. Inside, the formal dining room sits to the left of the foyer and gives easy access to the angled kitchen. A spacious gathering room offers a fireplace, built-ins, a wall of windows, and access to a covered terrace. Located on the first floor for privacy, the master bedroom is lavish with its amenities, including His and Hers walk-in closets and basins, a garden tub, and a compartmented toilet. Upstairs, two suites offer private baths and share a linkside retreat that includes a fairway veranda.

plan# HPK0900178

Style: Bungalow
First Floor: 1,661 sq. ft.
Second Floor: 951 sq. ft.
Total: 2,612 sq. ft.
Bedrooms: 3
Bathrooms: 3½
Width: 59' - 0"
Depth: 58' - 11"
Foundation: Crawlspace

SEARCH ONLINE @ EPLANS.COM

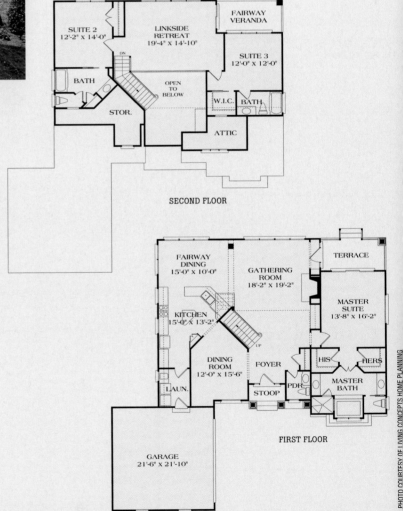

SECOND FLOOR

FIRST FLOOR

ORDER BLUEPRINTS 24 HOURS, 7 DAYS A WEEK, AT 1-800-521-6797

An attractive combination of styles creates a lovely exterior for this transitional home. The first floor offers a raised foyer and open great room leading to the dining room with a sloped ceiling. Exposed on two sides, a fireplace warms the formal gathering area. A less formal space is created in the island kitchen and breakfast/hearth room combination. The master bedroom is located on the main floor, featuring a sloped ceiling through the private bath with a large walk-in closet, dressing area, dual vanities and an angled soaking tub

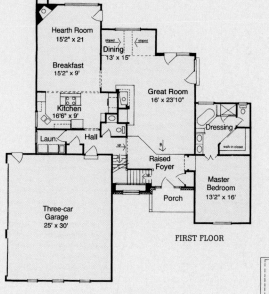

FIRST FLOOR

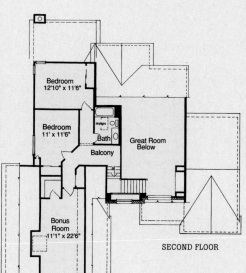

SECOND FLOOR

plan # HPK0900179

Style: Craftsman
First Floor: 1,784 sq. ft.
Second Floor: 566 sq. ft.
Total: 2,350 sq. ft.
Bonus Space: 336 sq. ft.
Bedrooms: 3
Bathrooms: 2½
Width: 59' - 0"
Depth: 67' - 0"
Foundation: Unfinished Basement

SEARCH ONLINE @ EPLANS.COM

Craftsman stylings grace this two-story traditional home, designed for a narrow lot. Shingles and siding present a warm welcome; the front porch opens to the dining room and the gathering room, allowing great entertainment options. The kitchen connects to the living areas with a snack bar and works hard with an island and lots of counter space. The master suite is on this level and delights in a very private bath. Two bedrooms on the upper level have private vanities and a shared bath. Extra storage or bonus space is available for future development.

plan ⊞ HPK0900180

Style: Craftsman
First Floor: 1,392 sq. ft.
Second Floor: 708 sq. ft.
Total: 2,100 sq. ft.
Bedrooms: 3
Bathrooms: 2½
Width: 32' - 0"
Depth: 55' - 0"
Foundation: Crawlspace

SEARCH ONLINE @ EPLANS.COM

FIRST FLOOR

SECOND FLOOR

Relax in this vacation home in the mountains or by a lake. Simple rooflines and a small footprint make this home affordable. A flexible living, dining, and kitchen space work together to offer comfort and a sense of openness. The first-floor master suite features a closet and is near a full bath. The entry acts as a mud room for messy boots and coats. Upstairs, two secondary bedrooms access large storage spaces.

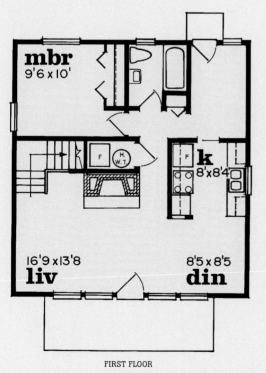

FIRST FLOOR

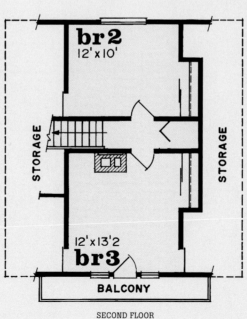

SECOND FLOOR

plan# HPK0900181

Style: Country Cottage
First Floor: 728 sq. ft.
Second Floor: 350 sq. ft.
Total: 1,078 sq. ft.
Bedrooms: 3
Bathrooms: 1
Width: 26' - 0"
Depth: 28' - 0"
Foundation: Crawlspace

SEARCH ONLINE @ EPLANS.COM

Interesting arches, columns, and cantilevers adorn this elegant home. A dining room with a tray ceiling flanks the foyer to the left, and a den/study is to the right. The large living room enjoys rear views and a covered porch. The island kitchen has an abundance of counter space and flows directly into a bayed breakfast nook. The hearth-warmed family room boasts easy access to the kitchen. The master bedroom resides on the right side of the plan; amenities include His and Hers walk-in closets and sinks, a garden tub, separate shower, compartmented toilet, and a sitting bay that looks to the rear porch.

plan# HPK0900182

Style: Country Cottage
Square Footage: 2,713
Bonus Space: 440 sq. ft.
Bedrooms: 3
Bathrooms: 3
Width: 66' - 4"
Depth: 80' - 8"
Foundation: Slab

SEARCH ONLINE @ EPLANS.COM

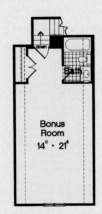

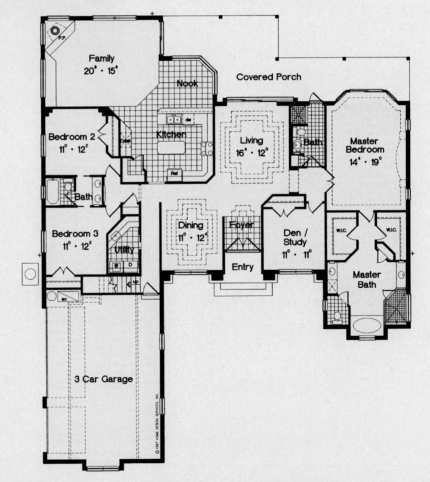

Shingles, stone, and shutters all combine to give this attractive manor a warm and welcoming feel. The two-story foyer presents the formal living room on the right—complete with a fireplace. The spacious family room also features a fireplace, along with a built-in media center, a wall of windows, and a 10-foot ceiling. Open to the family room, the efficient kitchen provides plenty of cabinet and counter space, as well as a nearby bayed nook. A study is available, with built-in bookshelves. Upstairs, the master suite is sure to please. It includes a large walk-in closet, a pampering bath with dual vanities and a tub set in a bay, a 10-foot ceiling, and a corner fireplace. Bedrooms 3 and 4 share a bath, while Bedroom 2 offers privacy. A bonus room is available for future expansion.

SECOND FLOOR

plan# HPK0900183

Style: Chateau Style
First Floor: 2,451 sq. ft.
Second Floor: 1,762 sq. ft.
Total: 4,213 sq. ft.
Bonus Space: 353 sq. ft.
Bedrooms: 4
Bathrooms: 3½
Width: 92' - 6"
Depth: 46' - 0"
Foundation: Crawlspace

SEARCH ONLINE @ EPLANS.COM

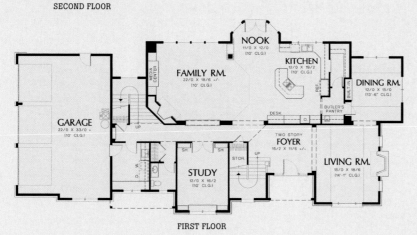

FIRST FLOOR

ORDER BLUEPRINTS 24 HOURS, 7 DAYS A WEEK, AT 1-800-521-6797

The Essington is a quaint transitional home option. A combination of exterior materials is artistically showcased on this exciting home, offering impressive curb appeal. Amenities such as a covered porch, sloped ceilings, angles, skylights, a snack bar in the spacious kitchen, and a deluxe bath in the master suite offer stylish luxury to this moderate-sized home. The bonus room above the garage offers the option of creating a second-story game room, home office, or fourth bedroom.

plan# HPK0900184

Style: Transitional
First Floor: 1,432 sq. ft.
Second Floor: 464 sq. ft.
Total: 1,896 sq. ft.
Bonus Space: 153 sq. ft.
Bedrooms: 3
Bathrooms: 2½
Width: 49' - 6"
Depth: 53' - 6"
Foundation: Basement

SEARCH ONLINE @ EPLANS.COM

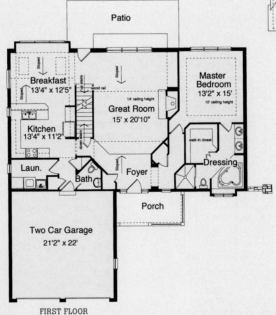

SECOND FLOOR

FIRST FLOOR

With vaulted ceilings in the dining room and the great room, a tray ceiling in the master suite, and a sunlit two-story foyer, this inviting design offers a wealth of light and space. The counter-filled kitchen opens to a large breakfast area with backyard access. The master suite is complete with a walk-in closet and pampering bath. Upstairs, two secondary bedrooms share a hall bath and access to an optional bonus room. Note the storage space in the two-car garage.

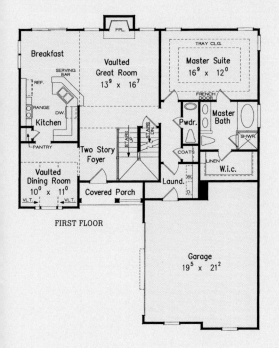

FIRST FLOOR

- Breakfast
- FPL.
- SERVING BAR
- REF.
- Vaulted Great Room 13⁹ x 16⁷
- TRAY CLG.
- Master Suite 16⁹ x 12⁰
- RANGE
- DW.
- Kitchen
- PANTRY
- STAIRS UP
- STAIRS DN
- Pwdr.
- FRENCH DOOR
- Master Bath
- SH'WR.
- COATS
- LINEN
- Two Story Foyer
- Vaulted Dining Room 10⁰ x 11⁰
- VLT.
- VLT.
- Covered Porch
- Laund.
- W. D.
- W.i.c.
- Garage 19⁵ x 21²

SECOND FLOOR

- VAULT
- Great Room Below
- OPEN RAIL
- LINEN
- Bath
- W.i.c.
- Bedroom 2 10⁰ x 12²
- OVERLOOK
- STAIRS DN
- Bedroom 3 13⁰ x 10⁰
- Foyer Below
- PLANT SHELF
- Opt. Bonus Room 12⁰ x 23⁰

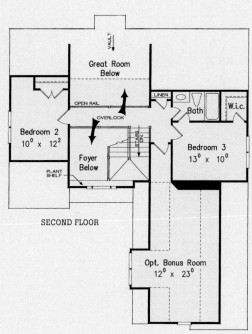

plan# HPK0900185

Style: Country Cottage
First Floor: 1,179 sq. ft.
Second Floor: 460 sq. ft.
Total: 1,639 sq. ft.
Bonus Space: 338 sq. ft.
Bedrooms: 3
Bathrooms: 2½
Width: 41' - 6"
Depth: 54' - 4"
Foundation: Crawlspace, Slab, Basement

SEARCH ONLINE @ EPLANS.COM

© 2002 Donald A. Gardner, Inc.

plan# HPK0900186

Style: Country
Square Footage: 1,827
Bonus Space: 384 sq. ft.
Bedrooms: 3
Bathrooms: 2
Width: 61' – 8"
Depth: 62' – 8"

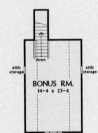

BONUS RM.
14-4 x 23-4

attic storage | attic storage

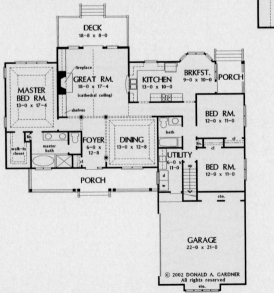

© 2002 DONALD A. GARDNER
All rights reserved

© 2002 Donald A. Gardner, Inc.

plan# HPK0900187

Style: Traditional
Square Footage: 1,700
Bonus Space: 333 sq. ft.
Bedrooms: 3
Bathrooms: 2
Width: 49' – 0"
Depth: 65' – 4"

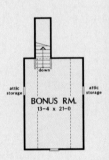

BONUS RM.
13-4 x 21-0

attic storage | attic storage

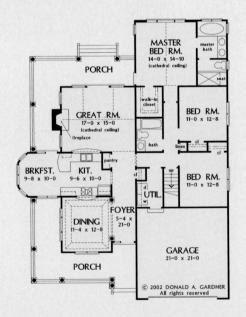

© 2002 DONALD A. GARDNER
All rights reserved

This eye-pleasing beauty with its clerestory window and front columns has an interior uniquely designed for enjoyment and comfort. Enter the foyer and the dining room is to the right, very elegant with its octagonal-shaped ceiling. Straight ahead, the main living room enjoys a warming fireplace and vault ceiling. The roomy kitchen surrounded by counter space opens to a sunlit breakfast alcove. On the left side of the plan, the dazzling master suite embraces a huge walk-in closet and sumptuous bath with a double-sink vanity. To the right, two more bedrooms share a bath and are conveniently located near the laundry. Over the two-car garage, additional space is available to be used as you want.

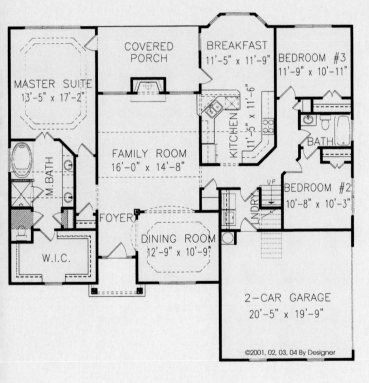

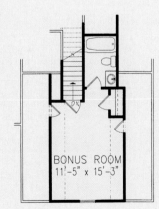

plan # HPK0900188

Style: Country Cottage
Square Footage: 1,821
Bonus Space: 191 sq. ft.
Bedrooms: 3
Bathrooms: 2
Width: 54' - 0"
Depth: 54' - 0"
Foundation: Slab

SEARCH ONLINE @ EPLANS.COM

An endearing and enduring American original that is straightforward and of spare design, yet warm, cozy, and uncomplicated, this home brings the past into sharp focus. The openness of the floor plan pairs the great room with the dining area for convenience and a modern flow. The island kitchen enjoys a view of the front property. The master suite features a large master bath with dual vanities, a compartmented toilet, and separate shower and tub. Two family bedrooms share a bath upstairs. Above the garage is future space that is easily converted into livable space as needed.

plan# HPK0900189

Style: Country Cottage
First Floor: 1,211 sq. ft.
Second Floor: 551 sq. ft.
Total: 1,762 sq. ft.
Bonus Space: 378 sq. ft.
Bedrooms: 3
Bathrooms: 2½
Width: 64' - 4"
Depth: 39' - 4"
Foundation: Crawlspace, Basement

SEARCH ONLINE @ EPLANS.COM

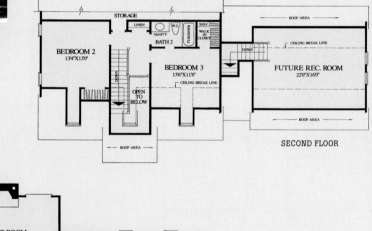

SECOND FLOOR

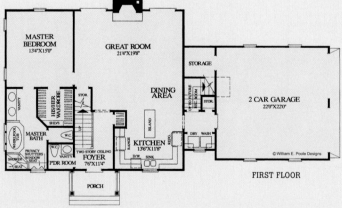

FIRST FLOOR

© William E. Poole Designs

ORDER BLUEPRINTS 24 HOURS, 7 DAYS A WEEK, AT 1-800-521-6797

This unique design presents an open, yet cozy floor plan. A built-in entertainment center and a cathedral ceiling create a spacious great room that leads to the breakfast area and island kitchen. The terrace is accessible from the breakfast area. Privacy is afforded to the master bedroom, placed to the far right of the design; it's complemented by a master bath built for two and a walk-in closet with a window seat. At the top of the stairs, a balcony and a hall lead to a future recreation room. Three bedrooms, each with a full bath, are also available on thesecond floor.

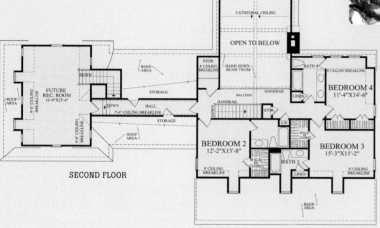

SECOND FLOOR

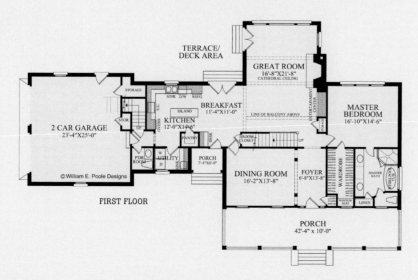

FIRST FLOOR

plan# **HPK0900190**

Style: Country Cottage
First Floor: 1,904 sq. ft.
Second Floor: 1,098 sq. ft.
Total: 3,002 sq. ft.
Bonus Space: 522 sq. ft.
Bedrooms: 4
Bathrooms: 4½
Width: 88' - 2"
Depth: 54' - 0"
Foundation: Crawlspace, Basement

SEARCH ONLINE @ EPLANS.COM

plan# HPK0900191

Style: Craftsman
First Floor: 2,477 sq. ft.
Second Floor: 742 sq. ft.
Total: 3,219 sq. ft.
Bonus Space: 419 sq. ft.
Bedrooms: 4
Bathrooms: 4
Width: 100' - 0"
Depth: 66' - 2"

SEARCH ONLINE @ EPLANS.COM

plan# HPK0900192

Style: Country Cottage
First Floor: 2,891 sq. ft.
Second Floor: 1,336 sq. ft.
Total: 4,227 sq. ft.
Bonus Space: 380 sq. ft.
Bedrooms: 4
Bathrooms: 3½ + ½
Width: 90' - 8"
Depth: 56' - 4"
Foundation: Crawlspace,
Basement

SEARCH ONLINE @ EPLANS.COM

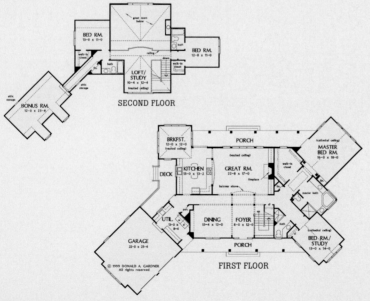

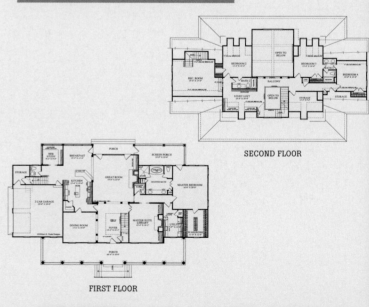

This gigantic country farmhouse is accented by exterior features that really stand out—a steep roof gable, shuttered muntin windows, stone siding, and the double-columned, covered front porch. Inside, the entry is flanked by the study/Bedroom 2 and the dining room. Across the tiled gallery, the great room provides an impressive fireplace and overlooks the rear veranda. The island kitchen opens to a bayed breakfast room. The right side of the home includes a utility room and a three-car garage, and two family bedrooms that share a bath. The master wing of the home enjoys a bayed sitting area, a sumptuous bath, and an enormous walk-in closet. The second-floor bonus room is cooled by a ceiling fan and is perfect for a guest suite.

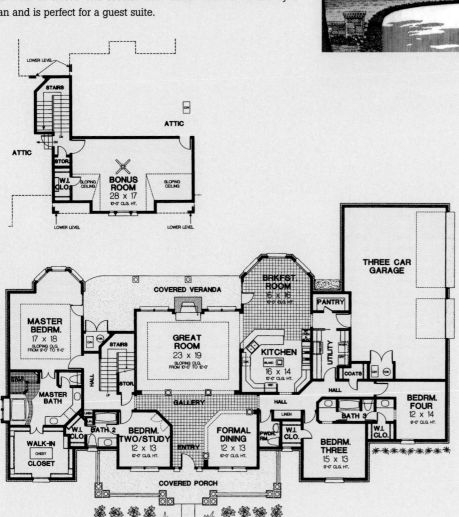

plan# HPK0900193

Style: Farmhouse
Square Footage: 3,439
Bonus Space: 514 sq. ft.
Bedrooms: 4
Bathrooms: 3½
Width: 100' - 0"
Depth: 67' - 11"
Foundation: Crawlspace,
Slab, Basement

SEARCH ONLINE @ EPLANS.COM

An oversized dormer above the entryway and a steep, side-gabled roof bring an interesting front perspective to this Craftsman style vacation home. Inside, a wood-burning fireplace warms the family room, overlooked by the second-floor walkway. To the left, the master suite is attended by a large walk-in closet and double vanities in the bathroom. Owners will also appreciate the private access to the deck. The full-sized garage at the right of the plan features a bonus room on the upper floor.

plan# HPK0900194

Style: Craftsman
First Floor: 1,799 sq. ft.
Second Floor: 709 sq. ft.
Total: 2,508 sq. ft.
Bonus Space: 384 sq. ft.
Bedrooms: 3
Bathrooms: 2½
Width: 77' - 4"
Depth: 41' - 4"
Foundation: Basement

SEARCH ONLINE @ EPLANS.COM

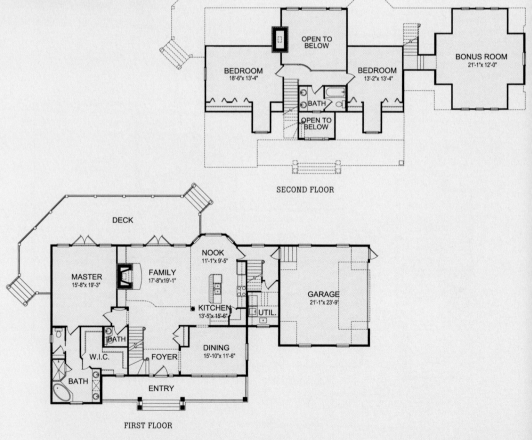

ORDER BLUEPRINTS 24 HOURS, 7 DAYS A WEEK, AT 1-800-521-6797

Beautiful wood details frame the windows and front entry of this appealing design. The foyer introduces the dining room to the right and the family room at the rear. An open island kitchen and adjoining nook create a welcoming and versatile space with the family room. Privacy and comfort can be found in the first-floor master suite. Upstairs, two family bedrooms share a full hall bath. A bonus room sits above the garage and is accessible from the garage entry.

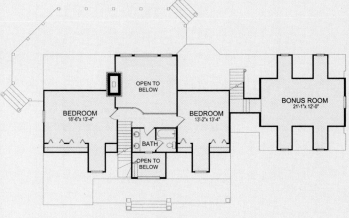

SECOND FLOOR

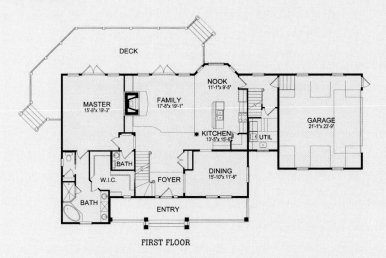

FIRST FLOOR

plan # HPK0900195

Style: Craftsman
First Floor: 1,799 sq. ft.
Second Floor: 709 sq. ft.
Total: 2,508 sq. ft.
Bonus Space: 384 sq. ft.
Bedrooms: 3
Bathrooms: 2½
Width: 77' - 4"
Depth: 41' - 4"
Foundation: Basement

SEARCH ONLINE @ EPLANS.COM

Perfect seaside summer cottage or year-round home, this design creates a comfortable space in a small footprint. An open, vaulted family room features a fireplace that can be enjoyed from the adjoining dining room, and is a warm center for entertaining. A secluded first-floor master suite enjoys a tray ceiling and a full bath. Two family bedrooms, bonus space, and a full compartmented bath round out the second floor.

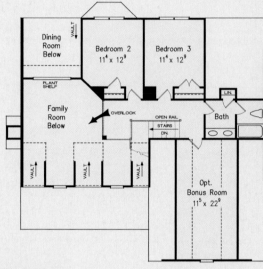

SECOND FLOOR

plan⊕ HPK0900196

Style: Country Cottage
First Floor: 1,299 sq. ft.
Second Floor: 564 sq. ft.
Total: 1,863 sq. ft.
Bonus Space: 276 sq. ft.
Bedrooms: 3
Bathrooms: 2½
Width: 48' - 4"
Depth: 49' - 0"
Foundation: Crawlspace, Basement

SEARCH ONLINE @ EPLANS.COM

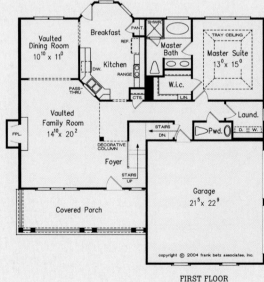

FIRST FLOOR

An appealing mixture of exterior building materials combines with decorative wood brackets in the gables to create undeniable Craftsman style for this four-bedroom home. Special ceiling treatments create volume and add interest throughout the home: tray ceilings in the foyer, dining room, bedroom/study, and master bedroom and a stunning cathedral ceiling in the great room. The great room is further enhanced by a rear clerestory dormer window and back-porch access.

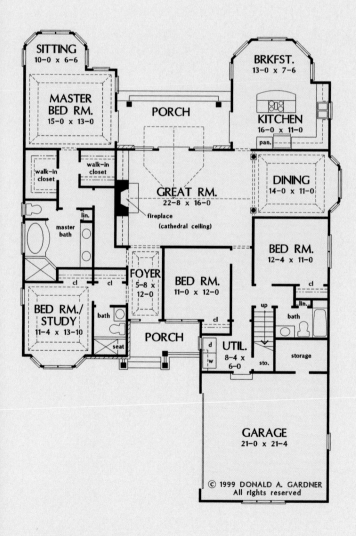

SITTING
10-0 x 6-6

MASTER
BED RM.
15-0 x 13-0

PORCH

BRKFST.
13-0 x 7-6

KITCHEN
16-0 x 11-0

pan.

walk-in closet

walk-in closet

DINING
14-0 x 11-0

GREAT RM.
22-8 x 16-0

fireplace
(cathedral ceiling)

master bath

lin.

BED RM.
12-4 x 11-0

cl

FOYER
5-8 x 12-0

BED RM.
11-0 x 12-0

cl

bath

cl

up

lin.

bath

BED RM./
STUDY
11-4 x 13-10

bath

cl

PORCH

seat

d
w

UTIL.
8-4 x 6-0

sto.

storage

GARAGE
21-0 x 21-4

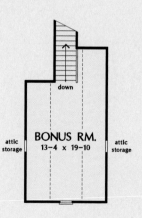

BONUS RM.
13-4 x 19-10

down

attic storage

attic storage

plan # HPK0900197

Style: Craftsman
Square Footage: 2,290
Bonus Space: 355 sq. ft.
Bedrooms: 4
Bathrooms: 3
Width: 53' - 0"
Depth: 77' - 10"

SEARCH ONLINE @ EPLANS.COM

© 2001 Donald A. Gardner, Inc.

This incredible home evokes images of stately Southwestern ranches with classic wood detailing and deep eaves. An arched entryway mimics the large clerestory above it, and a trio of dormers and multiple gables add architectural interest. Equally impressive, the interior boasts three fireplaces—one within a scenic screened porch—and a long cathedral ceiling extends from the great room to the screened porch and is highlighted by exposed beams. An art niche complements the foyer, and a wet bar enhances the great room. Columns help distinguish rooms without enclosing space. The extraordinary master suite features a large study/sitting area, bedroom with exposed beams in a hipped cathedral ceiling, huge walk-in closet, and spacious master bath.

plan # HPK0900198

Style: Craftsman
Square Footage: 3,188
Bonus Space: 615 sq. ft.
Bedrooms: 3
Bathrooms: 2½
Width: 106' - 4"
Depth: 104' - 1"

SEARCH ONLINE @ EPLANS.COM

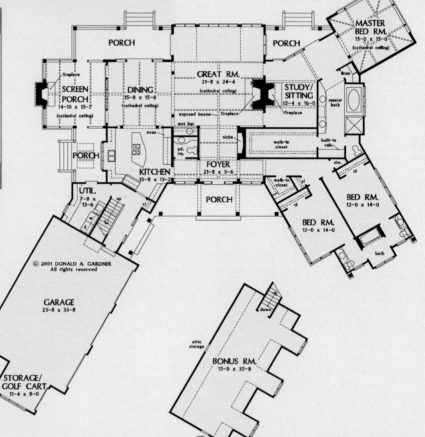

Using materials that combine the rugged frontier with stately elegance, this home has a grand, majestic facade. Four towering columns frame the dramatic barrel-vault entrance, and clerestories mimic the arched theme. Cedar shake, stone, and siding complement a metal roof over the front porch. The two-story foyer has impressive views of the study, dining room, living room, and balcony. Cathedral ceilings top the family room and master bedroom, and a vaulted ceiling tops the living room. Built-ins, three fireplaces, and a walk-in pantry add special touches. The master suite on the first floor and two family bedrooms upstairs each boast private baths and walk-in closets. A library and flexible bonus space round out the second level.

© 2003 Donald A. Gardner, Inc.

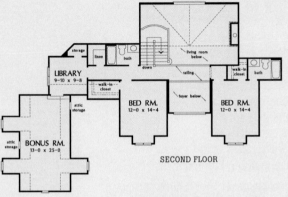

SECOND FLOOR

plan# **HPK0900199**

Style: Craftsman
First Floor: 2,766 sq. ft.
Second Floor: 881 sq. ft.
Total: 3,647 sq. ft.
Bonus Space: 407 sq. ft.
Bedrooms: 3
Bathrooms: 3½
Width: 92' - 5"
Depth: 71' - 10"

SEARCH ONLINE @ EPLANS.COM

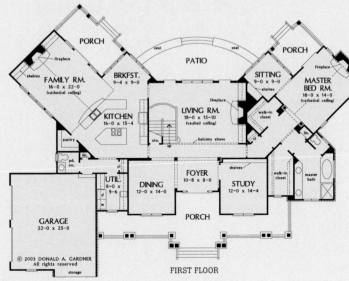

FIRST FLOOR

plan# HPK0900200

Style: Craftsman
First Floor: 1,846 sq. ft.
Second Floor: 1,309 sq. ft.
Total: 3,155 sq. ft.
Bonus Space: 563 sq. ft.
Bedrooms: 4
Bathrooms: 3½
Width: 77' – 6"
Depth: 48' – 8"
Foundation: Crawlspace

SEARCH ONLINE @ EPLANS.COM

SECOND FLOOR

FIRST FLOOR

plan# HPK0900201

Style: Plantation
First Floor: 2,578 sq. ft.
Second Floor: 1,277 sq. ft.
Total: 3,855 sq. ft.
Bedrooms: 4
Bathrooms: 4
Width: 53' – 6"
Depth: 97' – 0"
Foundation: Pier (same as Piling)

SEARCH ONLINE @ EPLANS.COM

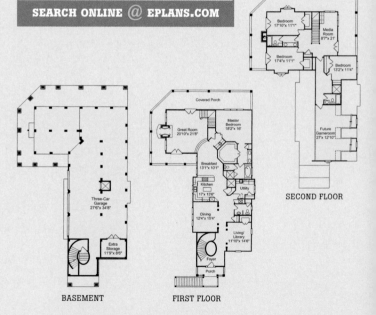

BASEMENT   FIRST FLOOR   SECOND FLOOR

Horizontal siding, double-hung windows, and European gables lend a special charm to this contemporary home. The formal dining room opens from the foyer and offers a wet bar and a box-bay window. The great room features a fireplace and opens to a golf porch as well as a charming side porch. A well-lit kitchen contains a cooktop island counter and two pantries. The first-floor master suite has a tray ceiling, a box-bay window, and a deluxe bath with a garden tub and an angled shower. Both of the upper-level bedrooms privately access a full bath.

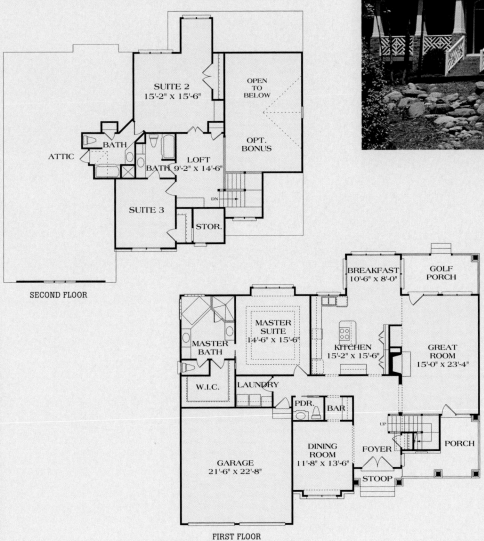

SECOND FLOOR

FIRST FLOOR

plan# HPK0900202

Style: Country Cottage
First Floor: 1,824 sq. ft.
Second Floor: 842 sq. ft.
Total: 2,666 sq. ft.
Bonus Space: 267 sq. ft.
Bedrooms: 3
Bathrooms: 3½
Width: 59' - 0"
Depth: 53' - 6"
Foundation: Crawlspace

SEARCH ONLINE @ EPLANS.COM

Lattice walls, pickets, and horizontal siding

complement a relaxed Key West design that's perfect for waterfront properties. The grand room with a fireplace, the dining room, and Bedroom 2 open through French doors to the veranda. The master suite occupies the entire second floor and features access to a private balcony through double doors. This pampering suite also includes a spacious walk-in closet and a full bath with a whirlpool tub. Enclosed storage/bonus space and a garage are available on the lower level.

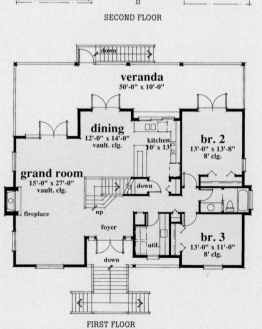

SECOND FLOOR

plan# HPK0900203

Style: Floridian
First Floor: 1,586 sq. ft.
Second Floor: 601 sq. ft.
Total: 2,187 sq. ft.
Bedrooms: 3
Bathrooms: 2
Width: 50' - 0"
Depth: 44' - 0"
Foundation: Pier (same as Piling)

SEARCH ONLINE @ EPLANS.COM

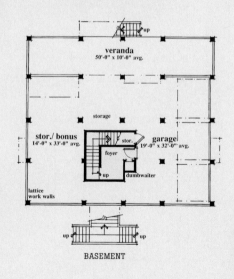

BASEMENT

FIRST FLOOR

©OSCAR THOMPSON PHOTOGRAPHY

ORDER BLUEPRINTS 24 HOURS, 7 DAYS A WEEK, AT 1-800-521-6797

This fabulous Key West home blends interior space with the great outdoors. Designed for a balmy climate, this home boasts expansive porches and decks—with outside access from every area of the home. A sun-dappled foyer leads via a stately midlevel staircase to a splendid great room, which features a warming fireplace tucked in beside beautiful built-in cabinetry. Highlighted by a wall of glass that opens to the rear porch, this two-story living space opens to the formal dining room and a well-appointed kitchen. Spacious secondary bedrooms on the main level open to outside spaces and share a full bath. Upstairs, a 10-foot tray ceiling highlights a private master suite, which provides French doors to an upper-level porch.

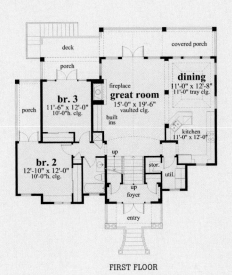

SECOND FLOOR

Rear Exterior

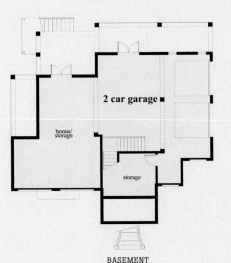

BASEMENT

FIRST FLOOR

plan# HPK0900204

Style: Seaside
First Floor: 1,383 sq. ft.
Second Floor: 595 sq. ft.
Total: 1,978 sq. ft.
Bonus Space: 617 sq. ft.
Bedrooms: 3
Bathrooms: 2
Width: 48' - 0"
Depth: 42' - 0"
Foundation: Basement

SEARCH ONLINE @ EPLANS.COM

ORDER BLUEPRINTS 24 HOURS, 7 DAYS A WEEK, AT 1-800-521-6797

Arches, columns, and French doors pay homage to a captivating Key West style that's light, airy, and fully au courant. French doors lead to a study or parlor, which features a wall of built-in shelves and a view of the front property through an arch-topped window. Built-ins frame the fireplace in the great room too, providing an anchor for a wall of glass that brings in a sense of the outdoors. The main level includes a secluded secondary bedroom that's thoughtfully placed near a full bath, coat closet, and linen storage. Upstairs, a balcony hall allows interior vistas of the living area below, and connects a secondary bedroom and bath with the master suite. French doors open from both bedrooms to a wrapping deck. The master bath provides a bumped-out garden tub and a walk-in closet designed for two.

plan # HPK0900205

Style: Tidewater
First Floor: 1,542 sq. ft.
Second Floor: 971 sq. ft.
Total: 2,513 sq. ft.
Bedrooms: 3
Bathrooms: 3
Width: 46' - 0"
Depth: 51' - 0"
Foundation: Basement

SEARCH ONLINE @ EPLANS.COM

SECOND FLOOR

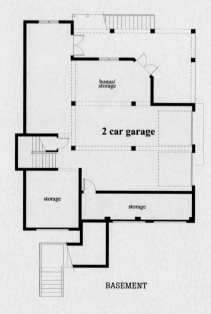

BASEMENT

FIRST FLOOR

Sunny Days:
Homes with Patios or Decks

Warm weather, sunny skies, and starry nights send everyone out to the backyard for a cookout, a party, or just to relax. Patios and decks are some of the most coveted spots in a getaway house and they can help blend the inside and the outside into one big comfortable space, regardless of the size of the floor plan. Blur the line even more with substantial furnishings, some protection from the sun, and distinct areas for various family activities. Furnish a deck or patio the same way interior spaces are planned and furnished, and they become outside rooms. Decks and patios can be added after a house is designed and built, but why wait? Finding plans that already include these exterior living spaces will help transform the backyard of your retreat into a mini escape right away.

Enjoy this home's deck off the main level or the patio downstairs (page 255).

A symmetrical facade gives this Southern-inspired home plenty of curb appeal.

Fresh Air

A front porch and spacious back deck take advantage of the outdoors and make this home the perfect escape

This luxurious waterfront design sings of Southern island influences. Outdoor spaces define the home, from the front porch that's begging for rocking chairs to the wraparound deck in back, perfect for cookouts and sunbathing. Easy transitions from indoors to out have been emphasized as well, particularly in back where a screened porch extends the width of the living room.

The home is no less luxurious inside, with an open plan that connects the living and dining rooms to the kitchen. The result is a friendly space that feels comfortable whether you are entertaining a crowd, or just a couple of relatives.

The master bedroom includes double French doors that open to the deck. In the master bath, a separate tub and shower occupy two corners

Gorgeous dark hardwood floors connect the family spaces on the first floor.

The kitchen enjoys plenty of natural light through the breakfast nook.

The dock provides a perfect lure when viewing this home from the water.

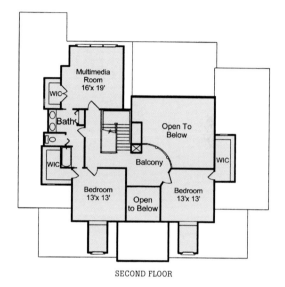

SECOND FLOOR

The wraparound deck helps make this an ideal waterfront home. **Left:** The kitchen opens easily to the living room, and a balcony connects the space to upstairs.

plan ⊕ HPK0900206

Style: Country Cottage
First Floor: 2,390 sq. ft.
Second Floor: 1,200 sq. ft.
Total: 3,590 sq. ft.
Bedrooms: 4
Bathrooms: 3
Width: 61' - 0"
Depth: 64' - 4"
Foundation: Pier (same as Piling)

SEARCH ONLINE @ EPLANS.COM

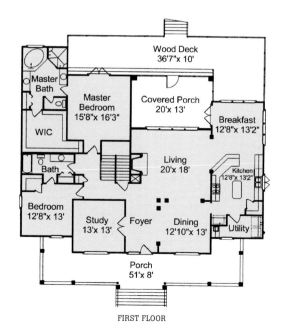

FIRST FLOOR

of the room; at the opposite end you'll find the spacious walk-in closet.

A second bedroom resides on the first floor as well, and two more can be found upstairs. Also upstairs is a multimedia room—perfect for enjoying your favorite DVDs, and also available for use as an extra bedroom if needed. After all, this home—with luxury inside and out—is sure to draw a crowd. ∎

ORDER BLUEPRINTS 24 HOURS, 7 DAYS A WEEK, AT 1-800-521-6797

This enticing European villa boasts an Italian charm and a distinct Mediterranean feel. The foyer steps lead up to the formal living areas. To the left, a study is expanded by a vaulted ceiling and double doors that open to the front balcony. The island kitchen is conveniently open to a breakfast nook. The guest quarters reside on the right side of the plan— one suite boasts a private bath; the other uses a full hall bath. The secluded master suite features two walk-in closets and a pampering whirlpool master bath. The home is completed by a basement-level garage.

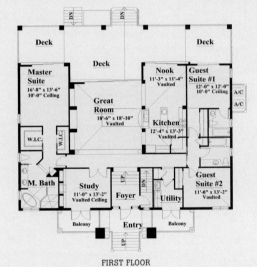

FIRST FLOOR

plan # HPK0900207

Style: Italianate
Square Footage: 2,385
Bedrooms: 3
Bathrooms: 3
Width: 60' - 0"
Depth: 52' - 0"
Foundation: Slab

SEARCH ONLINE @ EPLANS.COM

Rear Exterior

(FRONT) PHOTO COURTESY OF SATER DESIGN COLLECTION, INC. (REAR) PHOTO BY: TOM HARPER

BASEMENT

ORDER BLUEPRINTS 24 HOURS, 7 DAYS A WEEK, AT 1-800-521-6797

Dramatic balconies and spectacular window treatments enhance this stunning luxury home. Inside, a through-fireplace warms the formal living room and a restful den. Both living spaces open to a balcony that invites quiet reflection on starry nights. The banquet-sized dining room is easily served from the adjacent kitchen. Here, space is shared with an eating nook that provides access to the rear grounds and a family room with a corner fireplace—perfect for casual gatherings. The upper level contains two family bedrooms and a luxurious master suite that enjoys its own private balcony. The basement accommodates a shop and a bonus room for future development.

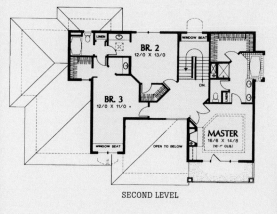

SECOND LEVEL

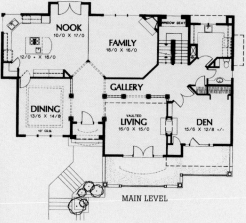

MAIN LEVEL

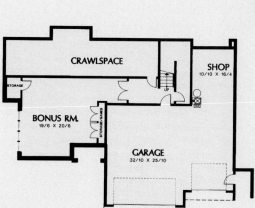

LOWER LEVEL

plan# HPK0900208

Style: NW Contemporary
Main Level: 1,989 sq. ft.
Second Level: 1,349 sq. ft.
Lower Level: 105 sq. ft.
Total: 3,443 sq. ft.
Bonus Space: 487 sq. ft.
Bedrooms: 3
Bathrooms: 2½
Width: 63' - 0"
Depth: 48' - 0"
Foundation: Basement

SEARCH ONLINE @ EPLANS.COM

A split staircase adds flair to this European-style coastal home, where a fireplace brings warmth on chilly evenings. The foyer opens to the expansive living/dining area and island kitchen. A multitude of windows fills the interior with sunlight and ocean breezes. The wrap-around rear deck finds access near the kitchen. The utility room is conveniently tucked between the kitchen and the two first-floor bedrooms. The second-floor master suite offers a private deck and a luxurious bath with a garden tub, shower, and walk-in closet.

SECOND FLOOR

plan # HPK0900209

Style: Seaside
First Floor: 1,552 sq. ft.
Second Floor: 653 sq. ft.
Total: 2,205 sq. ft.
Bedrooms: 3
Bathrooms: 2
Width: 60' - 0"
Depth: 50' - 0"
Foundation: Pier (same as Piling)

SEARCH ONLINE @ EPLANS.COM

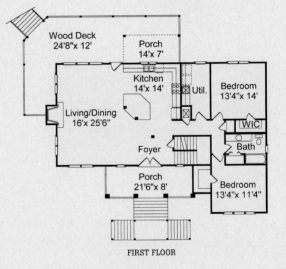

Rear Exterior

FIRST FLOOR

ORDER BLUEPRINTS 24 HOURS, 7 DAYS A WEEK, AT 1-800-521-6797

This waterfront home offers classic seaboard details with louvered shutters, covered porches, and an open floor plan. The lower level comprises two single-car garages, a game room with an accompanying full bath, and a utility room. The U-shaped staircase leads to the main living areas where the island kitchen is open to the dining room. The living room offers a wall of windows with access to the rear porch and deck. Two bedrooms lie to the left and share a full bath. On the right are the master suite and a fourth bedroom—each with private baths. Upstairs, a fifth bedroom with a bath completes the plan.

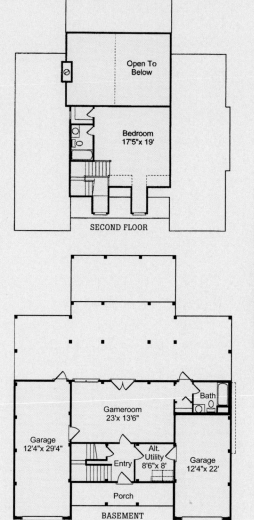

SECOND FLOOR

Open To Below

Bedroom
17'5"x 19'

BASEMENT

Garage
12'4"x 29'4"

Gameroom
23'x 13'6"

Entry

Alt. Utility
8'6"x 8'

Garage
12'4"x 22'

Bath

Porch

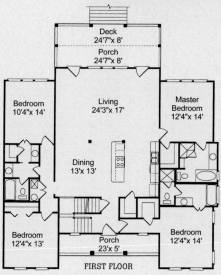

FIRST FLOOR

Deck
24'7"x 8'

Porch
24'7"x 8'

Bedroom
10'4"x 14'

Living
24'3"x 17'

Master Bedroom
12'4"x 14'

Dining
13'x 13'

Bedroom
12'4"x 13'

Porch
23'x 5'

Bedroom
12'4"x 14'

plan # HPK0900210

Style: Seaside
First Floor: 464 sq. ft.
Second Floor: 2,061 sq. ft.
Total: 2,525 sq. ft.
Basement: 452 sq. ft.
Bedrooms: 5
Bathrooms: 4
Width: 50' - 0"
Depth: 63' - 0"
Foundation: Pier (same as Piling)

SEARCH ONLINE @ EPLANS.COM

This pier-foundation home has an abundance of amenities to offer, not the least being the loft lookout. Inside, the living room is complete with a corner gas fireplace. The spacious kitchen features a cooktop island, an adjacent breakfast nook, and easy access to the dining room. From this room, a set of French doors leads out to a small deck—perfect for dining alfresco. Upstairs, the sleeping zone consists of two family bedrooms sharing a full hall bath, and a deluxe master suite. Amenities in this suite include two walk-in closets and a private bath.

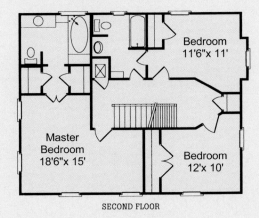

SECOND FLOOR

plan # HPK0900211

Style: Seaside
First Floor: 731 sq. ft.
Second Floor: 935 sq. ft.
Total: 1,666 sq. ft.
Bedrooms: 3
Bathrooms: 3
Width: 35' - 0"
Depth: 38' - 0"
Foundation: Pier (same as Piling)

SEARCH ONLINE @ EPLANS.COM

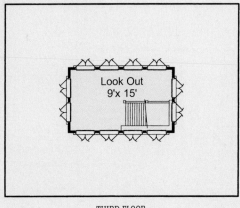

THIRD FLOOR

FIRST FLOOR

ORDER BLUEPRINTS 24 HOURS, 7 DAYS A WEEK, AT 1-800-521-6797

A stately tower adds a sense of grandeur to contemporary high-pitched rooflines on this dreamy Mediterranean-style villa. Surrounded by outdoor views, the living space extends to a veranda through three sets of French doors. Decorative columns announce the dining area, which boasts a 10-foot ceiling and views of its own. Tall arch-top windows bathe a winding staircase with sunlight or moonlight. The upper-level sleeping quarters include a master retreat that offers a bedroom with views and access to the observation deck. Secondary bedrooms share a full bath and linen storage. Bedroom 3 features a walk-in closet and French doors to the deck.

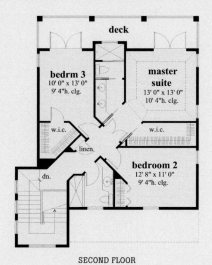

SECOND FLOOR

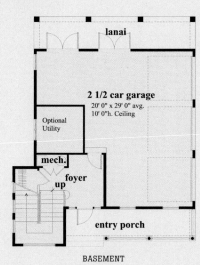

BASEMENT

FIRST FLOOR

plan# **HPK0900212**

Style: Italianate
First Floor: 874 sq. ft.
Second Floor: 880 sq. ft.
Total: 1,754 sq. ft.
Bedrooms: 3
Bathrooms: 2½
Width: 34' - 0"
Depth: 43' - 0"
Foundation: Basement

SEARCH ONLINE @ EPLANS.COM

This elegant Charleston townhouse is enhanced by Southern grace and three levels of charming livability. Covered porches offer outdoor living space at every level. The first floor offers a living room warmed by a fireplace, an island kitchen serving a bayed nook, and a formal dining room. A first-floor guest bedroom is located at the front of the plan, along with a laundry and powder room. The second level offers a sumptuous master suite boasting a private balcony, a master bath, and enormous walk-in closet. Two other bedrooms sharing a Jack-and-Jill bath are also on this level. The basement level includes a three-car garage and game room warmed by a fireplace.

plan # HPK0900213

Style: Country Cottage
First Floor: 1,901 sq. ft.
Second Floor: 1,874 sq. ft.
Total: 3,775 sq. ft.
Bedrooms: 4
Bathrooms: 3½
Width: 50' - 0"
Depth: 70' - 0"
Foundation: Pier (same as Piling)

SEARCH ONLINE @ EPLANS.COM

SECOND FLOOR

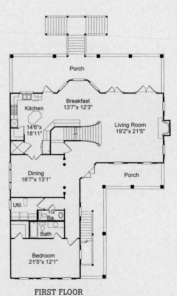

FIRST FLOOR

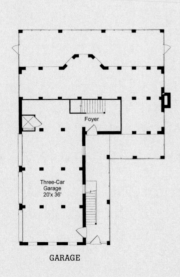

GARAGE

plan# **HPK0900214**

Style: NW Contemporary
Square Footage: 2,412
Bedrooms: 3
Bathrooms: 2½
Width: 60' - 0"
Depth: 59' - 0"
Foundation: Slab

SEARCH ONLINE @ EPLANS.COM

plan# **HPK0900215**

Style: Seaside
Square Footage: 2,190
Bedrooms: 3
Bathrooms: 2
Width: 60' - 0"
Depth: 54' - 0"
Foundation: Basement

SEARCH ONLINE @ EPLANS.COM

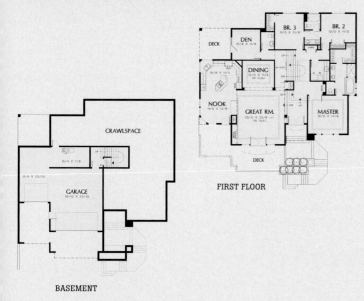

BASEMENT

FIRST FLOOR

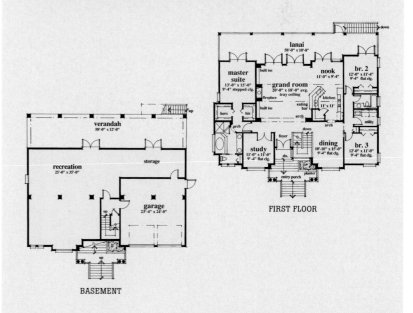

BASEMENT

FIRST FLOOR

plan # HPK0900216

Style: Seaside
First Floor: 1,342 sq. ft.
Second Floor: 511 sq. ft.
Total: 1,853 sq. ft.
Bedrooms: 3
Bathrooms: 2½
Width: 44' - 0"
Depth: 40' - 0"
Foundation: Basement

SEARCH ONLINE @ EPLANS.COM

plan # HPK0900217

Style: Tidewater
First Floor: 1,855 sq. ft.
Second Floor: 901 sq. ft.
Total: 2,756 sq. ft.
Bedrooms: 3
Bathrooms: 3½
Width: 66' - 0"
Depth: 50' - 0"
Foundation: Basement

SEARCH ONLINE @ EPLANS.COM

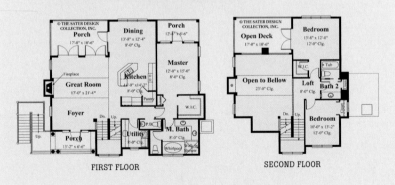

FIRST FLOOR   SECOND FLOOR

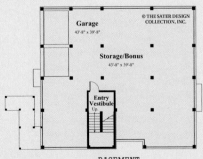

BASEMENT

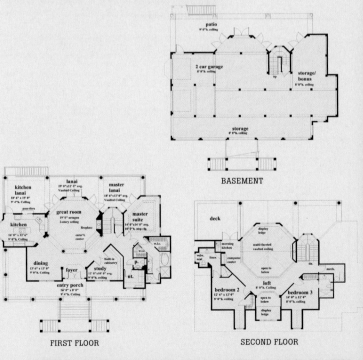

BASEMENT

FIRST FLOOR   SECOND FLOOR

ORDER BLUEPRINTS 24 HOURS, 7 DAYS A WEEK, AT 1-800-521-6797

plan# HPK0900218

Style: Tidewater
First Floor: 2,146 sq. ft.
Second Floor: 952 sq. ft.
Total: 3,098 sq. ft.
Bedrooms: 3
Bathrooms: 3½
Width: 52' - 0"
Depth: 65' - 4"
Foundation: Basement

SEARCH ONLINE @ EPLANS.COM

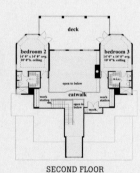

SECOND FLOOR

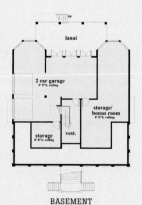

BASEMENT

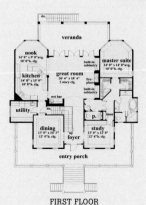

FIRST FLOOR

plan# HPK0900219

Style: Bungalow
First Floor: 1,855 sq. ft.
Second Floor: 901 sq. ft.
Total: 2,756 sq. ft.
Bedrooms: 3
Bathrooms: 3½
Width: 66' - 0"
Depth: 50' - 0"
Foundation: Basement

SEARCH ONLINE @ EPLANS.COM

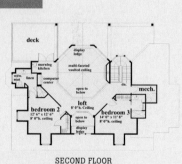

SECOND FLOOR

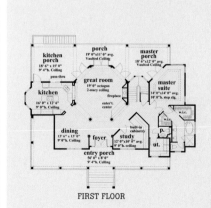

FIRST FLOOR

BASEMENT

This traditional country cabin is a vacationer's dream. Stone and vertical wood siding rustically camouflage the exterior; the inside pampers in lavish style. An elegant entryway extends into the foyer, where straight ahead, the two-story great room visually expands the lofty interior. This room provides a warming fireplace and offers built-in cabinetry. Double doors open to a fresh veranda, which wraps around to the rear deck—a perfect place to enjoy the outdoors. Upstairs, a vaulted ceiling enhances the master suite and its private bath. A private deck from the master suite can be accessed through a set of double doors. The loft area overlooking the great room accesses a second deck. The basement level hosts a bonus room, storage area, and two-car garage.

plan# HPK0900220

Style: Bungalow
First Floor: 1,143 sq. ft.
Second Floor: 651 sq. ft.
Total: 1,794 sq. ft.
Bonus Space: 651 sq. ft.
Bedrooms: 2
Bathrooms: 2½
Width: 32' - 0"
Depth: 57' - 0"
Foundation: Basement

SEARCH ONLINE @ EPLANS.COM

SECOND FLOOR

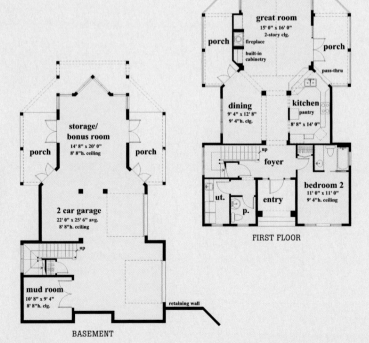

FIRST FLOOR

BASEMENT

Perfect for a narrow lot, this shingle-and-stone Nantucket Cape home caters to the casual lifestyle. The side entrance gives direct access to the wonderfully open living areas: gathering room with fireplace and an abundance of windows; island kitchen with angled, pass-through snack bar; and dining area with sliding glass doors to a covered eating area. Note also the large deck that further extends the living potential. Also on this floor is the large master suite with a compartmented bath, private dressing room, and walk-in closet. Upstairs, you'll find the three family bedrooms. Of the two bedrooms that share a bath, one features a private balcony.

Rear Exterior

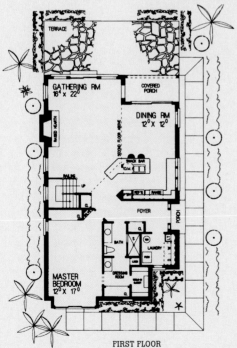

FIRST FLOOR

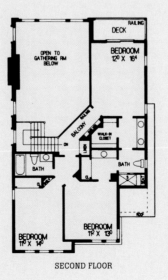

SECOND FLOOR

plan# HPK0900221

Style: Cape Cod
First Floor: 1,387 sq. ft.
Second Floor: 929 sq. ft.
Total: 2,316 sq. ft.
Bedrooms: 4
Bathrooms: 3
Width: 30' - 0"
Depth: 51' - 8"
Foundation: Crawlspace

SEARCH ONLINE @ EPLANS.COM

This three-level beach house offers spectacular views all around. With three deck levels accessible from all living areas, the outside sea air will surround you. The first level enjoys a living room, three bedrooms, a full bath, and a laundry area. The second level expands to a family area, a dining room, and a kitchen with an island snack bar and nearby half-bath. The master suite enjoys a walk-through closet and an amenity-filled bath with dual vanities and a separate tub and shower. The third level is a private haven—perfect for another bedroom—complete with a bath, walk-in closet, and sitting area.

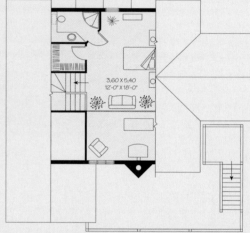

THIRD FLOOR

plan # HPK0900222

Style: Cape Cod
First Floor: 967 sq. ft.
Second Floor: 1,076 sq. ft.
Third Floor: 342 sq. ft.
Total: 2,385 sq. ft.
Bedrooms: 5
Bathrooms: 3½
Width: 39' - 8"
Depth: 36' - 8"
Foundation: Pier (same as Piling)

SEARCH ONLINE @ EPLANS.COM

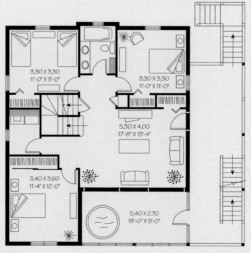

FIRST FLOOR

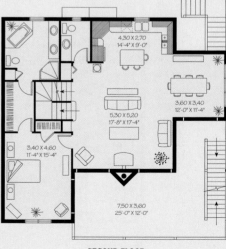

SECOND FLOOR

plan# HPK0900223

Style: Country Cottage
First Floor: 728 sq. ft.
Second Floor: 420 sq. ft.
Total: 1,148 sq. ft.
Bedrooms: 1
Bathrooms: 1½
Width: 28' - 0"
Depth: 26' - 0"
Foundation: Basement

SEARCH ONLINE @ EPLANS.COM

plan# HPK0900224

Style: Cape Cod
First Floor: 1,024 sq. ft.
Second Floor: 456 sq. ft.
Total: 1,480 sq. ft.
Bedrooms: 2
Bathrooms: 2
Width: 32' - 0"
Depth: 40' - 0"
Foundation: Basement

SEARCH ONLINE @ EPLANS.COM

FIRST FLOOR

SECOND FLOOR

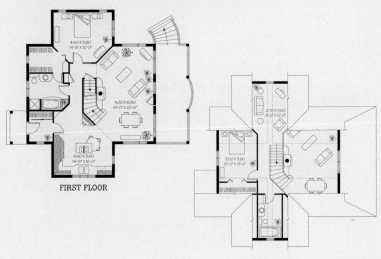

FIRST FLOOR

SECOND FLOOR

ORDER BLUEPRINTS 24 HOURS, 7 DAYS A WEEK, AT 1-800-521-6797

Horizontal siding, plentiful windows, and a wraparound porch grace this comfortable home. The great room is aptly named, with a fireplace, built-in seating, and access to the rear deck. Meal preparation is a breeze with a galley kitchen designed for efficiency. A screened porch is available for sipping lemonade on warm summer afternoons. The first floor contains two bedrooms and a unique bath to serve family and guests. The second floor offers a private getaway with a master suite that supplies panoramic views from its adjoining sitting area. A master bath with His and Hers walk-in closets and a private deck completes the second floor.

plan # HPK0900225

Style: Vacation
First Floor: 1,341 sq. ft.
Second Floor: 598 sq. ft.
Total: 1,939 sq. ft.
Bedrooms: 3
Bathrooms: 2
Width: 50' - 3"
Depth: 46' - 3"
Foundation: Crawlspace

SEARCH ONLINE @ EPLANS.COM

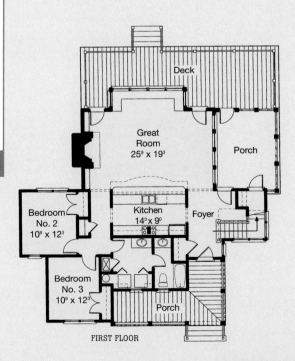

SECOND FLOOR

FIRST FLOOR

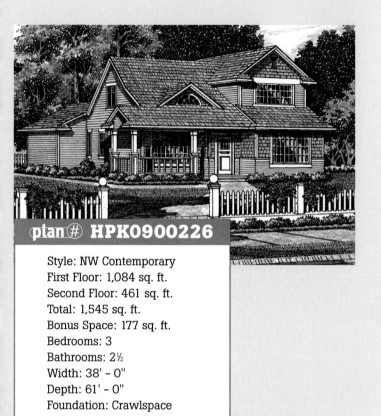

plan # **HPK0900226**

Style: NW Contemporary
First Floor: 1,084 sq. ft.
Second Floor: 461 sq. ft.
Total: 1,545 sq. ft.
Bonus Space: 177 sq. ft.
Bedrooms: 3
Bathrooms: 2½
Width: 38' – 0"
Depth: 61' – 0"
Foundation: Crawlspace

SEARCH ONLINE @ EPLANS.COM

plan # **HPK0900227**

Style: Farmhouse
Square Footage: 1,937
Bonus Space: 414 sq. ft.
Bedrooms: 3
Bathrooms: 2
Width: 76' – 4"
Depth: 73' – 4"
Foundation: Crawlspace

SEARCH ONLINE @ EPLANS.COM

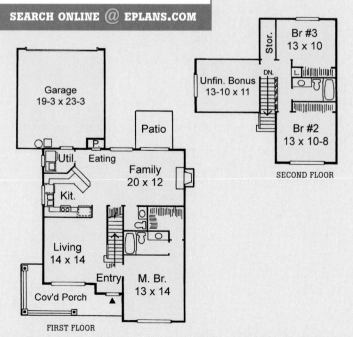

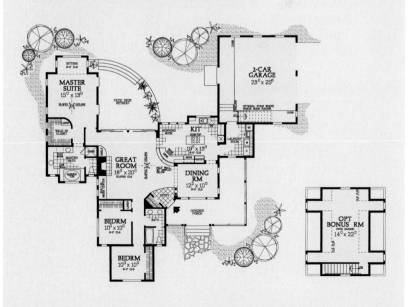

This combination of stone and siding creates an appealing facade to complement any neighborhood. Inside, the dining room is defined by columns and features a tray ceiling. A fireplace warms up the great room and provides access to the rear deck. In the kitchen, the cooktop island and extended counter space make meal preparation simple and organized. Two family bedrooms—one that can be used as a study—share a full hall bath. The master bedroom provides a private bath with double-bowl sinks, His and Hers closets, a tub, and a separate shower. The utility room is located near the garage entrance.

plan # HPK0900228

Style: Craftsman
Square Footage: 1,753
Bonus Space: 389 sq. ft.
Bedrooms: 3
Bathrooms: 2
Width: 49' - 4"
Depth: 64' - 4"

SEARCH ONLINE @ EPLANS.COM

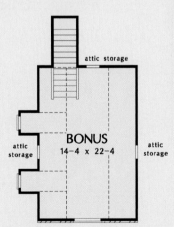

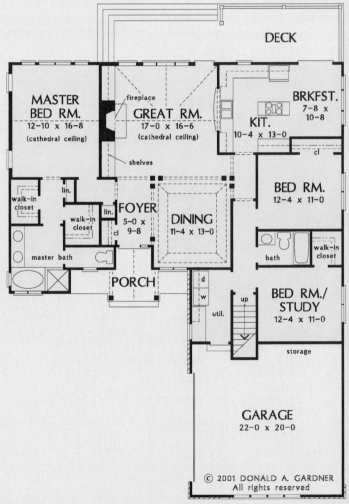

Interesting window treatments highlight this stone-and-shake facade, but don't overlook the columned porch to the left of the portico. Arches outline the formal dining room and the family room, both of which are convenient to the island kitchen. Household chores are made easier by the placement of a pantry, powder room, laundry room, and office between the kitchen and the entrances to the side porch and garage. If your goal is relaxation, the breakfast room, screened porch, and covered deck are also nearby. The master suite features a beautiful bay. Three secondary bedrooms and a recreation room are on the lower level.

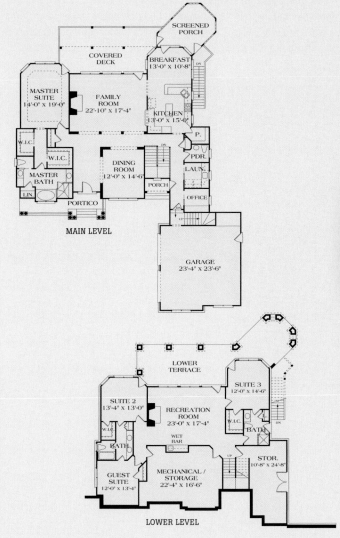

MAIN LEVEL

LOWER LEVEL

Rear Exterior

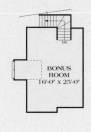

BONUS ROOM
16'-0" X 25'-0"

plan# HPK0900229

Style: Country Cottage
Main Level: 2,213 sq. ft.
Lower Level: 1,333 sq. ft.
Total: 3,546 sq. ft.
Bonus Space: 430 sq. ft.
Bedrooms: 4
Bathrooms: 3½
Width: 67' - 2"
Depth: 93' - 1"
Foundation: Basement

SEARCH ONLINE @ EPLANS.COM

Traditional classics come and go—but this stunning estate tops the rest, with a breathtakingly pretty facade and award-winning rooms. An intelligent layout arranges the formal rooms off the foyer. French doors open to an elegant dining room. A privacy door leads from the dining room to the gourmet kitchen. Decorative columns and an exposed-beam ceiling define the family room. Tall windows frame a massive stone fireplace. A French door leads out to the rear deck and wraparound arbor. An extraordinary master suite boasts an open sitting area in the bedroom. Twin windows brighten this space. This bright reprieve leads to a roomy bath with a garden tub, separate lavatories, and a walk-in closet large enough for two. Upstairs, each bedroom offers ample linen storage, a walk-in closet, and a triple window that brightens the vanity in each private bath. Dormer windows add a sitting area in each of the suites.

plan # HPK0900230

Style: Cape Cod
First Floor: 2,660 sq. ft.
Second Floor: 815 sq. ft.
Total: 3,475 sq. ft.
Bedrooms: 3
Bathrooms: 3½
Width: 76' - 6"
Depth: 58' - 0"
Foundation: Basement

SEARCH ONLINE @ EPLANS.COM

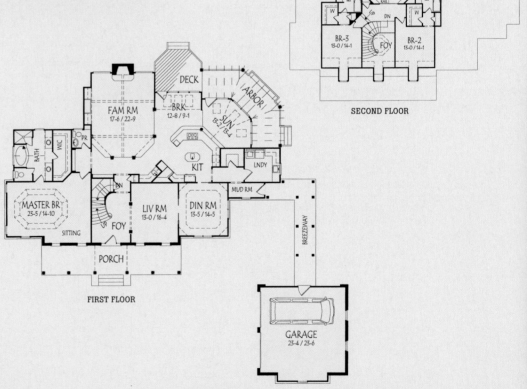

SECOND FLOOR

FIRST FLOOR

ORDER BLUEPRINTS 24 HOURS, 7 DAYS A WEEK, AT 1-800-521-6797

A distinctive exterior, complete with siding, stone, and brick, presents a welcoming facade on this four-bedroom home. The large family room includes a cathedral ceiling, a fireplace, and built-ins. The island kitchen has plenty of work space and direct access to a sunny, bay-windowed breakfast room. A study and formal dining room flank the tiled entryway, which leads straight into a formal living room. Three family bedrooms are arranged across the front of the house. The master suite offers plenty of seclusion as well as two walk-in closets, a lavish bath, and direct access to the rear patio. A stairway leads to the attic.

plan # HPK0900231

Style: Traditional
Square Footage: 3,270
Bedrooms: 4
Bathrooms: 3½
Width: 101' – 0"
Depth: 48' – 1"
Foundation: Crawlspace, Slab

SEARCH ONLINE @ EPLANS.COM

Patio

Brkfst 16x12

Patio

Cov. Patio

Roof line

Entertainment Center

FamilyRm 20x16

W.I. Closet

niche

MstrBth

Three-Car Garage 21x30

CATHEDRAL CEILING FROM 9'- 0"

42" ht. snack bar

Kitchen 16x14

MstrBed 17x15
PULLMAN CEILING TO 10'- 0"

W.I. Closet

Books

54"x24" Work Island

LivRm 17x15
10'- 0" CLG. HT.

Util 10x10

Stairs To Attic

Strg

Linen

W.I. Closet

Linen

Bth #2

chest

W.I. Closet

Pantry

Gallery 10'- 0" CLG. HT.

W.I. Closet

chest

Bed#4 11x14

Bed#3 13x12

Pwdr.

FmlDin 13x14
10'- 0" CLG. HT.

Ent 10'- 0" CLG. HT.

Study 13x14
10'- 0" CLG. HT.

Bed#2 15x13

Bth#3

W.I.Closet

Cov. Porch

©1999 Donald A. Gardner, Inc.

plan# HPK0900232

Style: Bungalow
Square Footage: 1,927
Bonus Space: 413 sq. ft.
Bedrooms: 3
Bathrooms: 2½
Width: 60' - 0"
Depth: 64' - 8"

SEARCH ONLINE @ EPLANS.COM

BONUS RM.
14-8 x 23-4

©1998 Donald A. Gardner, Inc.

plan# HPK0900233

Style: Bungalow
First Floor: 2,755 sq. ft.
Second Floor: 735 sq. ft.
Total: 3,490 sq. ft.
Bonus Space: 481 sq. ft.
Bedrooms: 3
Bathrooms: 3½
Width: 92' - 6"
Depth: 69' - 10"

SEARCH ONLINE @ EPLANS.COM

SECOND FLOOR

FIRST FLOOR

plan# **HPK0900234**

Style: Resort Lifestyles
First Floor: 1,620 sq. ft.
Second Floor: 770 sq. ft.
Total: 2,390 sq. ft.
Bedrooms: 3
Bathrooms: 3½
Width: 49' - 0"
Depth: 58' - 8"

SEARCH ONLINE @ EPLANS.COM

plan# **HPK0900235**

Style: Bungalow
Main Level: 1,810 sq. ft.
Lower Level: 1,146 sq. ft.
Total: 2,956 sq. ft.
Bedrooms: 4
Bathrooms: 3
Width: 68' - 4"
Depth: 60' - 10"

SEARCH ONLINE @ EPLANS.COM

FIRST FLOOR

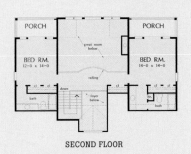

SECOND FLOOR

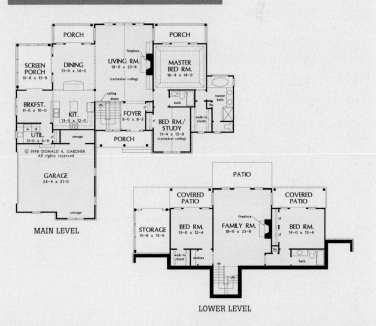

MAIN LEVEL

LOWER LEVEL

©1998 Donald A. Gardner, Inc.

This Craftsman-style home takes advantage of hillside views with its deck, patio, and an abundance of rear windows. An open floor plan enhances the home's spaciousness. The great room features a cathedral ceiling, a fireplace with built-in cabinets and shelves, and access to the generous rear deck. Designed for ultimate efficiency, the kitchen serves the great room, dining room, and breakfast area with equal ease. A tray ceiling lends elegance to the master bedroom, which features deck access, twin walk-in closets, and an extravagant bath with dual vanities, a large linen closet, and separate tub and shower.

plan# HPK0900236

Style: Bungalow
Main Level: 2,068 sq. ft.
Lower Level: 930 sq. ft.
Total: 2,998 sq. ft.
Bedrooms: 3
Bathrooms: 3½
Width: 72' - 4"
Depth: 66' - 0"

SEARCH ONLINE @ EPLANS.COM

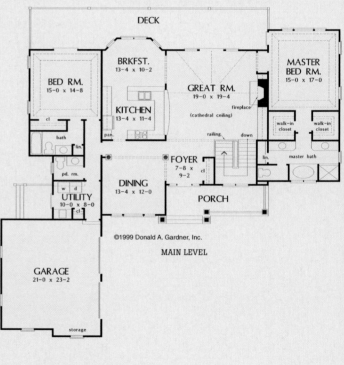

MAIN LEVEL

©1999 Donald A. Gardner, Inc.

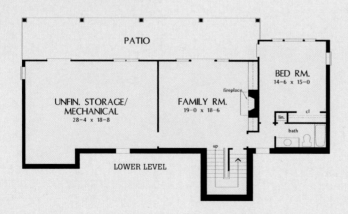

LOWER LEVEL

ORDER BLUEPRINTS 24 HOURS, 7 DAYS A WEEK, AT 1-800-521-6797

Stone, siding, and multiple gables combine beautifully on the exterior of this hillside home. Taking advantage of rear views, the home's most oft-used rooms are oriented at the back with plenty of windows. Augmented by a cathedral ceiling, the great room features a fireplace, built-in shelves, and access to the rear deck. Twin walk-in closets and a private bath infuse the master suite with luxury. The nearby powder room offers an optional full-bath arrangement, allowing the study to double as a bedroom. Downstairs, a large media/recreation room with a wet bar and fireplace separates two more bedrooms, each with a full bath and walk-in closet.

©1998 Donald A. Gardner, Inc.

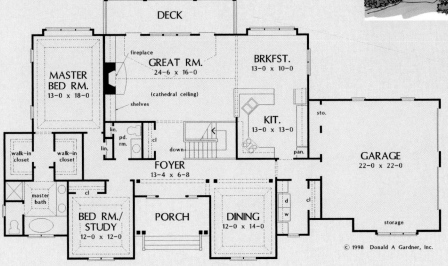

MAIN LEVEL

© 1998 Donald A Gardner, Inc.

plan# HPK0900237

Style: Bungalow
Main Level: 2,065 sq. ft.
Lower Level: 1,216 sq. ft.
Total: 3,281 sq. ft.
Bedrooms: 4
Bathrooms: 3½
Width: 82' - 2"
Depth: 43' - 6"

SEARCH ONLINE @ EPLANS.COM

(optional bath)

OPTIONAL LAYOUT

LOWER LEVEL

A wraparound covered porch is just one of many luxurious touches that fill this bungalow design. Columns add elegance to the entry, living room, and dining room, and built-ins and a fireplace enhance the living room. A covered deck and screened porch, accessible from the living room, offer opportunities for outdoor gatherings. Conveniently near the kitchen, a walk-in pantry and butler's pantry allow for easy storage and service. A master suite and two additional bedrooms cluster to the right of the plan; the splendid master bath features a corner tub and shower and a large walk-in closet. Bonus space offers room to grow.

plan # HPK0900238

Style: Farmhouse
Square Footage: 2,405
Bonus Space: 375 sq. ft.
Bedrooms: 3
Bathrooms: 2½
Width: 70' - 7"
Depth: 89' - 5"
Foundation: Crawlspace, Slab

SEARCH ONLINE @ EPLANS.COM

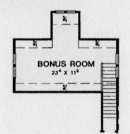

BONUS ROOM
23⁴ X 11⁹

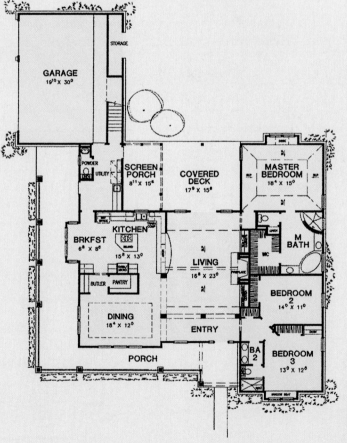

PHOTO BY: GEORGE ANDERSON

Two gables, supported by pillars and accented with rafter tails, are fine examples of Craftsmanship presented on this three-bedroom home. Inside, a den opens to the left of the foyer, providing a quiet place for relaxing. A living room with a fireplace flanked by windows welcomes casual times. The unique kitchen offers a small, yet cozy nook as well as ease in serving the dining room. The master suite is also on this floor and features a walk-in closet and a pampering bath. Downstairs, a huge recreation room is available for fun and stylish entertainment.

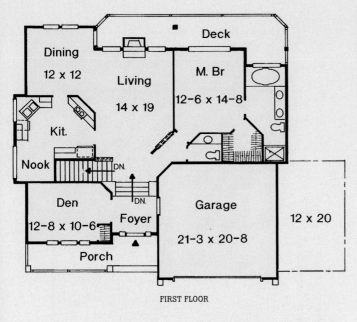

FIRST FLOOR

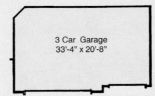

3 Car Garage
33'-4" x 20'-8"

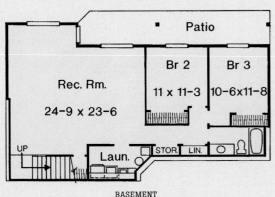

BASEMENT

plan # HPK0900239

Style: NW Contemporary
Main Level: 1,416 sq. ft.
Lower Level: 1,300 sq. ft.
Total: 2,716 sq. ft.
Bedrooms: 3
Bathrooms: 2½
Width: 50' - 0"
Depth: 46' - 0"
Foundation: Basement

SEARCH ONLINE @ EPLANS.COM

sunny days

This transitional-style home is a great narrow-lot design. Inside, the foyer opens to the great room/dining area combination—here, a corner fireplace warms crisp evenings. The kitchen easily serves the dining area and optional screened porch, which is great for seasonal outdoor meals. The first-floor master suite includes a whirlpool bath and a walk-in closet. The laundry room leads to the two-car garage. Optional basement-level fixtures include a spacious recreation room, a hall bath, and two additional bedrooms—one easily converts to a library. Basement storage and unexcavated space is reserved for future developments.

plan # HPK0900240

Style: Transitional
Square Footage: 1,462
Basement: 1,007 sq. ft.
Bedrooms: 3
Bathrooms: 2½
Width: 46' - 0"
Depth: 59' - 4"
Foundation: Basement

SEARCH ONLINE @ EPLANS.COM

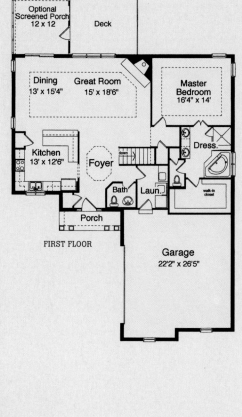

FIRST FLOOR

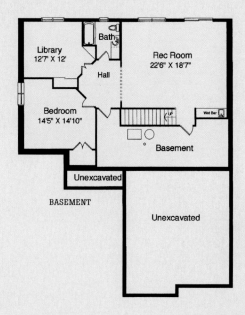

BASEMENT

plan # HPK0900241

Style: Cape Cod
First Floor: 873 sq. ft.
Second Floor: 481 sq. ft.
Total: 1,354 sq. ft.
Bedrooms: 3
Bathrooms: 2
Width: 51' – 6"
Depth: 31' – 8"
Foundation: Basement

SEARCH ONLINE @ EPLANS.COM

plan # HPK0900242

Style: Cape Cod
First Floor: 1,251 sq. ft.
Second Floor: 505 sq. ft.
Total: 1,756 sq. ft.
Bonus Space: 447 sq. ft.
Bedrooms: 3
Bathrooms: 2½
Width: 50' – 0"
Depth: 39' – 0"
Foundation: Basement, Crawlspace

SEARCH ONLINE @ EPLANS.COM

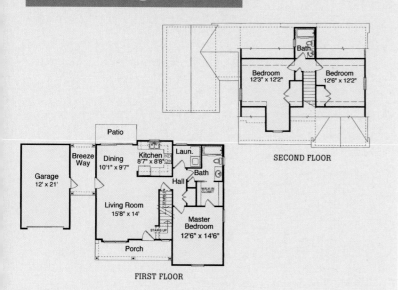

SECOND FLOOR

FIRST FLOOR

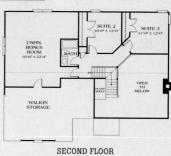

SECOND FLOOR

FIRST FLOOR

sunny days

This cozy cottage offers all of the comforts of a first home in a one-story, efficient design. The bedrooms sit to either side of the plan, with the master suite on the left, and two additional family bedrooms on the right. The great room is at the heart of the home, outfitted with a corner fireplace. The U-shaped kitchen with serving bar offers added convenience. The breakfast nook enjoys a pleasant view of the rear covered patio. A two-car garage completes this plan.

plan# HPK0900243

Style: Mediterranean
Square Footage: 1,550
Bedrooms: 3
Bathrooms: 2
Width: 50' - 0"
Depth: 55' - 0"
Foundation: Slab

SEARCH ONLINE @ EPLANS.COM

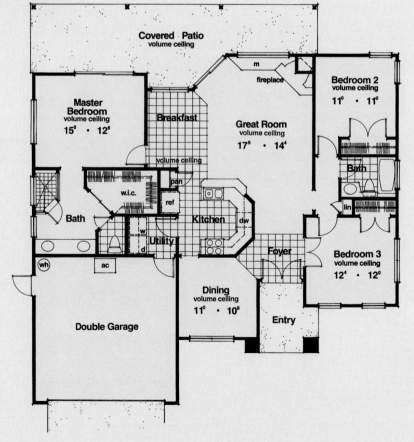

This smart, traditional plan packs a lot of living space into its modest square footage. A stately columned porch leads to the foyer, which boasts a convenient coat closet to its left. Just ahead, the great room's cathedral ceiling amplifies elegance; its cozy hearth offers the warmth of home. The kitchen features ample counter space and is book-ended by a formal dining room and a sunny breakfast nook. The rear deck will provide many seasons of fun and relaxation. Two bedrooms—one that could be converted to a study—share a full bath on the left of the plan. A divine master suite is secluded behind the garage, with a vaulted ceiling, stunning master bath, and walk-in closet. The utility room is convenient to both the kitchen and the garage. Bonus space awaits expansion upstairs.

plan # HPK0900244

Style: Traditional
Square Footage: 1,606
Bonus Space: 338 sq. ft.
Bedrooms: 3
Bathrooms: 2
Width: 50' - 0"
Depth: 54' - 0"

SEARCH ONLINE @ EPLANS.COM

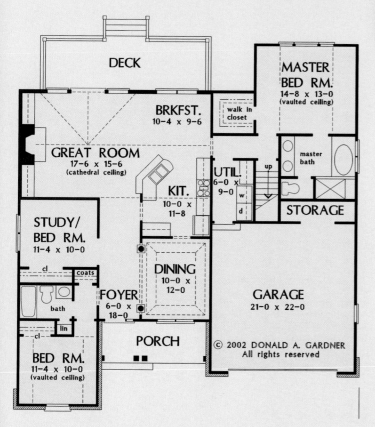

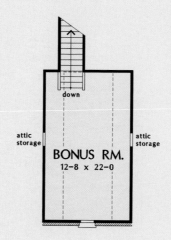

This refined hillside home is designed for lots that fall off toward the rear and works especially well with a view out the back. The kitchen and eating nook wrap around the vaulted family room where arched transom windows flank the fireplace. Formal living is graciously centered in the living room that's directly off the foyer and the adjoining dining room. A grand master suite is located on the main level for convenience and privacy. Downstairs, three family bedrooms share a compartmented hall bath.

plan # HPK0900245

Style: NW Contemporary
Main Level: 2,196 sq. ft.
Lower Level: 1,542 sq. ft.
Total: 3,738 sq. ft.
Bedrooms: 4
Bathrooms: 2½
Width: 72' - 0"
Depth: 56' - 0"
Foundation: Crawlspace, Basement

SEARCH ONLINE @ EPLANS.COM

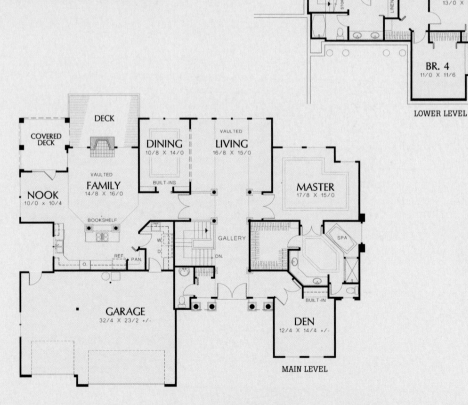

ORDER BLUEPRINTS 24 HOURS, 7 DAYS A WEEK, AT 1-800-521-6797

The fine exterior features of this European-style home accurately suggest the gracious comforts that are found inside. Four bedrooms, one a master suite with a private porch, provide ample sleeping quarters. The kitchen is a delight, with a long island counter and a peninsular bar that swings into the sunlit breakfast nook. The living room, which enjoys a fireplace and built-in shelves, opens to a rear porch through two sets of French doors. Beyond the porch, a patio will be a great place for barbecues, or just to sit and catch some rays. A laundry/utility room opens to the two-car garage, as does the kitchen.

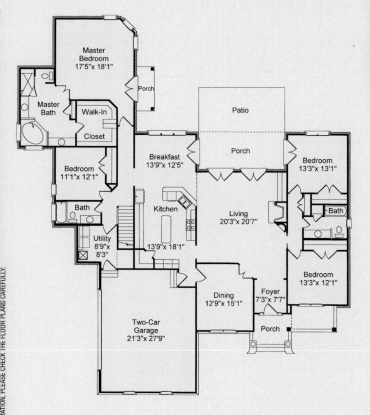

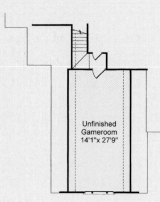

plan# HPK0900246

Style: Mediterranean
Square Footage: 2,903
Bedrooms: 4
Bathrooms: 3
Width: 80' - 0"
Depth: 95' - 6"
Foundation: Slab

SEARCH ONLINE @ EPLANS.COM

Master Bedroom 17'5"x 18'1"
Porch
Master Bath
Walk-In
Closet
Patio
Porch
Breakfast 13'9"x 12'5"
Bedroom 13'3"x 13'1"
Bedroom 11'1" x 12'1"
Bath
Kitchen
Living 20'3"x 20'7"
Bath
13'9"x 18'1"
Utility 8'9"x 8'3"
Bedroom 13'3"x 12'1"
Two-Car Garage 21'3"x 27'9"
Dining 12'9"x 15'1"
Foyer 7'3"x 7'7"
Porch
Porch
Unfinished Gameroom 14'1"x 27'9"

Arts and Crafts has never looked so appealing! A steeply pitched front gable accented with cedar shingles and stone is set-off by gentle porch arches. Inside find the desirable great room/kitchen combination with an adjacent breakfast nook. A first-floor master suite offers a walk-in closet, compartmented bath, and decorative ceiling. Conveniently placed, the den functions as a perfect office or library. Two family bedrooms, a gallery library, and the game room share a spacious hall bath.

SECOND FLOOR

plan # HPK0900247

Style: Craftsman
First Floor: 2,172 sq. ft.
Second Floor: 824 sq. ft.
Total: 2,996 sq. ft.
Bedrooms: 3
Bathrooms: 2½
Width: 67' - 0"
Depth: 68' - 0"
Foundation: Crawlspace

SEARCH ONLINE @ EPLANS.COM

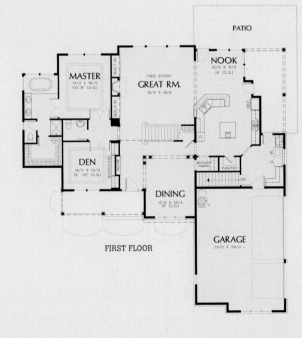

FIRST FLOOR

Plentiful outdoor living spaces make this an ideal home for entertaining. Inside, the open floor plan allows easy interaction between rooms. The spacious island kitchen conveniently serves the family room and dining room. At the rear of the first floor, a fireplace warms the living room. Upstairs houses the master bedroom, outfitted with tray ceilings, a dual-sink vanity, a garden tub and separate shower, and a compartmented toilet. The adjacent home office is an added convenience. Two additional family bedrooms share a full bath. A three-car garage completes this plan.

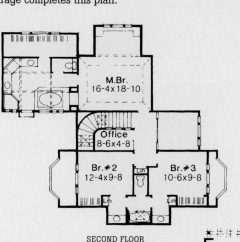

SECOND FLOOR

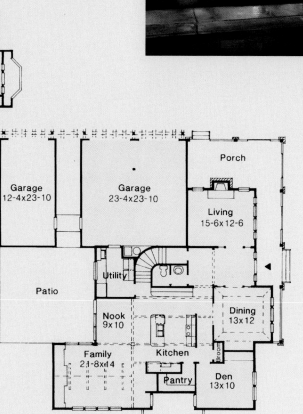

FIRST FLOOR

plan# HPK0900248

Style: Bungalow
First Floor: 1,706 sq. ft.
Second Floor: 1,123 sq. ft.
Total: 2,829 sq. ft.
Bedrooms: 3
Bathrooms: 2½
Width: 71' - 2"
Depth: 64' - 6"
Foundation: Crawlspace

SEARCH ONLINE @ EPLANS.COM

Looking a bit like a mountain resort, this fine rustic-style home is sure to be the envy of your neighborhood. Entering through the elegant front door, one finds an open staircase to the right and a spacious great room directly ahead. Here, a fireplace and a wall of windows give a cozy welcome. A lavish master suite begins with a sitting room complete with a fireplace and continues to a private porch, large walk-in closet, and sumptuous bedroom area. The gourmet kitchen adjoins a sunny dining room that offers access to a screened porch.

plan⊕ HPK0900249

Style: Craftsman
Main Level: 3,040 sq. ft.
Lower Level: 1,736 sq. ft.
Total: 4,776 sq. ft.
Bedrooms: 5
Bathrooms: 4½ + ½
Width: 106' - 5"
Depth: 104' - 2"

SEARCH ONLINE @ EPLANS.COM

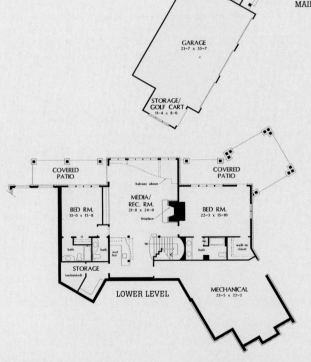

The strong impact of its exterior design will make this home look good in the country or the suburbs. Upon entering, guests are greeted with the expansive great room's cathedral ceiling and cozy fireplace. The kitchen has a snack-counter island with a breakfast nook that opens to a deck. Located on the first floor for privacy, the master suite contains plenty of windows, two walk-in closets, and a whirlpool tub with views out a bayed window. The immaculate second floor overlooks the great room and entryway. A lounge area is flanked by Bedrooms 2 and 3. A full bath with dual vanities completes the plan.

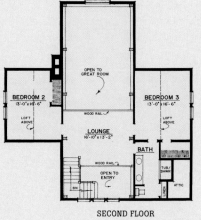

SECOND FLOOR

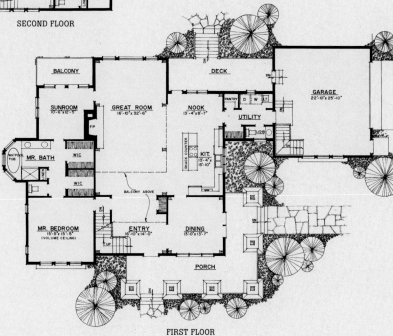

FIRST FLOOR

plan# HPK0900250

Style: Bungalow
First Floor: 2,078 sq. ft.
Second Floor: 823 sq. ft.
Total: 2,901 sq. ft.
Bedrooms: 3
Bathrooms: 2½
Width: 88' - 5"
Depth: 58' - 3"
Foundation: Basement

SEARCH ONLINE @ EPLANS.COM

Alternate exteriors—both European style!

Stone quoins and shutters give one facade the appearance of a French Country cottage. The other, with keystone window treatment and a copper roof over the bay window, creates the impression of a stately French chateau. From the entry, formal living areas are entered through graceful columned openings—living room to the left and dining room to the right. Straight ahead, the comfortable family room awaits with its warming fireplace and cathedral ceiling, offering room to relax and enjoy casual gatherings. The private master suite features a Pullman ceiling, a luxurious bath, and twin walk-in closets. A private lanai is accessed from the master bath. Located nearby, Bedroom 2 serves nicely as a guest room or easily converts to a nursery or study. Two family bedrooms, a connecting bath, handy kitchen, breakfast room, and utility room complete the floor plan.

plan# HPK0900251

Style: Country Cottage
Square Footage: 2,888
Bedrooms: 4
Bathrooms: 3
Width: 68' - 6"
Depth: 78' - 1"
Foundation: Slab

SEARCH ONLINE @ EPLANS.COM

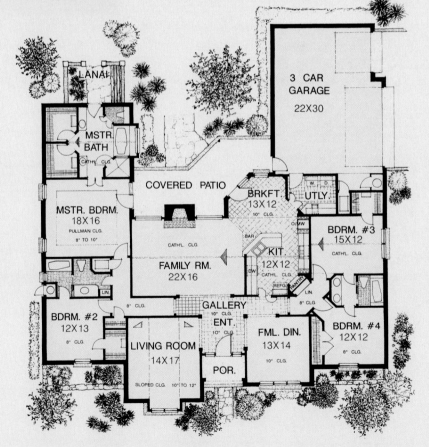

An eye-catching shed dormer is both lovely and functional, bringing light into the foyer. A mud room is the perfect casual entry off the garage, right next to the main-level laundry and optional third-car garage. The open kitchen works with the keeping, breakfast, and grand rooms. A study—or living room—and formal dining room flank the foyer for entertaining guests.

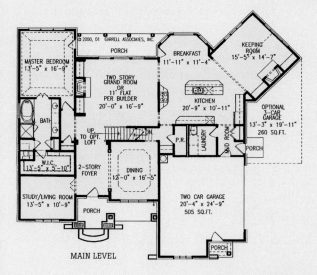

MAIN LEVEL

plan # HPK0900252

Style: Bungalow
Main Level: 2,160 sq. ft.
Lower Level: 919 sq. ft.
Total: 3,079 sq. ft.
Bedrooms: 3
Bathrooms: 2½
Width: 68' - 3"
Depth: 60' - 11"
Foundation: Basement

SEARCH ONLINE @ EPLANS.COM

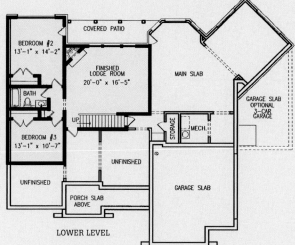

LOWER LEVEL

plan # HPK0900253

Style: Craftsman
Square Footage: 3,055
Bedrooms: 3
Bathrooms: 3
Width: 80' - 0"
Depth: 68' - 11"
Foundation: Basement, Crawlspace

SEARCH ONLINE @ EPLANS.COM

Inspired by nature and Asian

design, the Prairie style has become a beloved American tradition. Windows invite the outdoors in and enhance the amount of natural light throughout the home. Formal spaces are not overlooked; a dining room sits just off the foyer and is open with a carefully placed defining wall. Decorative columns discern the living room space without overwhelming it. A central fireplace can be enjoyed by any spot in the room. The grand master suite is set aside in the left wing of the home. This position will maintain privacy and comfort with twin walk-in closets, a soothing bath with garden tub, separate shower, His and Hers vanities, and a compartmented toilet. The right wing contains the casual living spaces and family bedrooms. A large utility room functions as laundry and mud room. The gourmet kitchen is the heart of the home, with a large center island, eating nook, adjoining family room with fireplace, and extended media room.

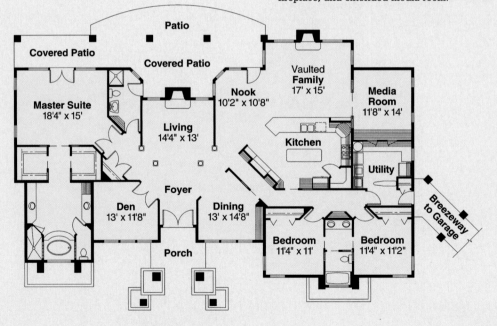

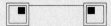

ORDER BLUEPRINTS 24 HOURS, 7 DAYS A WEEK, AT 1-800-521-6797

Sand-finished stucco, distinctive columns, and oversized circle-top windows grace this luxurious three-bedroom home. A sunken living room features a two-sided gas fireplace that it shares with the formal dining room. The den is warmed by a fireplace and features double doors to the front porch. The family room is also sunken and shares a two-sided fireplace with an indoor spa and a glazed roof overhead. Two secondary bedrooms and a master suite are on the second floor. The master suite enjoys a through-fireplace between the bath and the bedroom.

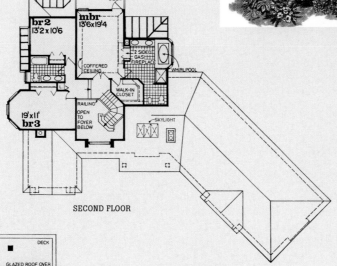

SECOND FLOOR

FIRST FLOOR

plan# HPK0900254

Style: SW Contemporary
First Floor: 2,132 sq. ft.
Second Floor: 1,295 sq. ft.
Total: 3,427 sq. ft.
Bedrooms: 3
Bathrooms: 3
Width: 91' - 6"
Depth: 75' - 6"
Foundation: Crawlspace, Basement

SEARCH ONLINE @ EPLANS.COM

With more than 50 years of experience in the industry and millions of blueprints sold, Hanley Wood is a trusted source of high-quality, high-value pre-drawn home plans.

Using pre-drawn home plans is a **reliable, cost-effective way** to build your dream home, and our vast selection of plans is second-to-none. The nation's finest designers craft these plans that builders know they can trust. Meanwhile, our friendly, knowledgeable customer service representatives can help you every step of the way.

WHAT YOU'LL GET WITH YOUR ORDER

The contents of each designer's blueprint package is unique, but all contain detailed, high-quality working drawings. You can expect to find the following standard elements in most sets of plans:

1. FRONT PERSPECTIVE

This artist's sketch of the exterior of the house gives you an idea of how the house will look when built and landscaped.

2. FOUNDATION AND BASEMENT PLANS

This sheet shows the foundation layout including concrete walls, footings, pads, posts, beams, and bearing walls, and foundation notes. If the home features a basement, the first-floor framing details may also be included on this plan. If your plan features slab construction rather than a basement, the plan shows footings and details for a monolithic slab. This page, or another in the set, may include a sample plot plan for locating your house on a building site. Additional sheets focus on foundation cross-sections and other details.

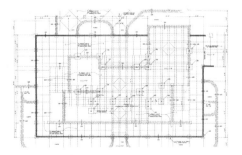

3. DETAILED FLOOR PLANS

These plans show the layout of each floor of the house. Rooms and interior spaces are carefully dimensioned, doors and windows located, and keys are given for cross-section details provided elsewhere in the plans.

4. HOUSE AND DETAIL CROSS-SECTIONS

Large-scale views show sections or cutaways of the foundation, interior walls, exterior walls, floors, stairways, and roof details. Additional cross-sections may show important changes in floor, ceiling, or roof heights, or the relationship of one level to another. These sections show exactly how the various parts of the house fit together and are extremely valuable during construction. Additional sheets may include enlarged wall, floor, and roof construction details.

5. ROOF AND FLOOR STRUCTURAL SUPPORTS

The roof and floor framing plans provide detail for these crucial elements of your home. Each includes floor joist, ceiling joist, rafter and roof joist size, spacing, direction, span, and specifications. Beam and window headers, along with necessary details for framing connections, stairways, skylights, or dormers are also included.

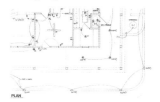

6. ELECTRICAL PLAN

The electrical plan offers a detailed outline of all wiring for your home, with notes for all lighting, outlets, switches, and circuits. A layout is provided for each level, as well as basements, garages, or other structures.

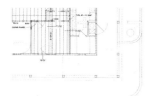

7. EXTERIOR ELEVATIONS

In addition to the front exterior, your blueprint set will include drawings of the rear and sides of your house as well. These drawings give notes on exterior materials and finishes. Particular attention is given to cornice detail, brick and stone accents, or other finish items that make your home unique.

BEFORE YOU CALL

You are making a terrific decision to use a pre-drawn house plan—it is one you can make with confidence, knowing that your blueprints are crafted by national-award-winning certified residential designers and architects, and trusted by builders.

Once you've selected the plan you want—or even if you have questions along the way—our experienced customer service representatives are available 24 hours a day, seven days a week to help you navigate the home-building process. To help them provide you with even better service, please consider the following questions before you call:

■ Have you chosen or purchased your lot?
If so, please review the building setback requirements of your local building authority before you call. You don't need to have a lot before ordering plans, but if you own land already, please have the width and depth dimensions handy when you call.

■ Have you chosen a builder?
Involving your builder in the plan selection and evaluation process may be beneficial. Luckily, builders know they can have confidence with pre-drawn plans because they've been designed for livability, functionality, and typically are builder-proven at successful home sites across the country.

■ Do you need a construction loan?
Construction loans are unique because they involve determining the value of something that is not yet constructed. Several lenders offer convenient contstruction-to-permanent loans. It is important to choose a good lending partner—one who will help guide you through the application and appraisal process. Most will even help you evaluate your contractor to ensure reliability and credit worthiness. Our partnership with IndyMac Bank, a nationwide leader in construction loans, can help you save on your loan, if needed.

■ How many sets of plans do you need?
Building a home can typically require a number of sets of blueprints—one for yourself, two or three for the builder and subcontractors, two for the local building department, and one or more for your lender. For this reason, we offer 5- and 8-set plan packages, but your best value is the Reproducible Plan Package. Reproducible plans are accompanied by a license to make modifications and typically up to 12 duplicates of the plan so you have enough copies of the plan for everyone involved in the financing and construction of your home.

■ Do you want to make any changes to the plan?
We understand that it is difficult to find blueprints for a home that will meet all of your needs. That is why Hanley Wood is glad to offer plan Customization Services. We will work with you to design the modifications you'd like to see and to adjust your blueprint plans accordingly—anything from changing the foundation; adding square footage, redesigning baths, kitchens, or bedrooms; or most other modifications. This simple, cost-effective service saves you from hiring an outside architect to make alterations. Modifications may only be made to Reproducible Plan Packages that include the license to modify.

■ Do you have to make any changes to meet local building codes?
While all of our plans are drawn to meet national building codes at the time they were created, many areas required that plans be stamped by a local engineer to certify that they meet local building codes. Building codes are updated frequently and can vary by state, county, city, or municipality. Contact your local building inspection department, office of planning and zoning, or department of permits to determine how your local codes will affect your construction project. The best way to assure that you can make changes to your plan, if necessary, is to purchase a Reproducible Plan Package.

■ Has everyone—from family members to contractors—been involved in selecting the plan?
Building a new home is an exciting process, and using pre-drawn plans is a great way to realize your dreams. Make sure that everyone involved has had an opportunity to review the plan you've selected. While Hanley Wood is the only plans provider with an exchange policy, it's best to be sure all parties agree on your selection before you buy.

CALL TOLL-FREE 1-800-521-6797

Source Key
HPK09

CUSTOMIZE YOUR PLAN –
HANLEY WOOD CUSTOMIZATION SERVICES

Creating custom home plans has never been easier and more directly accessible. Using state-of-the-art technology and top-performing architectural expertise, Hanley Wood delivers on a long-standing customer commitment to provide world-class home-plans and customization services. Our valued customers—professional home builders and individual home owners—appreciate the convenience and accessibility of this interactive, consultative service.

With the Hanley Wood Customization Service you can:

■ Save valuable time by avoiding drawn-out and frequently repetitive face-to-face design meetings
■ Communicate design and home-plan changes faster and more efficiently
■ Speed-up project turn-around time
■ Build on a budget without sacrificing quality
■ Transform master home plans to suit your design needs and unique personal style

All of our design options and prices are impressively affordable. A detailed quote is available for a $50 consultation fee. Plan modification is an interactive service. Our skilled team of designers will guide you through the customization process from start to finish making recommendations, offering ideas, and determining the feasibility of your changes. This level of service is offered to ensure the final modified plan meets your expectations. If you use our service the $50 fee will be applied to the cost of the modifications.

You may purchase the customization consultation before or after purchasing a plan. In either case, it is necessary to purchase the Reproducible Plan Package and complete the accompanying license to modify the plan before we can begin customization.

Customization Consultation...$50

TOOLS TO WORK WITH YOUR BUILDER

Two Reverse Options For Your Convenience –
Mirror and Right-Reading Reverse (as available)

Mirror reverse plans simply flip the design 180 degrees—keep in mind, the text will also be flipped. For a minimal fee you can have one or all of your plans shipped mirror reverse, although we recommend having at least one regular set handy. Right-reading reverse plans show the design flipped 180 degrees but the text reads normally. When you choose this option, we ship each set of purchased blueprints in this format.

Mirror Reverse Fee (indicate the number of sets when ordering).........$55
Right Reading Reverse Fee (all sets are reversed).............................$175

A Shopping List Exclusively for Your Home – Materials List

A customized Materials List helps you plan and estimate the cost of your new home, outlining the quantity, type, and size of materials needed to build your house (with the exception of mechanical system items). Included are framing lumber, windows and doors, kitchen and bath cabinetry, rough and finished hardware, and much more.

Materials List...$75 each
Additional Materials Lists (at original time of purchase only).......$20 each

Plan Your Home-
Building Process – Specification Outline

Work with your builder on this step-by-step chronicle of 166 stages or items crucial to the building process. It provides a comprehensive review of the construction process and helps you choose materials.
Specification Outline..$10 each

Get Accurate Cost Estimates for Your Home –
Quote One® Cost Reports

The Summary Cost Report, the first element in the Quote One® package, breaks down the cost of your home into various categories based on building materials, labor, and installation, and includes three grades of construction: Budget, Standard, and Custom. Make even more informed decisions about your project with the second element of our package, the Material Cost Report. The material and installation cost is shown for each of more than 1,000 line items provided in the standard-grade Materials List, which is included with this tool. Additional space is included for estimates from contractors and subcontractors, such as for mechanical materials, which are not included in our packages.

Quote One® Summary Cost Report..$35
Quote One® Detailed Material Cost Report...........................$140*
***Detailed material cost report includes the Materials List**

Learn the Basics of Building – Electrical, Plumbing, Mechanical, Construction Detail Sheets

If you want to know more about building techniques—and deal more confidently with your subcontractors—we offer four useful detail sheets. These sheets provide non-plan-specific general information, but are excellent tools that will add to your understanding of Plumbing Details, Electrical Details, Construction Details, and Mechanical Details.

Electrical Detail Sheet...$14.95
Plumbing Detail Sheet..$14.95
Mechanical Detail Sheet..$14.95
Construction Detail Sheet...$14.95

SUPER VALUE SETS:
Buy any 2: $26.95; Buy any 3: $34.95; Buy All 4: $39.95

Best Value

MAKE YOUR HOME TECH-READY – HOME AUTOMATION UPGRADE

Building a new home provides a unique opportunity to wire it with a plan for future needs. A Home Automation-Ready (HA-Ready) home contains the wiring substructure of tomorrow's connected home. It means that every room—from the front porch to the backyard, and from the attic to the basement—is wired for security, lighting, telecommunications, climate control, home computer networking, whole-house audio, home theater, shade control, video surveillance, entry access control, and yes, video gaming electronic solutions.

Along with the conveniences HA-Ready homes provide, they also have a higher resale value. The Consumer Electronics Association (CEA), in conjunction with the Custom Electronic Design and Installation Association (CEDIA), have developed a TechHome™ Rating system that quantifies the value of HA-Ready homes. The rating system is gaining widespread recognition in the real estate industry.

Developed by CEDIA-certified installers, our Home Automation Upgrade package includes everything you need to work with an installer during the construction of your home. It provides a short explanation of the various subsystems, a wiring floor plan for each level of your home, a detailed materials list with estimated costs, and a list of CEDIA-certified installers in your local area.

Home Automation Upgrade.......................\$250

GET YOUR HOME PLANS PAID FOR!

IndyMac Bank, in partnership with Hanley Wood, will reimburse you up to \$600 toward the cost of your home plans simply by financing the construction of your new home with IndyMac Bank Home Construction Lending.

IndyMac's construction and permanent loan is a one-time close loan, meaning that one application—and one set of closing fees—provides all the financing you need.

Apply today at www.indymacbank.com, call toll free at 1-866-237-3478, or ask a Hanley Wood customer service representative for details.

DESIGN YOUR HOME – INTERIOR AND EXTERIOR FINISHING TOUCHES

Be Your Own Interior Designer! – Home Furniture Planner

Effectively plan the space in your home using our Hands-On Home Furniture Planner. It's fun and easy—no more moving heavy pieces of furniture to see how the room will go together. The kit includes reusable peel-and-stick furniture templates that fit on a 12"x18" laminated layout board—enough space to lay out every room in your house.

Home Furniture Planning Kit.......................\$15.95

Enjoy the Outdoors! – Deck Plans

Many of our homes have a corresponding deck plan, sold separately, which includes a Deck Plan Frontal Sheet, Deck Framing and Floor Plans, Deck Elevations, and a Deck Materials List. A Standard Deck Details Package, also available, provides all the how-to information necessary for building any deck. Get both the Deck Plan and the Standard Deck Details Package for one low price in our Complete Deck Building Package. See the price tier chart below and call for deck plan availability.

Deck Details (only).......................\$14.95
Deck Building Package.......................Plan price + \$14.95

Create a Professionally Designed Landscape – Landscape Plans

Many of our homes have a front-yard Landscape Plan that is complementary in design to the house plan. These comprehensive Landscape Blueprint Packages include a Frontal Sheet, Plan View, Regionalized Plant & Materials List, a sheet on Planting and Maintaining Your Landscape, Zone Maps, and a Plant Size and Description Guide. Each set of blueprints is a full 18" x 24" with clear, complete instructions in easy-to-read type. Our Landscape Plans are available with a Plant & Materials List adapted by horticultural experts to eight regions of the country. Please specify your region when ordering your plan—see region map below. Call for more information about landscape plan availability and applicable regions.

LANDSCAPE & DECK PRICE SCHEDULE

PRICE TIERS	1-SET STUDY PACKAGE	5-SET BUILDING PACKAGE	8-SET BUILDING PACKAGE	1-SET REPRODUCIBLE*
P1	\$25	\$55	\$95	\$145
P2	\$45	\$75	\$115	\$165
P3	\$75	\$105	\$145	\$195
P4	\$105	\$135	\$175	\$225
P5	\$145	\$175	\$215	\$275
P6	\$185	\$215	\$255	\$315

TERMS & CONDITIONS

OUR EXCHANGE POLICY

HANLEY WOOD EXCLUSIVE!

Hanley Wood is committed to ensuring your satisfaction with your blueprint order, which is why we're the only provider of pre-drawn house plans to offer an exchange policy. With the exception of Reproducible Plan Package orders, we will exchange your entire first order for an equal or greater number of blueprints from our plan collection within 90 days of the original order. The entire content of your original order must be returned before an exchange will be processed. Please call our customer service department at 1-888-690-1116 for your return authorization number and shipping instructions. If the returned blueprints look used, redlined, or copied, we will not honor your exchange. Fees for exchanging your blueprints are as follows: 20% of the amount of the original order, plus the difference in cost if exchanging for a design in a higher price bracket or less the difference in cost if exchanging for a design in a lower price bracket. (Because they can be copied, Reproducible blueprints are not exchangeable or refundable.) Please call for current postage and handling prices. Shipping and handling charges are not refundable.

ARCHITECTURAL AND ENGINEERING SEALS

Some cities and states now require that a licensed architect or engineer review and "seal" a blueprint, or officially approve it, prior to construction. Prior to application for a building permit or the start of actual construction, we strongly advise that you consult your local building official who can tell you if such a review is required.

LOCAL BUILDING CODES AND ZONING REQUIREMENTS

Each plan was designed to meet or exceed the requirements of a nationally recognized model building code in effect at the time and place the plan was drawn. Typically plans designed after the year 2000 conform to the International Residential Building Code (IRC 2000 or 2003). The IRC is comprised of portions of the three major codes below. Plans drawn before 2000 conform to one of the three recognized building codes in effect at the time: Building Officials and Code

Administrators (BOCA) International, Inc.; the Southern Building Code Congress International, (SBCCI) Inc.; the International Conference of Building Officials (ICBO); or the Council of American Building Officials (CABO).

Because of the great differences in geography and climate throughout the United States and Canada, each state, county, and municipality has its own building codes, zone requirements, ordinances, and building regulations. Your plan may need to be modified to comply with local requirements. In addition, you may need to obtain permits or inspections from local governments before and in the course of construction. We authorize the use of the blueprints on the express condition that you consult a local licensed architect or engineer of your choice prior to beginning construction and strictly comply with all local building codes, zoning requirements, and other applicable laws, regulations, ordinances, and requirements. Notice: Plans for homes to be built in Nevada must be redrawn by a Nevada-registered professional. Consult your local building official for more information on this subject.

TERMS AND CONDITIONS

These designs are protected under the terms of United States Copyright Law and may not be copied or reproduced in any way, by any

means, unless you have purchased a Reproducible Plan Package and signed the accompanying license to modify and copy the plan, which clearly indicates your right to modify, copy, or reproduce. We authorize the use of your chosen design as an aid in the construction of ONE (1) single- or multifamily home only. You may not use this design to build a second dwelling or multiple dwellings without purchasing another blueprint or blueprints or paying additional design fees. Multi-use fees vary by designer—please call one of experienced sales representatives for a quote.

DISCLAIMER

The designers we work with have put substantial care and effort into the creation of their blueprints. However, because we cannot provide on-site consultation, supervision, and control over actual construction, and because of the great variance in local building requirements, building practices, and soil, seismic, weather, and other conditions, WE MAKE NO WARRANTY OF ANY KIND, EXPRESS OR IMPLIED, WITH RESPECT TO THE CONTENT OR USE OF THE BLUEPRINTS, INCLUDING BUT NOT LIMITED TO ANY WARRANTY OF MERCHANTABILITY OR OF FITNESS FOR A PARTICULAR PURPOSE. ITEMS, PRICES, TERMS, AND CONDITIONS ARE SUBJECT TO CHANGE WITHOUT NOTICE.

CALL TOLL-FREE
1-800-521-6797
OR VISIT EPLANS.COM

IMPORTANT COPYRIGHT NOTICE

From the Council of Publishing Home Designers

Blueprints for residential construction (or working drawings, as they are often called in the industry) are copyrighted intellectual property, protected under the terms of the United States Copyright Law and, therefore, cannot be copied legally for use in building. The following are some guidelines to help you get what you need to build your home, without violating copyright law:

1. HOME PLANS ARE COPYRIGHTED

Just like books, movies, and songs, home plans receive protection under the federal copyright laws. The copyright laws prevent anyone, other than the copyright owner, from reproducing, modifying, or reusing the plans or design without permission of the copyright owner.

2. DO NOT COPY DESIGNS OR FLOOR PLANS FROM ANY PUBLICATION, ELEC-TRONIC MEDIA, OR EXISTING HOME

It is illegal to copy, change, or redraw home designs found in a plan book, CD-ROM, or on the Internet. The right to modify plans is one of the exclusive rights of copyright. It is also illegal to copy or redraw a constructed home that is protected by copyright, even if you have never seen the plans for the home. If you find a plan or home that you like, you must purchase a set of plans from an authorized source. The plans may not be lent, given away, or sold by the purchaser.

3. DO NOT USE PLANS TO BUILD MORE THAN ONE HOUSE

The original purchaser of house plans is typically licensed to build a single home from the plans. Building more than one home from the plans without permission is an infringement of the home designer's copyright. The purchase of a multiple-set package of plans is for the construction of a single home only. The purchase of additional sets of plans does not grant the right to construct more than one home.

4. HOUSE PLANS IN THE FORM OF BLUEPRINTS OR BLACKLINES CANNOT BE COPIED OR REPRODUCED

Plans, blueprints, or blacklines, unless they are reproducibles, cannot be copied or reproduced without prior written consent of the copyright owner. Copy shops and blueprinters are prohibited from making copies of these plans without the copyright release letter you receive with reproducible plans.

5. HOUSE PLANS IN THE FORM OF BLUE-PRINTS OR BLACKLINES CANNOT BE REDRAWN

Plans cannot be modified or redrawn without first obtaining the copyright owner's permission. With your purchase of plans, you are licensed to make non-structural changes by "red-lining" the purchased plans. If you need to make structural changes or need to redraw the plans for any reason, you must purchase a reproducible set of plans (see topic 6) which includes a license to modify the plans. Blueprints do not come with a license to make structural changes or to redraw the plans. You may not reuse or sell the modified design.

6. REPRODUCIBILE HOME PLANS

Reproducible plans (for example sepias, mylars, CAD files, electronic files, and vellums) come with a license to make modifications to the plans. Once modified, the plans can be taken to a local copy shop or blueprinter to make up to 10 or 12 copies of the plans to use in the construction of a single home. Only one home can be constructed from any single purchased set of reproducible plans either in original form or as modified. The license to modify and copy must be completed and returned before the plan will be shipped.

7. MODIFIED DESIGNS CANNOT BE REUSED

Even if you are licensed to make modifications to a copyrighted design, the modified design is not free from the original designer's copyright. The sale or reuse of the modified design is prohibited. Also, be aware that any modification to plans relieves the original designer from liability for design defects and voids all warranties expressed or implied.

8. WHO IS RESPONSIBLE FOR COPYRIGHT INFRINGEMENT?

Any party who participates in a copyright violation may be responsible including the purchaser, designers, architects, engineers, drafters, homeowners, builders, contractors, sub-contractors, copy shops, blueprinters, developers, and real estate agencies. It does not matter whether or not the individual knows that a violation is being committed. Ignorance of the law is not a valid defense.

9. PLEASE RESPECT HOME DESIGN COPYRIGHTS

In the event of any suspected violation of a copyright, or if there is any uncertainty about the plans purchased, the publisher, architect, designer, or the Council of Publishing Home Designers (www.cphd.org) should be contacted before proceeding. Awards are sometimes offered for information about home design copyright infringement.

10. PENALTIES FOR INFRINGEMENT

Penalties for violating a copyright may be severe. The responsible parties are required to pay actual damages caused by the infringement (which may be substantial), plus any profits made by the infringer commissions to include all profits from the sale of any home built from an infringing design. The copyright law also allows for the recovery of statutory damages, which may be as high as $150,000 for each infringement. Finally, the infringer may be required to pay legal fees which often exceed the damages.

BLUEPRINT PRICE SCHEDULE

PRICE TIERS	1-SET STUDY PACKAGE	5-SET BUILDING PACKAGE	8-SET BUILDING PACKAGE	1-SET REPRODUCIBLE*
A1	$450	$500	$555	$675
A2	$490	$545	$595	$735
A3	$540	$605	$665	$820
A4	$590	$660	$725	$895
C1	$640	$715	$775	$950
C2	$690	$760	$820	$1025
C3	$735	$810	$875	$1100
C4	$785	$860	$925	$1175
L1	$895	$990	$1075	$1335
L2	$970	$1065	$1150	$1455
L3	$1075	$1175	$1270	$1600
L4	$1185	$1295	$1385	$1775
SQ1				.40/SQ. FT.
SQ3				.55/SQ. FT.
SQ5				.80/SQ. FT.

PRICES SUBJECT TO CHANGE

* REQUIRES A FAX NUMBER

PLAN #	PRICE TIER	PAGE	MATERIALS LIST	QUOTE ONE:	DECK	DECK PRICE	LANDSCAPE	LANDSCAPE PRICE	REGIONS
HPK0900001	C1	26							
HPK0900002	C3	30	Y						
HPK0900003	A4	31							
HPK0900004	A4	32							
HPK0900005	A4	33							
HPK0900006	A4	34							
HPK0900007	C1	35							
HPK0900008	L2	36							
HPK0900009	C2	37							
HPK0900010	A2	38	Y						
HPK0900011	A4	39							
HPK0900012	A4	40	Y						
HPK0900013	A3	41	Y						
HPK0900014	A3	42		Y		OLA003	P3	123568	
HPK0900015	C1	43	Y						
HPK0900016	C1	44	Y						
HPK0900017	C1	45	Y						
HPK0900018	A3	46	Y						
HPK0900019	A3	47	Y						
HPK0900020	A3	48	Y						
HPK0900021	A4	49							
HPK0900022	C2	50							
HPK0900023	C4	51							
HPK0900024	C1	52							
HPK0900025	C2	53							
HPK0900026	C2	54							
HPK0900027	C2	55							
HPK0900028	A4	56	Y						
HPK0900029	A4	57							
HPK0900030	C2	58	Y						

PLAN #	PRICE TIER	PAGE	MATERIALS LIST	QUOTE ONE:	DECK	DECK PRICE	LANDSCAPE	LANDSCAPE PRICE	REGIONS
HPK0900031	C2	59	Y						
HPK0900032	SQ1	60							
HPK0900033	C1	61							
HPK0900034	A4	62							
HPK0900035	A3	63							
HPK0900036	A3	64	Y						
HPK0900037	SQ1	65	Y						
HPK0900038	C1	66							
HPK0900039	C3	66	Y						
HPK0900040	A3	67							
HPK0900041	C3	67							
HPK0900042	A3	68	Y						
HPK0900043	A4	69							
HPK0900044	A4	70	Y						
HPK0900045	A3	70							
HPK0900046	C1	71							
HPK0900047	A4	72	Y						
HPK0900048	A3	73	Y						
HPK0900049	A2	73	Y						
HPK0900050	A1	74							
HPK0900051	A2	75	Y						
HPK0900052	A3	76							
HPK0900053	SQ1	78	Y						
HPK0900054	SQ1	82							
HPK0900055	C2	83							
HPK0900056	C2	83							
HPK0900057	C1	84	Y						
HPK0900058	C4	85	Y						
HPK0900059	C3	86	Y	Y		OLA038	P3	7	
HPK0900060	C3	87	Y	Y		OLA034	P3	347	

PLAN #	PRICE TIER	PAGE	MATERIALS LIST	QUOTE ONE:	DECK	DECK PRICE	LANDSCAPE	LANDSCAPE PRICE	REGIONS
HPK0900061	C2	88	Y						
HPK0900062	SQ1	89							
HPK0900063	C2	90	Y	Y	ODA012	P3	OLA024	P4	123568
HPK0900064	C1	90	Y						
HPK0900065	C3	91	Y						
HPK0900066	C1	92							
HPK0900067	C1	93							
HPK0900068	C1	94							
HPK0900069	SQ1	95							
HPK0900070	C2	96	Y						
HPK0900071	C3	97							
HPK0900072	A3	98	Y						
HPK0900073	L1	99							
HPK0900074	C1	100	Y						
HPK0900075	C4	101							
HPK0900076	C3	102							
HPK0900077	C3	103							
HPK0900078	A4	104	Y						
HPK0900079	C4	105							
HPK0900080	A4	106							
HPK0900081	A2	107							
HPK0900082	A3	108	Y						
HPK0900083	C3	109	Y						
HPK0900084	C4	110							
HPK0900085	C3	111							
HPK0900086	C1	112							
HPK0900087	A4	113							
HPK0900088	C1	114							
HPK0900089	L1	115							
HPK0900090	SQ1	116							

PLAN #	PRICE TIER	PAGE	MATERIALS LIST	QUOTE ONE:	DECK	DECK PRICE	LANDSCAPE	LANDSCAPE PRICE	REGIONS
HPK0900091	CI	117							
HPK0900092	C2	118	Y						
HPK0900093	C3	119							
HPK0900094	CI	120							
HPK0900095	CI	121							
HPK0900096	A2	122							
HPK0900097	CI	123							
HPK0900098	A4	124							
HPK0900099	CI	125							
HPK0900100	C4	126							
HPK0900101	C3	127							
HPK0900102	C4	128							
HPK0900103	SQI	130							
HPK0900104	SQI	134							
HPK0900105	C2	135							
HPK0900106	A4	135							
HPK0900107	SQI	136							
HPK0900108	SQI	137							
HPK0900109	C2	138							
HPK0900110	C4	139					OLA004	P3	123568
HPK0900111	A4	140							
HPK0900112	CI	141							
HPK0900113	CI	142							
HPK0900114	A4	143							
HPK0900115	CI	144							
HPK0900116	C2	145	Y	Y	ODA013	P2	OLA018	P3	12345678
HPK0900117	CI	146	Y	Y			OLA037	P4	347
HPK0900118	C3	147	Y	Y			OLA021	P3	123568
HPK0900119	SQI	148							
HPK0900120	SQI	149							
HPK0900121	SQI	150	Y						
HPK0900122	LI	151							
HPK0900123	CI	152							
HPK0900124	CI	153	Y						
HPK0900125	CI	154							
HPK0900126	L2	155							
HPK0900127	SQI	156							
HPK0900128	SQI	157							
HPK0900129	LI	158							
HPK0900130	LI	159							
HPK0900131	L2	160							
HPK0900132	A3	161							
HPK0900133	A4	161							
HPK0900134	CI	162							
HPK0900135	A4	163							
HPK0900136	CI	164							
HPK0900137	CI	165							
HPK0900138	CI	166							
HPK0900139	CI	167							
HPK0900140	A4	168							
HPK0900141	A2	169							
HPK0900142	A3	170							
HPK0900143	CI	171							
HPK0900144	A3	172	Y						
HPK0900145	C2	173	Y						

PLAN #	PRICE TIER	PAGE	MATERIALS LIST	QUOTE ONE:	DECK	DECK PRICE	LANDSCAPE	LANDSCAPE PRICE	REGIONS
HPK0900146	C2	173	Y						
HPK0900147	CI	174	Y						
HPK0900148	C4	174							
HPK0900149	A4	175	Y		ODA016	P2	OLA001	P3	123568
HPK0900150	A4	176	Y		ODA013	P2			
HPK0900151	A4	177	Y						
HPK0900152	C2	178							
HPK0900153	C2	179							
HPK0900154	CI	180							
HPK0900155	SQI	182							
HPK0900156	A4	186							
HPK0900157	C2	187	Y						
HPK0900158	C3	188	Y						
HPK0900159	C3	189	Y						
HPK0900160	CI	190							
HPK0900161	C3	191	Y						
HPK0900162	C2	192	Y						
HPK0900163	C2	193	Y						
HPK0900164	CI	194							
HPK0900165	C2	195							
HPK0900166	CI	196	Y						
HPK0900167	C2	197	Y						
HPK0900168	C2	198							
HPK0900169	A4	199							
HPK0900170	CI	200	Y						
HPK0900171	C2	201							
HPK0900172	C3	202							
HPK0900173	C2	203							
HPK0900174	CI	204	Y						
HPK0900175	C2	205							
HPK0900176	CI	206	Y						
HPK0900177	CI	207	Y	Y					
HPK0900178	C3	208							
HPK0900179	A4	209							
HPK0900180	C2	210							
HPK0900181	A2	211							
HPK0900182	CI	212							
HPK0900183	SQI	213	Y						
HPK0900184	CI	214							
HPK0900185	CI	215							
HPK0900186	CI	216	Y						
HPK0900187	CI	216	Y						
HPK0900188	A3	217							
HPK0900189	CI	218							
HPK0900190	C3	219							
HPK0900191	SQI	220	Y						
HPK0900192	L2	220							
HPK0900193	C3	221	Y						
HPK0900194	CI	222							
HPK0900195	CI	223							
HPK0900196	CI	224							
HPK0900197	C2	225	Y						
HPK0900198	C4	226	Y						
HPK0900199	LI	227							
HPK0900200	C2	228							

PLAN #	PRICE TIER	PAGE	MATERIALS LIST	QUOTE ONE:	DECK	DECK PRICE	LANDSCAPE	LANDSCAPE PRICE	REGIONS
HPK0900201	LI	228							
HPK0900202	C3	229							
HPK0900203	A4	230							
HPK0900204	CI	231							
HPK0900205	C3	232	Y						
HPK0900206	SQI	234							
HPK0900207	A4	238	Y						
HPK0900208	SQI	239	Y	Y					
HPK0900209	A4	240							
HPK0900210	CI	241							
HPK0900211	A3	242							
HPK0900212	A3	243							
HPK0900213	LI	244							
HPK0900214	CI	245	Y						
HPK0900215	A4	245							
HPK0900216	A3	246	Y						
HPK0900217	CI	246	Y						
HPK0900218	C4	247							
HPK0900219	CI	247							
HPK0900220	A3	248							
HPK0900221	A4	249	Y						
HPK0900222	CI	250	Y						
HPK0900223	A3	251	Y						
HPK0900224	A2	251	Y						
HPK0900225	CI	252							
HPK0900226	A3	253							
HPK0900227	A4	253	Y	Y			OLA088	P4	12345678
HPK0900228	CI	254	Y						
HPK0900229	LI	255	Y						
HPK0900230	SQI	256							
HPK0900231	C3	257							
HPK0900232	CI	258	Y						
HPK0900233	C4	258	Y						
HPK0900234	C2	259	Y						
HPK0900235	C3	259	Y						
HPK0900236	C3	260	Y						
HPK0900237	SQI	261	Y						
HPK0900238	A4	262							
HPK0900239	CI	263							
HPK0900240	A4	264							
HPK0900241	A2	265							
HPK0900242	CI	265	Y						
HPK0900243	A3	266							
HPK0900244	CI	267	Y						
HPK0900245	C3	268	Y				OLA001	P3	123568
HPK0900246	CI	269							
HPK0900247	CI	270	Y						
HPK0900248	CI	271							
HPK0900249	SQI	272	Y						
HPK0900250	CI	273							
HPK0900251	C2	274							
HPK0900252	CI	275							
HPK0900253	C2	276							
HPK0900254	C2	277	Y						

Idyllic Escapes

Take the plunge and start building your perfect vacation home. No matter if you are seeking a breathtaking view, a relaxing retreat or a cozy cabin, HomePlanners has the house plan to fit your every fantasy.

If you are looking to build a vacation home, look to HomePlanners first.

pick up a copy today!

HOMES WITH A VIEW
ISBN 1-931131-25-2
$14.95 (192 PAGES)

175 Plans for Golf-Course, Waterfront and Mountain Homes
This stunning collection features homes as magnificent as the vistas they showcase. A 32-page, full-color gallery showcases the most spectacular homes—all designed specifically to accent the natural beauty of their surrounding landscapes.

COOL COTTAGES
ISBN 1-881955-91-5
$10.95 (256 PAGES)

245 Delightful Retreats 825 to 3,500 square feet
Cozy, inviting house plans designed to provide the ideal escape from the stress of daily life. This charming compilation offers perfect hideaways for every locale: mountaintops to foothills, woodlands to everglades.

VACATION AND SECOND HOMES, 3RD ED.
ISBN 1-881955-97-4
$9.95 (448 PAGES)

430 House Plans for Retreats and Getaways
Visit the cutting edge of home design in this fresh portfolio of getaway plans—ready to build anywhere. From sprawling haciendas to small rustic cabins, this collection takes on your wildest dreams with designs suited for waterfronts, cliffsides, or wide-open spaces.

Toll-Free: **800.322.6797**   Online: **http://books.eplans.com**

GETAWAY HOMES
ISBN 1-931131-37-6

$11.95 (288 PAGES)

250 Home Plans for Cottages, Bungalows & Capes
This is the perfect volume for anyone looking to create their own relaxing place to escape life's pressures—whether it's a vacation home or primary residence! Also included, tips to create a comfortable, yet beautiful atmosphere in a small space.

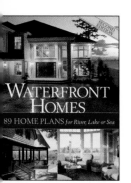

WATERFRONT HOMES
ISBN 1-931131-28-7

$10.95 (208 PAGES)

189 Home Plans for River, Lake or Sea
A beautiful waterfront setting calls for a beautiful home. Whether you are looking for a year-round home or a vacation getaway, this is a fantastic collection of home plans to choose from.

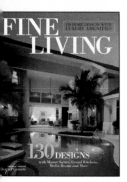

FINE LIVING
ISBN 1-931131-24-4

$17.95 (192 PAGES)

130 Home Designs with Luxury Amenities
The homes in this collection offer lovely exteriors, flowing floor plans and ample interior space, plus a stunning array of amenities that goes above and beyond standard designs. This title features gorgeous full-color photos, tips on furnishing and decorating as well as an extensive reference section packed with inspiring ideas.

Whether you are looking for a quaint cabin in the woods or a luxurious mansion on a rocky bluff, your perfect sanctuary is within reach with these collections from HomePlanners.

HANLEY WOOD CONSUMER GROUP
One Thomas Circle, NW, Suite 600, Washington, DC 20005

lasting impression

Day or night, this Key West-style home has an allure that's fitting for a getaway home. Its distinctive layout and abundance of outdoor living spaces will have you and your family counting the days until you get there. See page 231 for details.